STUDY GUIDE

Intr al

Fort Worth Philadelphia San Diego New York Orlando Austin San Antonio
Toronto Montreal London Sydney Tokyo

Cover Image: SPG International

Address for Editorial Correspondence
The Dryden Press, 301 Commerce Street, Suite 3700, Fort Worth, TX 76102

Address for Orders
The Dryden Press, 6277 Sea Harbor Drive, Orlando, FL 32887
1-800-782-4479, or 1-800-433-0001 (in Florida)

ISBN: 0-03-098077-1

Printed in the United States of America

9 0 1 2 3 4 082 9 8 7 6 5 4 3

The Dryden Press
Harcourt Brace College Publishers

PREFACE

This *Study Guide* is designed primarily to help you develop a working knowledge of the concepts and principles of financial management. Additionally, it will familiarize you with the types of true/false and multiple choice test questions that are being used with increasing frequency in introductory finance courses.

The *Study Guide* follows the outline of *Introduction to Financial Management*. You should read carefully the next section, "How To Use This *Study Guide*," to familiarize yourself with its specific contents and to gain some insights into how it can be used most effectively.

We would like to thank Dana Aberwald and Bob Karp for their considerable assistance in the preparation of this Edition, and Bob LeClair and Louis C. Gapenski for their helpful ideas that were incorporated into this *Study Guide*.

We have tried to make the *Study Guide* as clear and error-free as possible. However, some mistakes may have crept in, and there are almost certainly some sections that could be clarified. Any suggestions for improving the *Study Guide* would be greatly appreciated. Since instructors almost never read study guides, we address this call for help to students!

Bodie Dickerson
School of Business
Oregon State University
Corvallis, OR 97331

B.J. Campsey
School of Business
San Jose State University
San Jose, CA 95192-0066

Eugene F. Brigham
College of Business Administration
University of Florida
PO Box 117160
Gainesville, FL 32611-7160

HOW TO USE THIS STUDY GUIDE

Different people will tend to use the *Study Guide* in somewhat different ways. This is natural, because both introductory finance courses and individual students' needs vary widely. However, the tips contained in this section should help all students use the *Study Guide* more effectively, regardless of these differences.

Each chapter contains (1) an overview, (2) an outline, (3) definitional self-test questions, (4) some conceptual self-test questions, and (5) answers and solutions to the self-test questions and problems. You should begin your study by reading the overview; it will give you an idea of what is contained in the chapter and how this material fits into the overall scheme of things in financial management.

Next, read over the outline to get a better fix on the specific topics covered in the chapter. It is important to realize that the outline does not list every facet of every topic covered in the textbook--the *Study Guide* is intended to highlight and summarize the textbook, not to supplant it. Also, note that appendix material is clearly marked as such within the outline. Thus, if your instructor does not assign a particular appendix, you may not want to study that portion of the outline.

The definitional self-test questions are intended to test your knowledge of, and also to reinforce your ability to work with, the terms and concepts introduced in the chapter. If you do not understand the definitions thoroughly, review the outline prior to going on to the conceptual questions and problems.

The conceptual self-test questions focus on the same kinds of ideas that the textbook end-of-chapter questions address, but in the *Study Guide* the questions are set out in a true/false or multiple choice format. Thus, for many students these questions can be used to practice for the types of tests that are being used with increasing frequency. However, regardless of the types of tests you must take, working through the conceptual questions will help drive home the key concepts of financial management.

The numerical problems are also written in a multiple choice format. Generally, the problems are arranged in order of increasing difficulty. Also, note that some of the *Study Guide* problems are convoluted in the sense that information normally available to financial managers is withheld, and information normally unknown is given. Such problems are designed to test your knowledge of a subject, and you must work "backwards" to solve them. Furthermore, such problems are included in the *Study Guide* in part because they provide a good test of how well you understand the material, and in part because you may well be seeing similar problems on your exams.

Finally, each *Study Guide* chapter provides the answers and solutions to the self-test questions and problems. The rationale behind a question's correct answer is explained where necessary, but the problem solutions are always complete. Note that the problems generally provide both "table-based" and "financial calculator" solutions. You should not be concerned if your answer differs from ours by a small amount due to rounding.

Of course, each student must decide how to incorporate the *Study Guide* in his or her overall study program. Many students begin an assignment by reading the *Study Guide* overview and outline to get the "big picture," then read the chapter in the textbook. Naturally, the *Study Guide* overview and outline is also used extensively to review for exams. Most students work the textbook questions and problems, using the latter as a self-test and review tool. However, if you are stumped by a text problem, try the *Study Guide* problems first, because their detailed solutions can get you over stumbling blocks.

CONTENTS OF THE STUDY GUIDE

PREFACE iii

HOW TO USE THIS STUDY GUIDE v

CHAPTER

1 DEFINING FINANCIAL MANAGEMENT 1-1

2 TAXES AND THE FINANCIAL ENVIRONMENT 2-1

3 FINANCIAL INSTITUTIONS 3-1

4 INTEREST RATES 4-1

5 EXAMINING A FIRM'S FINANCIAL DATA 5-1

6 INTERPRETING FINANCIAL STATEMENTS 6-1

7 DETERMINING FUTURE FINANCIAL NEEDS 7-1

8 WORKING CAPITAL POLICY AND MANAGEMENT 8-1

9 MANAGING CASH AND MARKETABLE SECURITIES 9-1

10 ACCOUNTS RECEIVABLE AND INVENTORIES 10-1

11 SHORT-TERM FINANCING 11-1

12 RISK AND RETURN 12-1

13 TIME VALUE OF MONEY 13-1

14 THE PROCESS OF CAPITAL BUDGETING 14-1

15 DECISIONS IN CAPITAL BUDGETING 15-1

16 BONDS AND PREFERRED STOCK 16-1

17 COMMON STOCK 17-1

CHAPTER

18 HYBRID FINANCING: LEASING AND OPTION SECURITIES 18-1

19 THE COST OF CAPITAL 19-1

20 LEVERAGE AND THE TARGET CAPITAL STRUCTURE 20-1

21 DETERMINING THE DIVIDEND POLICY 21-1

22 MERGERS AND ACQUISITIONS 22-1

23 INTERNATIONAL FINANCIAL MANAGEMENT 23-1

CHAPTER 1
DEFINING FINANCIAL MANAGEMENT

OVERVIEW

This chapter provides an overview of financial management and should give you a better understanding of the following: (1) what forces will affect financial management in the future; (2) how businesses are organized; (3) how finance fits into the structure of a firm's organization; (4) how financial managers relate to their counterparts in other departments; and (5) what the goals of a corporation are and how financial managers can contribute to the attainment of these goals.

The evolution of financial management from 1900 to the present time has seen the financial manager playing an increasingly important role in the business organization. Decisions made by managers within the organization should be consistent with the goals of the corporation. The primary goal of most publicly owned firms is stock price maximization. Actions that result in stock price maximization not only are good for the corporation, but benefit society as well. Yet managers, because they usually do not own 100 percent of the firm's stock, are not always motivated to act in the best interest of the shareholders. However, there are reasons, such as proxy fights, hostile takeovers, and performance-linked compensation, which tend to force managers to respect the shareholders' interests. Ultimately, the combination of management's efforts along with external uncontrollable factors such as inflation, tax changes, and the general stock market interact to determine the stock price of the firm.

OUTLINE

I. **Finance consists of three interrelated areas: money and capital markets, investments, and financial management. Career opportunities within each field are varied and numerous, but financial managers must have a knowledge of all three areas.**

A. Many finance majors go to work for financial institutions, including banks, insurance companies, savings and loans, and credit unions. The bank officer trainee is the most common initial job in this area.

1. A knowledge of the factors that cause interest rates to rise and fall, the regulations to which financial institutions are subject, and the different types of financial instruments available is necessary.

B. Finance graduates who go into investments generally work for a brokerage house in sales or as a security analyst; for a bank, a mutual fund, or an insurance company in the management of their investment portfolios; or for a financial consulting firm, advising individual investors or pension funds on how to invest their funds.

C. Financial management, the broadest of the three areas, and the one with the greatest number of job opportunities, is important to all types of businesses. The types of jobs one encounters in this area range from decisions regarding plant expansions to the choice of stocks or bonds to finance expansion.

II. **Financial management has undergone significant changes over the years.**

A. During the early 1900s, the emphasis was on legalistic aspects of mergers, consolidations, the formation of new firms, and the various types of securities issued by corporations. At that time, capital markets were relatively primitive, and the critical problem firms faced was obtaining capital for expansion.

B. During the depression of the 1930s, the emphasis shifted from expansion to survival, and the focus was on bankruptcy and reorganization, corporate liquidity, and regulation of securities markets.

C. During the 1940s and early 1950s, finance continued to be taught as a descriptive subject viewed from the standpoint of an outsider rather than from that of management.

D. In the 1960s and 1970s, there was a movement toward theoretical analysis. The focus shifted to managerial decisions regarding the choice of assets and liabilities so as to maximize the firm's value.

E. In the 1980s, the following issues received emphasis:
1. Inflation and its implications for business decisions.
2. Increased recognition of social responsibilities of businesses.
3. Deregulation of financial institutions, and the trend away from specialized institutions toward broadly diversified financial service corporations.
4. Merger activity, ranging from friendly mergers to hostile takeovers and leveraged buyouts (LBOs).
5. An increased importance of global markets and global business operations.
6. The dramatic increase in the use of computers both for financial decisions analyses and use in the electronic transfer of funds and information.

III. **The five most important trends for financial management during the 1990s are likely to be: (1) continued globalization, (2) continued advances in computer and communications technology, (3) corporate restructuring and debt reduction, (4) a reversal of diversification into financial services, and (5) changes in corporate governance and shareholder rights.**

A. Four factors have made the trend toward globalization mandatory for many businesses.

1. Transportation and communications improvements have lowered shipping costs, lowered trade barriers, and increased competition.
2. Increased political clout of consumers has also helped lower trade barriers.
3. Due to increased technology, higher development costs have resulted, necessitating increased unit sales.
4. Competitive pressures have forced companies to shift manufacturing operations to lower-cost countries.

B. Continued advances in computer technology are revolutionizing the way financial decisions are made. Thus, the new generation of financial managers will need stronger computer and quantitative skills than were required in the past.

C. Corporate restructuring and debt reduction represents a reversal of the highly leveraged decade of the 1980s. This reversal was brought about in part by the 1990-1991 recession and renewed recognition by both firms and consumers of the risks associated with high debt levels.

D. There is a trend toward a reversal of the diversification into financial services. Firms that were not originally financial institutions are now rethinking their strategies.

E. Changes in corporate governance and shareholder rights is another developing trend in the 1990s. Boardroom reform may well do for the 1990s what LBOs did for the 1980s: Oust entrenched managements to make way for new ones who will better represent the interests of the firms' shareholders.

IV. The financial manager's primary task is to plan for the acquisition and use of funds in order to maximize the efficiency and value of the firm. Specific activities include the following: forecasting and planning, major investment and financing decisions, coordination and control, and dealing with the financial markets.

V. There has been a dramatic increase in the importance of financial management.

A. The financial manager is directly responsible for the control process and for corporate planning.

B. There are financial implications in virtually all business decisions, and nonfinancial executives must know enough about finance to incorporate these implications into their own specialized areas.

VI. The three major forms of business organization are the sole proprietorship, the partnership, and the corporation. About 80 percent of businesses operate as sole proprietorships, while the remainder are equally divided

between partnerships and corporations. By dollar value of sales, however, 80 percent of business is conducted by corporations, 13 percent by sole proprietorships, and about 7 percent by partnerships.

A. A sole proprietorship is an unincorporated business owned by one individual.

1. Advantages: (1) A sole proprietorship is easily and inexpensively formed since no formal charter is required, (2) it is subject to few government regulations, and (3) it pays no corporate income taxes. (However, all earnings of the business are taxed as personal income to the owner).

2. Disadvantages: (1) A sole proprietorship is limited in its ability to raise large sums of capital, (2) it has unlimited personal liability for business debts, and (3) it has a life limited to the life of the individual who created it.

B. A partnership exists when two or more persons associate to conduct a noncorporate business.

1. Advantage: Partnerships are easy and economical to form.

2. Disadvantages: (1) Each partner is exposed to unlimited personal liability for business debts, even for those unsatisfied claims other partners may have incurred, (2) the business's life is limited to the life of the owners, (3) there is difficulty in transferring ownership, and (4) it has difficulty raising large amounts of capital because of the disadvantages previously mentioned.

3. Taxation of a partnership is similar to that of a proprietorship. This is generally considered to be an advantage.

4. Limited partnerships differ from general partnerships in that each limited partner's liability extends only to the amount of the investment in the partnership. Limited partners are often called silent partners because they have no active voice in management.

C. A corporation is a legal entity created by a state, and it has allowed managers to become separate and distinct from the capital-providing owners of the firm.

1. Advantages: (1) A corporation has an unlimited life, (2) one can easily transfer ownership through the transfer of stock, and (3) it permits limited liability. The value of any business other than a very small one will probably be maximized if the business is organized as a corporation, because of these advantages.

2. Disadvantages: (1) Corporate earnings are subject to double taxation, and (2) setting up a corporation is more complex than forming a proprietorship or partnership.

   a. Double taxation occurs when the earnings of the corporation are taxed, and then any earnings paid out as dividends are taxed again as income to the stockholders.

   b. A charter must be filed with the state where the firm is incorporated and bylaws which govern the management of the company must be prepared.

D. Subchapter S of the Internal Revenue Code provides that some small, incorporated businesses may elect to be taxed as proprietorships or partnerships if certain technical requirements are met. Such a corporation is called an S corporation.

1. Advantages: (1) Owners enjoy the protection of limited liability and (2) they obtain some tax advantages, such as avoiding double taxation.

VII. Stockholder wealth maximization is the most important goal of most publicly traded firms, and it is a reasonable operative objective on which to build decision rules.

A. This goal translates into maximizing the price of the firm's common stock.

B. Other objectives--personal satisfaction, employee welfare, and the good of the community--also have an influence, but for publicly-owned companies they are less important than stock price maximization.

C. Tying management's compensation to company performance tends to reinforce stock price maximization as a goal.

D. Hostile takeovers and proxy fights have also stimulated management to maximize share price.

E. Social responsibility raises the question of whether businesses should operate strictly in their stockholders' best interests or also be responsible for the welfare of their employees, customers, and the communities in which they operate.

1. Any voluntary, socially responsible acts that raise costs will be difficult, if not impossible, in industries that are subject to keen competition.

2. Even firms with above-average profits will be constrained in exercising social responsibility by capital market forces because investors will normally prefer a firm that concentrates on profits over one excessively devoted to social action.

3. Socially responsible actions that increase costs may have to be put on a mandatory, rather than a voluntary, basis to insure that the burden falls uniformly on all businesses.

4. Industry and government must cooperate in establishing rules for fair hiring, product safety, environmental protection, and other programs that affect all businesses.

F. The same actions that maximize stock price also benefit society. To maximize stock price, a firm must provide a low-cost, high-quality product to consumers. This, in itself, is a benefit to society.

VIII. Business ethics can be thought of as a company's attitude and conduct towards its employees, customers, community, and stockholders.

A. A firm's commitment to business ethics can be measured by the tendency of the firm and its employees to adhere to laws and regulations relating to product safety and quality, fair employment practices, fair marketing and selling practices, and the use of confidential information for personal gain.

B. Most firms today have in place strong codes of ethical behavior; however, it is imperative that top management be openly committed to ethical behavior and that they communicate this commitment through their own personal actions as well as company policies.

IX. **An agency relationship exists when one or more persons (the principals) hire another person (the agent) to act on their behalf, delegating decision-making authority to that agent. Agency relationships exist (1) between stockholders and managers and (2) between stockholders and creditors (debtholders).**

A. A potential agency problem exists whenever a manager owns less than 100 percent of the firm's common stock.

1. Since the firm's earnings do not go solely to the manager, he or she may not concentrate exclusively on maximizing shareholder wealth.

2. Another potential conflict between management and stockholders arises in a leveraged buyout because management might attempt to minimize the firm's stock price just prior to the buyout. However, the Securities and Exchange Commission (SEC) now requires disclosure of material information relating to proposed deals where a conflict of interest exists.

B. Several mechanisms are used to ensure that managers act in shareholders' best interests: (1) the threat of firing, (2) the threat of takeover, and (3) the proper structuring of managerial compensation.

C. Another agency problem involves conflicts between stockholders and creditors (debtholders).

1. Conflicts arise if (a) management, acting for its stockholders, takes on projects that have greater risk than was anticipated by creditors or (b) the firm increases debt to a level higher than was anticipated. Both of these actions decrease the value of the debt outstanding.

2. It is in the firm's best interest to deal fairly with its creditors in order to assure future access to debt markets at reasonable interest costs.

X. **The financial manager can affect the firm's stock price by influencing the following factors: (1) projected earnings per share, (2) timing of the earnings stream, and (3) riskiness of these projected earnings. In turn, these factors are dependent on decisions regarding the use of debt in the firm's overall financing, its dividend policy, and numerous other policies and decisions.**

XI. **Financial managers must try to find that balance between risk and return which will maximize the price of the firm's common stock (and the value of the firm), and they must do so within external constraints, such as the social concerns and legislation discussed earlier.**

A. Although managerial actions affect the value of a firm's stock, external factors also influence stock prices. Included among them are legal constraints, the general level of economic activity, the tax laws, and conditions in the stock market.

DEFINITIONAL QUESTIONS

1. Finance consists of three interrelated areas: (1) _______ ___ _______ _______, which deals with many of the topics covered in macroeconomics; (2) ___________, which focuses on the decisions of individuals and financial institutions as they choose securities for their investment portfolios; and (3) _________ _________ or "business finance."

2. In the early 1900s, the finance function concentrated on ____________ matters such as mergers, consolidations, and the various types of securities issued by corporations.

3. The ___________ of the 1930s caused an emphasis on bankruptcy, liquidity, and ___________ securities markets.

4. During the 1960s and 1970s, the focus shifted to managerial decisions regarding the choice of ________ and ___________ so as to maximize the firm's value.

5. Some of the more important trends for financial management during the 1990s are likely to be: (1) continued _____________, (2) continued advances in ________ and communications technology, and (3) corporate _____________ and ____ reduction.

6. Modern financial theory operates on the assumption that the goal of management is the ____________ of shareholder ____________. This goal is accomplished if the firm's __________ __________ is maximized.

7. A firm's stock price depends on several factors. Among the most important of these are the level of projected ________ ______ ______ as well as the _________ of those projections.

8. Socially responsible activities that increase a firm's costs will be most difficult to initiate in those industries where _____________ is most intense.

9. Even firms with above-average profit levels will find social actions ___________ by capital market factors.

10. Sole proprietorships are easily formed, but often have difficulty raising _________, they subject proprietors to unlimited _______________, and they have a limited ________.

11. Partnership profits are taxed as _____________ income in proportion to each partner's proportionate ownership.

12. A partnership is dissolved upon the withdrawal or ________ of any one of the partners. In addition, the difficulty in ______________________ ownership is a major disadvantage of the partnership form of business organization.

13. A(n) ____________ is a legal entity created by a state, and it is separate from its owners and managers.

14. The concept of ________ ____________ means that a firm's stockholders are not personally liable for the debts of the business.

15. A(n) _____________ relationship exists when one or more persons (the principals) hire another person (the agent) to act on their behalf.

16. Potential agency problems exist between a firm's shareholders and its ____________ and also between shareholders and ____________.

CONCEPTUAL QUESTIONS

17. The primary objective of the firm is to maximize EPS.

    a. True b. False

18. The types of actions that help a firm maximize stock price are generally not directly beneficial to society at large.

    a. True b. False

19. There are factors that influence stock price over which managers have virtually no control.

    a. True b. False

20. Which of the following factors affect stock price?

    a. Level of projected earnings per share.
    b. Riskiness of projected earnings per share.
    c. Timing of the earnings stream.
    d. None of the above are factors.
    e. All of the above are factors.

21. Which of the following factors tend to encourage management to pursue stock price maximization as a goal?

a. Shareholders link management's compensation to company performance.
b. Managers react to the threat of hostile takeovers and proxy fights.
c. Managers do not have goals other than stock price maximization.
d. Statements a and b are both correct.
e. Statements a, b, and c are all correct.

22. The primary contribution of finance to total social welfare is its

a. Function as a productive resource.
b. Contribution to the efficient allocation and use of resources.
c. Role as an exogenous variable.
d. Positive impact on the externalities of "other variables."
e. Contribution to environmental protection.

23. Shareholder agency costs include

a. Expenditures to monitor managerial actions.
b. Managerial salaries.
c. Opportunity costs associated with managerial restrictions.
d. All of the above.
e. Answers a and c.

24. Which of the following represents a significant disadvantage to the corporate form of organization?

a. Difficulty in transferring ownership.
b. Exposure to taxation of corporate earnings and stockholder dividend income.
c. Degree of liability to which corporate owners and managers are exposed.
d. Level of difficulty corporations face in obtaining large amounts of capital in financial markets.

ANSWERS

1. money and capital markets; investments; financial management
2. legalistic
3. depression; regulating
4. assets; liabilities
5. globalization; computer; restructuring; debt
6. maximization; wealth; stock price
7. earnings per share; riskiness
8. competition
9. constrained
10. capital; liability; life
11. personal
12. death; transferring
13. corporation
14. limited liability
15. agency
16. managers; creditors (debtholders)

17. b. This is false because an increase in earnings per share will not necessarily increase stock price. For example, if the increase in earnings per share is accompanied by an increase in the riskiness of the firm, stock price might fall. The primary objective is the maximization of stock price.

18. b. This is false because the actions that maximize stock price generally also benefit society by promoting efficient, low-cost operations; encouraging the development of new technology, products and jobs; and requiring efficient and courteous service.

19. a. Managers have no control over factors such as (1) external constraints (for example, antitrust laws and environmental regulations), (2) the general level of economic activity, (3) taxes, and (4) conditions in the stock market, all of which affect the price of the firm's stock.

20. e. The firm's stock price is dependent on all the factors mentioned.

21. d. Mechanisms which tend to force managers to act in the shareholders' best interests include (1) the threat of firing, (2) the threat of takeover, and (3) the proper structuring of managerial compensation.

22. b. Financial management plays a crucial role in the operation of successful firms because of finance's contribution to the efficient allocation and use of resources. Successful firms are absolutely necessary for a healthy, productive economy.

23. e. Shareholder agency costs include expenditures to monitor managerial actions and the opportunity costs associated with restrictions placed on managers.

24. b. The double taxation of corporate earnings is a significant disadvantage of the corporate form of organization. The corporation's earnings are taxed, and then any earnings paid out as dividends are taxed again as income to the stockholders.

CHAPTER 2
TAXES AND THE FINANCIAL ENVIRONMENT

OVERVIEW

In the United States, income to both individuals and businesses is taxed by the federal government. Individuals pay income taxes on wages and salaries, on investment income, and on profits from proprietorships and partnerships. Corporations pay taxes on profits, as well as interest and dividends received by a corporation. Interest paid is a tax deductible expense, while dividends on common and preferred stock are not deductible. Depreciation of fixed assets reduces taxable income and is calculated using the Modified Accelerated Cost Recovery System (MACRS).

A developed economy relies on financial markets and institutions for efficient transfers of funds from savers to borrowers. In the United States, our stock markets include the organized exchanges, such as the New York Stock Exchange (NYSE), and the over-the-counter (OTC) market, which provides for all security transactions not conducted on the organized exchanges. The transfer of capital may take place through direct transfers, investment banking houses, or financial intermediaries. In order to promote quick and efficient access to all available information, the Securities and Exchange Commission (SEC) regulates almost all participants in the securities markets. The regulation helps ensure capital market efficiency and attempts to prevent fraud. However, it is the investor's responsibility to exercise good judgment when making investment decisions.

OUTLINE

I. **Individuals pay taxes on wages and salaries, on investment income (dividends, interest, and profits from the sale of securities), and on the profits of proprietorships and partnerships.**

A. U.S. income taxes are *progressive;* that is, the higher the income, the larger the percentage paid in taxes. Marginal tax rates begin at 15 percent and can go up to 39.6 percent.

1. The *marginal tax rate* is defined as the tax on the last unit of income.
2. The *average tax rate* is calculated as taxes paid divided by taxable income.
3. *Bracket creep* may occur when progressive tax rates combine with inflation to cause a greater portion of each taxpayer's real income to be paid as taxes.

B. Since dividends are paid from corporate income that has already been taxed (at rates going up as high as 39 percent), there is *double taxation* of corporate income. Interest on most state and local government securities, which are often called "municipals," is not subject to federal income taxes.

1. This allows state and local governments to borrow at lower rates than would otherwise be available to them.

2. Also, it creates a strong incentive for individuals in high tax brackets to purchase such securities.

C. Gains and losses on the sale of capital assets such as stocks, bonds, and real estate have historically received special tax treatment.

1. An asset purchased within one year produces a *short-term capital gain or loss,* while an asset held for more than one year, and then sold, produces a *long-term capital gain or loss.*

2. Short-term capital gains are taxed as ordinary income. Currently, all long-term capital gains income is taxed as if it were ordinary income, with a maximum tax rate capped at 28 percent.

II. Corporations pay taxes on profits.

A. Corporate tax rates are also progressive. Marginal tax rates are as follows:

1. 15 percent on the first $50,000 of taxable income.

2. 25 percent on the next $25,000.

3. 34 percent on the next $25,000.

4. 39 percent on income between $100,000 and $335,000.

5. 34 percent for income between $335,000 and $10,000,000.

6. 35 percent for income between $10,000,000 and $15,000,000.

7. 38 percent for income between $15,000,000 and $18,333,333.

8. 35 percent for income greater than $18,333,333.

B. Interest and dividends received by a corporation are taxed.

1. Interest is taxed as ordinary income at regular corporate tax rates.

2. However, 70 percent of the dividends received by one corporation from another is excluded from taxable income. The remaining 30 percent is taxed at the ordinary tax rate. Thus, the effective tax rate on dividends received by a 35 percent marginal tax bracket corporation is 0.30(35%) = 10.5%.

C. The tax system favors debt financing over equity financing.

1. Interest paid is a tax-deductible business expense.

2. Dividends on common and preferred stock are not deductible. Thus, a 40 percent federal-plus-state tax bracket corporation must earn $\$1/(1.0 - 0.40) = \$1/0.60 = \$1.67$ before taxes to pay $1 of dividends, but only $1 of pretax income is required to pay $1 of interest.

D. Before 1987, long-term corporate capital gains were taxed at lower rates than ordinary income. However, at present, long-term capital gains are taxed at the same rates as their operating income.

E. Ordinary corporate operating losses may first be carried back to each of the preceding 3 years and then forward for the next 15 years to offset taxable income, thus reducing taxes in those years. The purpose of permitting this loss treatment is to avoid penalizing corporations whose incomes fluctuate substantially from year to year.

F. The Internal Revenue Code imposes a penalty on corporations that improperly accumulate earnings if the purpose of the accumulation is to enable stockholders to avoid personal income tax on dividends.

G. If a corporation owns 80 percent or more of another corporation's stock, it can aggregate profits and losses and file a consolidated tax return. Thus, losses in one area can offset profits in another.

H. Small businesses which meet certain restrictions may be set up as *S corporations* which receive benefits of the corporate form--especially limited liability--yet are taxed as proprietorships or partnerships rather than as corporations. This treatment would be preferred by owners of small corporations in which all or most of the income earned each year is distributed as dividends because the income would be taxed only once at the individual level.

III. **Depreciation is the accounting process whereby the cost of a productive asset is allocated against the revenues that it helps to produce. However, depreciation is not a cash charge, so higher depreciation does not reduce cash flows. Indeed, higher depreciation increases cash flows, because the greater a firm's depreciation, the lower its tax bill.**

A. Depreciation is usually calculated by the straight line method when reporting income to investors, but for tax purposes, depreciation is calculated using the *Modified Accelerated Cost Recovery System (MACRS)*.

B. MACRS creates several classes of assets, each with a more or less arbitrarily prescribed life called a *recovery period* or *class life* which bears only a rough relationship to the expected useful economic life. For example, certain special manufacturing tools fall into the 3-year class life, while commercial buildings fall into the 39-year class life.

C. A major effect of the MACRS system has been to shorten the depreciable lives of assets, thus giving businesses larger tax deductions and thereby increasing cash flows available for reinvestment.

D. Once the class life of an asset is determined, MACRS specifies the percentage of the asset's depreciable basis that can be deducted each year as depreciation expense.

1. The *half-year convention* allows an asset to receive one-half of a year's depreciation in the first year, and the remaining half year's depreciation in the year following the last year of its class life, thus effectively extending the recovery period by one year.

E. The portion of an asset's value which can be depreciated for tax purposes is known as its *depreciable basis.* Under MACRS the depreciable basis is equal to the asset's cost plus any shipping and installation costs. The basis is *not* adjusted for *salvage value* (the estimated market value of the asset at the end of its useful life).

F. An *investment tax credit (ITC)* provides for a direct reduction of taxes, and its purpose is to stimulate business investment. ITCs were eliminated by the 1986 tax revision and were not brought back in 1993.

IV. Individuals and organizations wanting to raise capital are brought together with those having surplus funds in the financial markets. There are a great many different financial markets, each one consisting of many institutions, in a developed economy such as ours.

A. Within these markets, capital is allocated among firms by interest rates, which represent the price for borrowed capital.

B. Each market deals with a somewhat different security, serves a different set of customers, or operates in a different part of the country. Some of the major types of markets include the following:

1. *Financial asset markets* are those in which stocks, bonds, notes, mortgages, and other claims on assets are traded, while *physical asset markets* are those in which real (or tangible) assets are traded.
2. *Spot markets* and *futures markets* refer to whether the assets are being purchased or sold for "on the spot" delivery or for delivery at some future date.
3. *Money markets* are markets for short-term debt securities, those securities that mature in less than one year; while *capital markets* are for long-term debt and corporate stocks.
   a. Some money market instruments include: U.S. Treasury bills, negotiable certificates of deposit, commercial paper, and banker's acceptances.
   b. Some capital market instruments include: U.S Treasury notes and bonds, municipal bonds, corporate bonds, preferred stock, and common stock.
4. *Mortgage markets* deal with loans on residential, commercial, and industrial real estate, and on farmland, while *consumer credit markets* involve loans on automobiles and appliances, as well as loans for education, vacations, etc.
5. *Primary markets* are markets in which newly issued securities are bought and sold for the first time; while *secondary markets* are those in which existing, outstanding securities are traded among investors.

C. A healthy economy is dependent on efficient transfers of funds from savers to borrowers; that is, the economy depends on *efficient financial markets*.

V. Transfers of capital between savers and those who need funds take place in three different ways.

A. *Direct transfers* occur when businesses sell stocks or bonds directly to savers, without going through any type of intermediary or middleman.

B. Transfers through an *investment banking house* occur when a brokerage firm, such as Merrill Lynch, serves as a middleman. These middlemen help corporations design securities that will be attractive to investors, buy these securities from the corporations, and then resell them to savers in the primary markets.

C. Transfers may occur through a *financial intermediary*, such as a bank or mutual fund, which obtains funds from savers and then issues its own securities in exchange. For example, a saver might deposit dollars to a bank, receiving from it a certificate of deposit, and then the bank might lend the money to a small business in the form of a mortgage loan.
   1. Intermediaries literally create new forms of capital; this transformation of one financial claim into another increases general market efficiency.

D. The following major types of financial intermediaries are identified:
   1. *Commercial banks* are the traditional financial "department stores," serving a wide variety of savers and those with needs for funds.
   2. *Savings and loan associations (S&Ls)* serve individual savers and residential and commercial mortgage borrowers.
      a. One major economic function of the S&Ls is to "create liquidity."
   3. *Mutual savings banks*, found primarily in the Northeast, operate similarly to S&Ls.
   4. *Credit unions* are cooperative associations with members bonded by some common factor, such as the same employer.
   5. *Pension funds* are retirement plans funded by corporations or government agencies for the benefit of their employees.
   6. *Life insurance companies* invest the annual premiums of the insured to provide benefits upon retirement or to the beneficiaries of the insured upon death.
   7. *Mutual funds* pool the funds of investors into various types of securities designed to meet the desired risk-return levels of the investor.

E. Because of the recent changes in the regulation of financial institutions, there has been a blurring of the distinctions among the different types of institutions. This trend has resulted in the creation of huge *financial service corporations*, which own banks, S&Ls, insurance companies, pension fund operations, and mutual funds.
   1. Many large companies, hurt by the 1990-1991 recession, have recently had to consider either selling off financial service units to raise cash or have gone even further in a total dismantling of the "financial supermarkets" they had built in the 1980s.

VI. The stock market is the most important secondary market to financial managers, because it is here that the prices of firms' stocks are established.

A. The *organized security exchanges*, which include the New York Stock Exchange (NYSE), the American Stock Exchange (AMEX), and several regional stock exchanges, have actual physical market locations.

B. The *over-the-counter (OTC) market* consists of brokers and dealers connected by a computer and telephone network, but they have no central location.

C. Information pertaining to transactions on both the exchanges and in the over-the-counter market, as well as information regarding transactions in the bond markets can be found in the financial pages of daily newspapers.

D. The majority of bond transactions occur in the OTC market. Because bond holdings are concentrated in the hands of large financial institutions, it is relatively easy for OTC bond dealers to arrange the trade of large blocks of bonds among the comparatively few bondholders for one of their infrequent trades.

E. Sales of new securities, as well as operations in the secondary markets, are regulated by the *Securities and Exchange Commission (SEC)* and, to a lesser extent, by each of the fifty states.

F. Elements in the regulation of new issues by the SEC include the following:

1. The SEC has jurisdiction over all interstate offerings to the public in amounts of $1,500,000 or more.

2. Securities must be registered with the SEC at least 20 days before they are publicly offered. A *registration statement* and *prospectus* must also be filed.

3. After registration has become effective, the securities may be offered, but must be accompanied by the prospectus, the document summarizing the new security issue and the issuing company. Severe penalties may be imposed on the issuer if misrepresentations are found in its prospectus.

G. Some elements in the regulation of outstanding securities by the SEC include the following:

1. The SEC also regulates all national security exchanges. Firms listed on these exchanges must file annual reports with both the SEC and the exchanges, as well as periodic reports.

2. The SEC has control over *corporate insiders*, and requires officers, directors, and major stockholders to file monthly reports of changes in their holdings in the corporation's stock.

3. The SEC has control over the form of the *proxy* and the way the company uses it to solicit votes.

4. *Margin requirements* control the flow of credit into security transactions by stipulating the percentage of the security's purchase price that must be supplied by the purchaser.

H. The security industry itself realizes the importance of stable markets, sound brokerage firms, and the absence of stock manipulation. Therefore, the various exchanges and trade organizations work closely with the regulatory agencies to police the markets and protect customers.

I. The purpose of regulation is to insure that adequate and accurate information is available concerning securities offered to the public, and to prevent fraud. However, regulators cannot insure that investments will be successful or that investors will exercise good judgment.

VII. **An efficient capital market occurs when stock prices react quickly to new information and when stock prices reflect, at any point in time, all available information about the securities. The following requirements are necessary to insure an efficient capital market:**

A. There must be a reasonably large number of profit-seeking individuals who operate independently of one another.

B. Most investors should have quick and full access to any news about present and potential investments.

C. Investors are rational in that they will act (to buy or sell) quickly to adjust security prices in light of new information.

DEFINITIONAL QUESTIONS

1. A ______________ tax system is one in which tax rates are higher at higher levels of income.

2. ________ ________ may occur when progressive tax rates combine with ___________ to cause a greater portion of each taxpayer's real income to be paid as taxes.

3. The marginal tax rate on the largest corporations, those with taxable incomes exceeding $18,333,333, ___ percent, while that on the wealthiest individuals can go up as high as ___ percent.

4. Interest received on ___________ bonds is generally not subject to federal income taxes. This feature makes them particularly attractive to investors in ______ tax brackets.

5. In order to qualify as a long-term capital gain or loss, an asset must be held for more than ___ months.

6. Gains or losses on assets held less than 12 months are referred to as ______-______ transactions.

7. Interest income received by a corporation is taxed as ___________ income. However, only ___ percent of dividends received from another corporation is subject to taxation.

8. Another important distinction exists between interest and dividends paid by a corporation. Interest payments are ____ _____________, while dividend payments are not.

9. Ordinary corporate operating losses can first be carried back ___ years and then forward ___ years.

10. A firm that refuses to pay dividends in order to help stockholders avoid personal income taxes may be subject to a penalty for _________ _________________ of earnings.

11. A corporation that owns 80 percent or more of another corporation's stock may choose to file _______________ tax returns.

12. The Tax Code permits a corporation (that meets certain restrictions) to be taxed by the owners' personal tax rates and also avoids the impact of __________ taxation of dividends. This type of corporation is called an ___ corporation.

13. _____________ is the accounting process whereby the cost of a productive asset is allocated against the revenues that it helps to produce. The current system for calculating this expense for tax purposes is called ________ for short.

14. The portion of an asset's value which can be depreciated for tax purposes is known as its ______________ _______.

15. A(n) _____________ _____ ________ provides for a direct reduction of taxes, and its purpose is to stimulate business investment.

16. Markets for short-term debt securities are called ________ markets, while markets for long-term debt and equity are called _________ markets.

17. Newly issued securities are initially sold in the __________ markets, while existing, outstanding securities are traded in the __________ market.

18. An institution which issues its own securities in exchange for funds and then uses these funds to purchase other securities is called a ____________ ____________.

19. A(n) ____________ _________ _________ facilitates the transfer of capital between savers and borrowers by acting as a middleman.

20. The two basic types of stock markets are the __________ __________, such as the NYSE, and the ________-________-________ markets.

21. Before a large interstate issue of stock can be sold to the public, it must be ____________ with and approved by the ________.

22. A(n) __________ market is one in which security prices adjust rapidly to new information, reflecting all available information including the risk associated with a particular security.

CONCEPTUAL QUESTIONS

23. The fact that 70 percent of intercorporate dividends received by a corporation is excluded from taxable income has encouraged debt financing over equity financing.

a. True b. False

24. Although financial intermediaries aid in the transferral of funds from savers to borrowers, they must lend at higher rates than individual savers to account for their time and effort.

a. True b. False

25. Since intermediaries can enable savings to do more than just draw interest, they are able to attract more funds.

a. True b. False

26. The purpose of regulation is to ensure that investments will be successful or that investors will exercise good judgment.

a. True b. False

27. Because of the complexity of the investment world today, the efficient capital market requirements are unreachable and unrealistic.

a. True b. False

28. An individual with substantial personal wealth and income is considering the possibility of opening a new business. The business will have a relatively high degree of risk, and losses may be incurred for the first several years. Which legal form of business organization would probably be best?

a. Proprietorship
b. Corporation
c. Partnership
d. S corporation
e. Limited partnership

29. Which of the following statements is most *correct*?

a. In order to avoid double taxation and to escape the frequently higher tax rate applied to capital gains, stockholders generally prefer to have corporations pay dividends rather than to retain their earnings and reinvest the money in the business.
b. Under our current tax laws, when investors pay taxes on their dividend income, they are being subjected to a form of double taxation.
c. The fact that a percentage of the interest received by one corporation, which is paid by another corporation, is excluded from taxable income has encouraged firms to use more debt financing relative to equity financing.
d. If the tax laws stated that \$0.50 out of every \$1.00 of interest paid by a corporation was allowed as a tax-deductible expense, this would probably encourage companies to use more debt financing than they presently do, other things held constant.
e. None of the above statements are true.

30. Which of the following statements is most *correct*?

a. One of the major benefits of well-developed stock markets such as the New York Stock Exchange is that they increase liquidity, which makes it easier for firms to raise capital.
b. In the United States, we have a number of specialized financial institutions, but, according to the text, the trend is toward larger more diversified institutions which offer broad arrays of financial services.
c. Both statements a and b are true.
d. None of the above statements are true.

PROBLEMS

31. In 1993, Wayne Corporation had income from operations of \$385,000, it received interest payments of \$15,000, it paid interest of \$20,000, it received dividends from another corporation of \$10,000, and it paid \$40,000 in dividends to its common stockholders. What is Wayne's 1993 federal income tax?

a. \$122,760
b. \$130,220
c. \$141,700
d. \$155,200
e. \$163,500

32. A firm purchases $10 million of corporate bonds which paid a 16 percent interest rate, or $1.6 million in interest. If the firm's marginal tax rate is 35 percent, what is the after-tax interest yield?

a. 7.36%
b. 8.64%
c. 10.40%
d. 13.89%
e. 14.32%

33. Refer to the previous problem. The firm also invests in the common stock of another company having a 16 percent before-tax dividend yield. What is the after-tax dividend yield?

a. 7.36%
b. 8.64%
c. 10.40%
d. 13.89%
e. 14.32%

34. The Carter Company's taxable income and income tax payments are shown below for 1990 through 1993:

Year	Taxable Income	Tax Payment
1990	$10,000	$1,500
1991	5,000	750
1992	10,000	1,500
1993	5,000	750

Assume that Carter's tax rate for all 4 years was a flat 15 percent; that is, each dollar of taxable income was taxed at 15 percent. In 1994, Carter incurred a loss of $17,000. Using corporate loss carry-back, what is Carter's adjusted tax payment for 1993?

a. $850
b. $750
c. $610
d. $550
e. $450

35. A firm can undertake a new project which will generate a before-tax return of 20 percent or it can invest the same funds in the preferred stock of another company which yields 13 percent before taxes. If the only consideration is which alternative provides the highest relevant (after-tax) return, and the applicable tax rate is 35 percent, should the firm invest in the project or the preferred stock?

a. Preferred stock; its relevant return is 12 percent.
b. Project; its relevant return is 1.36 percentage points higher.
c. Preferred stock; its relevant return is 0.22 percentage points higher.

d. Project; its before-tax return is 20 percent.
e. Either alternative can be chosen; they have the same relevant return.

36. Wharton Wholesalers purchased an asset in 1993 for $100,000 which falls into the MACRS 5-year class life. What is the MACRS depreciation expense in Year 3?

a. $18,950
b. $19,000
c. $19,990
d. $20,900
e. $22,950

37. Carlisle Corporation has $20,000 which it plans to invest in securities. It is choosing between MCI bonds which yield 10 percent, state of Colorado municipal bonds which yield 7 percent, and MCI preferred stock with a dividend yield of 8 percent. Carlisle's corporate tax rate is 25 percent, and 70 percent of its dividends received are tax exempt. What is the after-tax rate of return on the *highest* yielding security?

a. 7.4%
b. 7.0%
c. 7.5%
d. 6.5%
e. 6.0%

ANSWERS AND SOLUTIONS

1. progressive
2. bracket creep; inflation
3. 35; 39.6
4. municipal; high
5. 12
6. short-term
7. ordinary; 30
8. tax deductible
9. 3; 15
10. improper accumulation
11. consolidated
12. double; S
13. depreciation; MACRS
14. depreciable basis
15. investment tax credit
16. money; capital
17. primary; secondary
18. financial intermediary
19. investment banking house
20. organized exchanges; over-the-counter(OTC)
21. registered; SEC
22. efficient

23. b. Debt financing is encouraged by the fact that interest payments are tax deductible while dividend payments are not.

24. b. Because they are able to gain economies of scale, they are able to lend at lower rates than individual savers.

25. a. This statement is correct.

26. b. The purpose of regulation is to insure that adequate and accurate information is available concerning securities offered to the public, and to prevent fraud.

27. b. Because of the efforts of the SEC, which insures that financial information is quickly and accurately provided, and because of the competition among many analysts, financial markets appear to be efficient in pricing securities relative to their risk.

28. d. The S corporation limits the liability of the individual, but permits losses to be deducted against personal income.

29. b. Statement a is incorrect. To avoid double taxation, stockholders would prefer that corporations retain more of their earnings because capital gains are taxed at a maximum tax rate of 28 percent. Statement b is correct. Statement c is incorrect. Debt financing has been encouraged by the fact that interest on debt is tax deductible. Statement d is incorrect. Currently, interest on debt is fully tax deductible; allowing 50 percent of interest to be tax deductible would discourage debt financing. Statement e is incorrect.

30. c. As discussed in the text, both statements a and b are correct.

31. b. The first step is to determine taxable income:

Income from operations	$385,000
Interest income (fully taxable)	15,000
Interest expense (fully deductible)	(20,000)
Dividend income (30% taxable)	3,000
Total taxable income	$383,000

(Note that dividends are paid from after-tax income and do not affect taxable income.)

Based on the current corporate tax table, the tax calculation is as follows:

Tax = $113,900 + ($383,000 - $335,000)(0.34) = $113,900 + $16,320 = $130,220.

32. c. The after-tax yield (or dollar return) equals the before-tax yield (or dollar return) multiplied by one minus the effective tax rate, or

$$\text{AT Yield} = \text{Pretax Yield}(1 - T).$$

Therefore,

AT Yield = 16%(1 - 35%) = 16%(1 - 0.35) = 16%(0.65) = 10.40%.

33. e. Since the dividends are received by a corporation, only 30 percent are taxable, and the Effective T = Tax rate x 30 percent:

$$\begin{aligned} AT &= BT(1 - \text{Effective T}) \\ &= 16\%[1 - 35\%(30\%)] \\ &= 16\%(1 - 0.105) \\ &= 16\%(0.895) \\ &= 14.32\%. \end{aligned}$$

34. e.

Year	Taxable Income	Tax Payment	Adjusted Taxable Income	Adjusted Tax Payment
1990	$10,000	$1,500	$10,000	$1,500
1991	5,000	750	0	0
1992	10,000	1,500	0	0
1993	5,000	750	3,000	450

The carry-back can only go back 3 years. Thus, there was no adjustment made in 1990. After $5,000 of adjustment in 1991 and $10,000 in 1992, there was a $2,000 loss remaining to apply to 1993. The 1993 adjusted tax payment is $3,000(0.15) = $450. Thus, Carter received a total of $2,550 in tax refunds after the adjustment.

35. b. The project is fully taxable; thus its after-tax return is as follows:

$$AT = 20\%(1 - 0.35) = 20\%(0.65) = 13.0\%.$$

But only 30 percent of the preferred stock dividends are taxable; thus its after-tax yield is

$$\begin{aligned} AT &= 13\%[(1 - 0.35(0.30)] \\ &= 13\%(1 - 0.105) \\ &= 13\%(0.895) = 11.64\%. \end{aligned}$$

Therefore, the new project should be chosen since its after-tax return is 1.36 percentage points higher.

36. b. First, note that the depreciable basis is the cost of $100,000.

Then, apply the MACRS recovery percentages for each year:

Year	Recovery Percentage	Depreciation Expense
1	20	$ 20,000
2	32	32,000
3	19	19,000
4	12	12,000
5	11	11,000
6	6	6,000
		$100,000

37. c. AT yield on Colorado bond = 7%.
AT yield on MCI bond = 10%(1 - T) = 10%(1 - 0.25) = 7.5%.
AT yield on MCI Preferred = 8%(1 - 0.3(T)) = 8%(1 - 0.075) = 7.4%.

CHAPTER 3
FINANCIAL INSTITUTIONS

OVERVIEW

In this chapter, we focus on the largest of the financial intermediaries, the commercial banking system. However, to understand the crucial role that commercial banks play in our economic system the functions of the central bank, the Federal Reserve System, are examined. In addition, how the Fed conducts its monetary policy through the commercial banking system, to influence the nation's money supply and the level of interest rates throughout the economy, is discussed. Specific monetary tools available to the Fed and their effectiveness are reviewed as well. Next, we examine the process by which commercial banks (and other depository institutions) "create money" through deposit expansion. The banking system's power to create money via the creation of demand deposits sets it apart from most financial intermediaries. All member deposit institutions are required to hold reserves against their deposits at the Fed. By affecting the reserves of commercial banks, the Federal Reserve System attempts to control the economic health of the nation. We also briefly take a look at bank balance sheets and banking regulation. We also examine the continuing bailout of the savings and loan industry--the crisis in the S&L industry is one example of the many disruptive changes occurring in many segments of the U.S. financial system. Finally, we stress some recent trends and developments within the commercial banking system, including the impact of globalization.

OUTLINE

I. **Of the number of regulatory agencies which have been developed to control the banking system and its ability to create credit, the Federal Reserve System is the most important. The Fed attempts to influence the ability of banks to create credit (and hence to influence the money supply) principally by increasing or reducing the reserves available to the banking system.**

A. The real decision-making authority in the Federal Reserve System is given to the Fed's seven-member *Board of Governors of the Federal Reserve System* in Washington, D.C.

B. All national banks are legally required to be members of the system.

1. Approximately 10 percent of all state banks are voluntary members of the Federal Reserve System.

C. The *Federal Open Market Committee (FOMC)* has the responsibility over open-market operations.
   1. *Open-market operations* are the purchase and sale of U.S. government securities conducted through the Federal Reserve Bank of New York.
   2. Open-market operations are the most effective monetary tool available to the Fed.
   3. The FOMC's committee of twelve members is at the heart of the Fed's powers.

D. By affecting reserves in the system, the Board of Governors can influence the money supply and hence interest rates. The principal tools of control are *changes in the reserve requirement, changes in the discount rate, and open-market operations.*
   1. The Federal Reserve System requires all deposit institutions to hold reserves against their deposits. The Fed, however, is reluctant to use the reserve requirement as an active tool of monetary policy because it is too powerful an instrument to be used in "fine tuning" the economy.
   2. The *discount rate* is the rate of interest the Fed charges to institutions which borrow reserves.
      a. The Federal Reserve System views these loans as a temporary mechanism for the adjustment of the institution's reserve position.
      b. Use of these funds for profit making is discouraged.
      c. Since these borrowings are considered a privilege and not a right, pressure is exerted by the Fed to limit borrowing.
         (1) Some banks, particularly large banks, avoid the Fed altogether as a source of credit by borrowing instead in the *Federal (Fed) funds market*, a market where banks borrow from other banks for short periods of time.
         (2) The *Federal funds rate* is the prevailing interest rate in the Federal (Fed) funds market.
      d. Although the discount rate was initially considered to be the principal instrument of monetary control authorized by Congress, evidence over time indicates otherwise because it has frequently *lagged behind* other short-term rates.
      e. Even though the discount rate is not the active monetary policy tool that the Fed's founders envisioned, announcements of changes in the discount rate have an important psychological effect in the financial community.
   3. The purchase and sale of government securities, called open-market operations, is the most powerful and useful instrument of monetary policy available to the Federal Reserve.
      a. Unlike changes in the reserve requirement, which trigger massive changes in bank reserves, purchases and sales of securities may be used in varying amounts to fine tune the economy.
      b. Open-market operations are an effective means of increasing or decreasing bank reserves. If these operations were purely cash transactions, they would have no effect on the banks' reserves;

however, when security dealers write or deposit checks as they buy and sell securities, the reserves of their banks are affected.

c. The purchase of government securities by the Fed increases the money supply and puts into motion events which lower interest rates, encourage additional borrowing and spending, and, thus, benefit a depressed economy.

d. The sale of securities by the Fed to brokers, who write checks on their bank accounts, reduces the ability of banks to lend and, therefore, results in higher interest rates, which discourage others from borrowing. The reduction in debt-financed spending is desirable for an economy faced with excessive inflationary expansion.

E. Banks are the most important element in our financial system for two reasons.

1. Demand deposits are money and banks can create demand deposits through the extension of credit in the form of loans.

a. In the United States, demand deposits, not currency, are the most important form of money.

b. Commercial banks are at the heart of the nation's financial system because of their ability to create money.

2. The Federal Reserve Board utilizes the banking system to affect the money supply and, therefore, interest rates.

a. The *money supply* consists of two elements: currency and bank deposits.

F. The banking system's ability to expand depends on the existence of excess reserves. By lending excess reserves, banks "create money." One can use the following formula to determine the maximum possible expansion in deposits:

$$\text{Maximum deposit expansion} = \frac{\text{Initial reserve infusion}}{\text{Reserve requirement}}.$$

G. Three factors could create "leakages" reducing the maximum deposit-expansion potential within the commercial banking system.

1. If customers decide to keep some of their newly created demand deposits as cash rather than in the bank, there will be less excess reserves available to lend.

2. The bank may decide, as a matter of policy, to keep some excess reserves in the bank in case of unexpected losses.

3. There may be a scarcity of qualified borrowers resulting in less than the entire excess reserves being lent out.

II. **Commercial banks are one of the largest of the U.S. financial institutions in terms of asset size, further demonstrating the importance of banks in our economy.**

A. The U.S. banking system is quite different from that of other countries, which usually have a few large banks with nationwide operations. In the U.S., there are approximately 11,500 separately chartered commercial banks, with restrictive banking regulations that limit the areas in which they may operate.

B. Another unique feature of the U.S. banking system is the dual (state and federal government) chartering system.

C. Many banks have become virtual financial supermarkets, offering a wide variety of services.

1. A *bank holding company* is an organizational structure which owns banks and nonbank subsidiaries. They were originally designed to circumvent bank regulations, but their activities are now restricted by the Bank Holding Company Acts of 1956 and 1970.

D. The banking system changed dramatically during the 1980s. A number of Congressional acts were passed which affected banking.

1. The *Depository Institutions Deregulation and Monetary Control Act (DIDMCA)* eliminated deposit rate and loan rate ceilings, removed differences between Fed member and non-member banks, and increased deposit insurance limits.
2. The *Garn-St. Germain Act* allowed banks to buy failing thrifts.
3. The *Competitive Equality in Banking Act (CEBA)* attempted to stem the growth of bank-like subsidiaries of companies such as Sears Roebuck.
4. The *Financial Institutions Reform, Recovery, and Enforcement Act (FIRREA)* of 1989 brought about a major restructuring of the thrift industry.

E. Deposits are a bank's primary source of funds and a major component of the economy's money supply. There are three types of deposits: *demand, savings, and time deposits.*

1. Demand deposits are deposits made by individuals, businesses, and government units that are available on demand. Demand deposits are the major source of liquidity for all economic units.
2. Savings and time deposits are the most important source of bank funds today. Savings accounts generally pay close to market interest rates and offer limited transaction services.
3. Time deposits offer higher rates but do not allow transactions. The most common time deposit is a CD, or certificate of deposit, which is a receipt for funds deposited in an institution for a specified time and interest rate.

F. Banks may choose to finance part of their assets with borrowed funds.

1. The primary source of borrowed funds is the *Federal funds market*, which is essentially the lending of excess reserves from one member bank to another member bank that has a temporary need for reserves.

2. A *repurchase agreement (or "repo")* is another source of short-term borrowing for a bank, in which the repo is a collateralized loan by one financial institution to another financial institution.
3. Banks may also borrow directly from the Federal Reserve or obtain funds by selling long-term bonds. However, banks are restricted in what they can do with funds obtained as loans from the Fed, and, consequently, they prefer not to borrow from the Fed unless absolutely necessary.

G. A bank's capital, which consists of common stock and retained earnings, provides a cushion to depositors from losses.
1. The typical commercial bank has only 5 to 10 percent of its assets financed by capital, while corporations are usually not considered financially sound unless at least 50 percent of their total financing has been provided by equity. Consequently, banks have much slimmer margins for error, and that by itself, is probably a good reason why banks should be subject to relatively strict regulations, especially since taxpayers bear the ultimate risk when banks fail.

H. In addition to vault cash, the cash account includes "items in process of collection" as well as funds which are required by law to be kept on deposit at the district Federal Reserve Bank.
1. Cash today (1993) accounts for less than 7 percent of a bank's total assets. This percentage is down substantially from earlier periods, signifying that banks have become more efficient cash managers.

I. The purchase of securities for investment purposes is a use of funds.
1. These securities are required by law to be of the highest investment quality.
2. State or other political subdivisions in the bank's geographic area issue the largest percentage of these securities.
3. The bank's investment portfolio serves to provide liquidity in case more required reserves are needed.

J. Banks are the major source of short-term credit for the business sector.
1. Because the greater proportion of funds now comes from time and savings deposits, banks are more willing to provide intermediate loans (3- to 7-year) maturities.
2. Recently, there has been a shift in bank assets--away from loans and toward investment in securities--due primarily to changes in the regulatory environment of banks which has contributed to the credit crunch of the early 1990s.

III. Savings and loan associations, known as "thrifts," originally began as institutions which accepted members' savings and then made mortgage loans to help people in the community buy houses.

A. Today, thrifts have no unique economic role because of the growth of mortgage-backed securities, through which institutional investors pump money into the home loan market and because other lenders are making loans directly to consumers.

B. Thrifts have been in trouble for the past two decades. Greed, political disputes, and volatile interest rates caused major problems in the industry.

1. When interest rates rose dramatically, loan interest rates did not keep up with deposit rates.

2. In 1982, Congress passed legislation which allowed S&Ls to take on nontraditional thrift investment activities like business loans and ownership of real estate projects.

3. Weak thrifts advertised high interest rates to obtain cash for risky assets; these high rates raised the entire industry's cost of funds.

4. The S&Ls' deposit insurance contributed greatly to the problem by adding to the reckless way money left some of these institutions.

5. By 1986 the institutions' insurance fund, the FSLIC, ran out of money. Congress approved some aid, but it was a case of too little, too late.

6. Congress ordered a complete reorganization of the thrift industry in 1989. The *Office of Thrift Supervision (OTS)* is responsible for taking over failing S&Ls and then handing them over to the *Resolution Trust Corporation (RTC)*, created to sell foreclosed property. The *Resolution Financing Corporation (RFC)* was created to raise the billions of dollars needed to pay off depositors in failed thrifts.

7. Currently (1993), low short-term interest rates have boosted the profitability of surviving S&Ls by widening their *interest-rate spreads*, the difference between the interest rate earned on loans and/or securities and the rate it pays, on average, to depositors.

IV. In recent years, questions have surfaced regarding the long-term strength of the U.S. financial system. The October 1987 stock market crash, the large losses that banks have incurred on a variety of loans, the S&L crisis, and the real estate market slump have signified profound changes in the economic environment of our financial institutions.

A. While it is difficult to pinpoint reasons for much of the chaos in our financial system, analysts have pointed to several reasons: bankers who are overly ambitious in lending to real estate developers, "takeover artists," and expansion-minded corporations; regulators who let things get out of control; and huge federal budget and trade deficits.

B. Because of increasing competition, increasing bad debts, higher deposit insurance premiums, tougher regulation, and more stringent capital adequacy regulation, commercial banks are restructuring themselves before they become victims of unwanted takeovers.

1. *The Federal Deposit Insurance Corporation Improvement Act (FDICIA) of 1991* effectively reversed the deregulatory banking climate of the 1980s. While the Fed was *easing credit* in 1991, this legislation virtually required banks to *tighten credit*.
2. As a result of risk-based capital standards, banks have shifted the composition of their assets from higher-risk weights to lower-risk weights.
3. Currently (1993), banks have been able to improve their profitability due to fewer bad loans and higher net interest margins.

C. Capital markets are becoming integrated into a global capital market, with universal banks competing directly with specialist banks.

D. *Universal (or global) banks* combine both commercial and investment banking services to their customers. These banks can cross-sell a wider range of products and can offer the customer a full range of products, thus encouraging customer loyalty. True universal banks exist only in Germany and Switzerland.
   1. Disadvantages include: Conflicts of interest, lower quality of service than that offered by specialist banks, and difficulty with coordination.

E. *Specialist banks* act only as investment banks, concentrating on the origination, distribution, and trading of securities. Examples would be the U.S. investment banking houses.

F. In order to survive, the U.S. commercial banking system must change. Different types of banks are likely to emerge. Trends influencing our commercial banking system in the next several years include:
   1. Constraints on asset growth
   2. Continued fierce competition
   3. An increase in nationwide branching
   4. A continued high level of banking mergers

DEFINITIONAL QUESTIONS

1. Of all financial institutions, the __________ ________ _______ is one of the largest in terms of asset size.

2. By extending credit in the form of loans, banks can create __________ ________.

3. The __________ __________ __________ affects the money supply and hence __________ __________ through the banking system.

4. ________ ________ are the major source of liquidity for all economic units.

5. The market in which excess reserves are lent by one bank to another bank which has a temporary shortage of reserves is called the ________ ________ ________.

6. The principal tools of monetary control that the Fed has available are changes in the _______ ____________, changes in the ________ rate, and ____-______ ____________.

7. Banks create money by lending excess __________.

8. __________ limit the deposit expansion potential within the commercial banking system.

9. The __________ attempts to influence the ability of banks to create credit (and hence to influence the money supply) principally by increasing or reducing the __________ available to the banking system.

10. ________-________ ____________ are the purchase and sale of U.S. government securities conducted through the Federal Reserve Bank of New York.

11. The ________ ________ ________ ________ has the responsibility over open market operations.

12. The __________ __________ is the rate of interest that the Fed charges to institutions which borrow reserves.

13. The most powerful instrument of monetary policy available to the Fed is ___________-__________ ____________.

14. ___________ _____ _______ _____________ originally began as institutions which accepted members' savings and then made mortgage loans to help people in the community buy houses.

15. Thrifts have been in trouble for the past decade. ________, __________ __________, and __________ __________ __________ caused major problems in the industry.

16. In recent years, questions have surfaced regarding the long-term strength of the U.S. financial system. The October 1987 __________ __________ __________, the large losses that banks have incurred on a variety of loans, the ________ ________, and the ______ ________ market slump have signified profound changes in the economic environment of our financial institutions.

17. __________ banks act only as investment banks, concentrating on the origination, distribution, and trading of securities.

18. Capital markets are becoming integrated into a __________ capital market, with _________ banks competing directly with specialist banks.

19. The _______ _________ consists of two elements: currency and bank deposits.

20. Deposits are a bank's primary source of funds and a major component of the economy's money supply. There are three types of deposits: ______, _______, and ______ deposits.

CONCEPTUAL QUESTIONS

21. Commercial banks are at the heart of the nation's financial system because of their ability to create money.

a. True b. False

22. The most common type of time deposit is a certificate of deposit, which is a receipt for funds deposited in an institution with a specified interest rate and for an unlimited period of time.

a. True b. False

23. The Federal funds market is a market where Federal certificates of deposit are sold.

a. True b. False

24. There is no limit to which deposits can expand.

a. True b. False

25. Loans from the Fed are usually long term in nature since they are used by most banks to obtain funds for investing.

a. True b. False

26. Although the discount rate was initially considered to be the principal instrument of monetary control authorized by Congress, evidence over time indicates otherwise because it has frequently lagged behind other short-term rates.

a. True b. False

27. Which of the following statements is *correct* in regards to the deposit expansion potential of the commercial banking system?

a. If a portion of newly credited demand deposits are kept in the form of cash, there would be less excess reserves to lend.
b. A bank may choose to keep some excess reserves in case of unexpected contingencies, thereby limiting the expansion potential.
c. There is no limit to its expansion.
d. Answers a and b are both correct.
e. None of the above is correct.

28. Which of the following statements is most *correct*?

a. Changes in the discount rate, the rate of interest the Fed charges to institutions which borrow reserves, is the most effective monetary tool available to the Fed.
b. The Fed actively uses the reserve requirement as a tool of monetary policy because it is an effective instrument in "fine tuning" the economy.
c. All state and national banks are legally required to be members of the Federal Reserve system.
d. The Board of Governors of the Federal Reserve System has the responsibility over open-market operations.
e. All of the statements are false.

29. Which of the following statements is most *correct*?

a. "Leakages" increase the maximum deposit-expansion potential within the commercial banking system by increasing the denominator of the maximum deposit expansion formula, reserve requirement.
b. In the United States, currency is the most important form of money.
c. One of the unique features of the U.S. banking system is the dual (state and federal government) chartering system.
d. A repurchase agreement, a collateralized loan by one financial institution to another financial institution, is one source of short-term borrowing available to a bank.
e. Both statements c and d are correct.

ANSWERS

1. commercial banking system
2. demand deposits
3. Federal Reserve System (Board of Governors); interest rates
4. Demand deposits
5. Federal funds market
6. reserve requirement; discount; open-market transactions
7. reserves
8. Leakages
9. Fed; reserves
10. Open-market operations
11. Federal Open Market Committee
12. discount rate
13. open-market operations
14. Savings and loan associations
15. Greed; political disputes; volatile interest rates
16. stock market crash; S&L crisis; real estate
17. Specialist
18. global; universal
19. money supply
20. demand; savings; time

21. a. This statement is correct.

22. b. Certificates of deposit are deposited for a specified period of time.

23. b. In the Federal funds market banks borrow from other banks for short periods of time.

24. b. The maximum deposit expansion equals the initial reserve infusion divided by the reserve requirement.

25. b. The Federal Reserve System views these loans as a temporary mechanism for the adjustment of the institution's reserve position; therefore, they are not long term.

26. a. This statement is correct.

27. d. Both statements a and b are correct.

28. e. Statement a is false; open-market operations are the most effective monetary tool available to the Fed. Statement b is false; changes in the reserve requirement are too powerful an instrument to "fine tune" the economy. Statement c is false; only national banks are legally required to be members of the Federal Reserve system. Statement d is false; the Federal Open Market Committee (FOMC) has responsibility for open-market operations. Thus, statement e is correct.

29. e. Statement a is false; leakages reduce the deposit-expansion potential within the commercial banking system. Statement b is false; in the U.S. demand deposits are the most important form of money. Statements c and d are both correct; thus, statement e is the correct choice.

CHAPTER 4
INTEREST RATES

OVERVIEW

One of the most important factors affecting the transfer of funds from savers to borrowers is interest rates. The interest rate is the price paid for the use of money, and it is determined by the combination of producers' expected rates of return on invested capital and consumers' time preferences for consumption. Many factors go into making up the actual interest rate. It is composed of the real, or risk-free rate, plus premiums to compensate investors for expected inflation, default risk, lack of liquidity, and maturity risk.

The term structure of interest rates is the relationship between long- and short-term interest rates, and this relationship, when plotted, produces a yield curve. The slope of the yield curve is important to corporate treasurers, who must make decisions regarding long-term and short-term borrowing. Since interest rates are very difficult to predict, sound financial policy calls for using a mix of securities that will enable a firm to survive in any interest rate environment.

OUTLINE

I. **Capital in a free economy is allocated through the price system. The interest rate is the price paid to borrow debt capital.**

   A. The interest rate paid to savers depends on four fundamental factors:
   1. The rate of return producers expect to earn on invested capital, which is based on production opportunities.
   2. Consumers'/savers' time preferences for current versus future consumption.
   3. The riskiness of the loan.
   4. The expected rate of inflation.

II. **The level of interest rates is determined not only by the Fed's monetary policy, but also by broader market forces--the supply of and demand for funds, risk factors, inflation, and overall investor expectations about the future.**

   A. The demand for investment capital is determined by production opportunities available, and the rates of return producers can expect to earn on invested capital.
   1. The supply of investment capital depends on consumers' time preferences for current versus future consumption.

B. The *equilibrium rate of return* is that rate which is required to induce savers to invest and, simultaneously, it is the rate which borrowers are willing to pay.

C. Long-term interest rates primarily reflect long-run expectations for the economy, especially inflation, while short-term interest rates are responsive to current economic conditions and the Fed's monetary policy moves. Thus, *short-term rates are more volatile than long-term rates.*

III. **The nominal interest rate on a debt security, k, is composed of the real risk-free rate of interest, k*, plus several premiums that reflect inflation (IP), default risk (DRP), lack of liquidity (LP), and maturity risk (MRP). While the nominal rate includes inflation, the real rate of interest is adjusted to remove the effects of inflation.**

A. The *nominal rate of interest (k)* can be expressed as $k = k^* + IP + DRP + LP + MRP$, where the values of the various premiums vary among debt securities.

B. The *real risk-free rate of interest (k^*)* is the interest rate that would exist on a riskless security if no inflation were expected. This rate may be thought of as the rate of interest on short-term U.S. Treasury securities in an inflation-free world.

1. This rate changes over time depending on the rate of return corporations and other borrowers can expect to earn on productive assets.
2. It will also vary in response to people's time preferences for current versus future consumption.
3. While difficult to measure precisely, most experts think the real risk-free rate in the U.S. has fluctuated in recent years from 1 to 4 percent.

C. The *nominal risk-free rate of interest (k_{RF})* is the real risk-free rate (k^*) plus a premium for expected inflation (IP): $k_{RF} = k^* + IP$. The actual rate of interest on short-term Treasury bills is generally used to measure k_{RF} since it is free of most risks.

1. When the term "risk-free rate" is used without a modifier, people generally mean the nominal rate, and this convention is followed in the text.
2. In general, we use the *T-bill rate* to approximate the *short-term* risk-free rate, while the *T-bond rate* is used to approximate the *long-term* risk-free rate.

D. The *inflation premium (IP)*, which is the average inflation rate expected over the life of the security, compensates investors for the expected loss of purchasing power.

1. Thus, for a default-free U.S. Treasury bill, the actual interest rate charged would be $k_{T\text{-bill}} = k^* + IP$.

2. Note that inflation built into interest rates is the average rate of inflation *expected in the future*, not the rate experienced in the past.
3. There has been a high correlation between inflation and interest rates over the years, although not a perfect one since the relationship is built upon expectations.
4. Expectations for future inflation are closely related to, although not perfectly correlated with, recent inflation experience.

E. The *default risk premium (DRP)* compensates investors for the risk that a borrower will default, or not pay the interest or the principal, on a loan.

1. Corporate bonds are rated according to their perceived default risk. *Bond ratings* range from Aaa or AAA for the most financially sound companies to D for those firms already in bankruptcy.
2. The difference between the quoted interest rate on a Treasury security and that on a corporate bond *with similar maturity, liquidity, and other features* is the premium added to the corporate bond to compensate for the possibility of default.

F. A security which can be sold and quickly converted into cash at a "fair market value" is said to be *liquid*. A *liquidity premium (LP)* compensates investors for securities that are not liquid.

1. Most financial assets are considered more liquid than real assets. However, less actively traded securities are said to have a *"thin market"* and are not very liquid.

G. Long-term securities are more price sensitive to interest rate changes than are short-term securities. Therefore, a *maturity risk premium (MRP)* is added to longer-term securities to compensate investors for interest rate risk.

1. *Interest rate risk* is the risk of incurring capital losses on a fixed-rate debt instrument due to changing interest rates over time. Two important points should be noted:
   a. Interest rate risk affects *all* fixed-rate debt securities.
   b. The problem arises when you want to trade a bond *prior to its maturity*. You are likely to have either a capital gain or loss on the investment. If you could hold the security until maturity, the assumption is that you would get back the original investment.
2. The longer the term to maturity, the more the security is subject to interest rate risk, and consequently, the higher the maturity risk premium.
3. Over time, the maturity risk premium varies, rising when interest rates are more volatile and uncertain and falling when interest rates are more stable.
4. While long-term bonds have interest rate risk, short-term bonds are subject to *reinvestment rate risk*. A decline in interest rates will lead to lower income when short-term bonds mature and funds are reinvested at the lower rate.

IV. **The term structure of interest rates is the relationship between long- and short-term interest rates on debt securities. Corporate treasurers and investors need to understand how long- and short-term rates are related to each other and what causes shifts in their relative positions.**

A. When plotted, this relationship produces a *yield curve.* The yield curve changes both in position and in slope over time.

B. Yield curves have different shapes depending on expected inflation rates and supply and demand conditions.
1. The *"normal" yield curve* is *upward sloping,* generally signifying that investors expect inflation to remain steady or increase in the future.
2. An *"inverted,"* or *downward sloping, yield curve* signifies that investors expect inflation to decrease.

C. Several theories have been proposed to explain the shape of the yield curve. The three major theories are (1) the market segmentation theory, (2) the liquidity preference theory, and (3) the expectations theory.

D. The *market segmentation theory* states that each lender and each borrower has a preferred maturity. Thus, the slope of the yield curve depends on supply and demand conditions in the long-term and short-term markets. The yield curve could, at any time, be flat, upward sloping, or downward sloping.
1. An upward-sloping yield curve would occur when there was a large supply of short-term funds relative to demand, but a shortage of long-term funds. A downward-sloping yield curve would indicate just the reverse.
2. A flat curve would indicate a balance between the two markets.

E. The *liquidity preference theory* states that the yield curve tends to be upward sloping for two reasons:
1. Investors prefer to hold short-term securities and accept lower yields because they are more liquid. They can be converted to cash with little danger of loss of principal.
2. Borrowers prefer long-term debt because short-term debt exposes them to the risk of having to repay the debt under adverse conditions; consequently, they are willing to pay a higher rate for long-term funds than short-term funds.

F. The *expectations theory* states that the yield curve depends upon expectations about future inflation rates. If the rate of inflation is expected to decline, the yield curve will be downward sloping, and if the rate of inflation is expected to increase, the yield curve will be upward sloping.

G. All three theories have merit; that is, actual yield curves are determined by all three sets of factors.

V. **Other factors influence the general level of interest rates. The four most important ones are (1) Federal Reserve policy, (2) the level of the federal budget deficit, (3) the foreign trade balance, and (4) the level of business activity.**

A. The money supply has a major effect on the level of economic activity and the inflation rate. In the U.S. the Federal Reserve System controls the money supply.
   1. To stimulate the economy the Fed takes steps to increase growth in the money supply, while when the Fed tightens monetary policy it reduces the money supply.
   2. During periods when the Fed is actively intervening in the markets, the yield curve will be distorted. Short-term rates will be temporarily "too high" if the Fed is tightening credit and "too low" if it is easing credit.
   3. Long-term rates are not affected as much by Fed intervention, except to the extent that such intervention affects expectations for long-term inflation.

B. When the federal government spends more than it takes in from tax revenues, it runs a *deficit*, and the deficit must be covered either by borrowing or by printing money.
   1. The larger the federal deficit, other things held constant, the higher the level of interest rates.
   2. Whether long- or short-term rates are affected more depends on how the deficit is financed, so we cannot state, in general, how deficits will affect the slope of the yield curve.

C. Businesses and individuals in the U.S. buy from and sell to people and firms in other countries. If we buy more than we sell, we are said to be running a *foreign trade deficit*.
   1. When trade deficits occur, they must be financed, and the main source of financing is debt.
   2. The larger our trade deficit, the more we must borrow, and as we increase our borrowing, this drives up interest rates.
   3. The existence of a deficit trade balance limits the Fed's ability to combat a recession through lower interest rates.

D. During recessions when both the demand for money and the inflation rate tend to fall, and the Federal Reserve tends to increase the money supply in an effort to stimulate the economy, there is a tendency for interest rates to decline.
   1. Short-term rates experience sharper declines than long-term rates.
      a. The Fed operates mainly in the short-term sector, and hence, its intervention has a major effect here.
      b. Long-term rates reflect the average expected inflation rate over the next 20 to 30 years, and that expectation generally

does not change much, even when the current inflation rate is low because of a recession.

VI. **The level of interest rates also has a significant effect on stock prices.**

A. Because interest is a cost, the higher the rate of interest, the lower a firm's profits, other things held constant.

B. Interest rates affect the level of economic activity, hence business profits.

C. Additionally, stocks and bonds compete in the marketplace for investors' capital. A rise in interest rates will increase the rate of return on bonds, causing investors to transfer funds from the stock market to the bond market. The resultant selling of stocks lowers stock prices.

VII. **Interest rate movements have a significant impact on business decisions.**

A. Wrong decisions, such as using short-term debt to finance long-term projects just before interest rates rise, can be very costly.

B. It is extremely difficult, if not impossible, to predict future interest rate levels.

C. Sound financial policy therefore calls for using a mix of long-term and short-term debt, and equity, so that the firm can survive in almost any interest rate environment.

   1. The optimal financial policy depends in an important way on the nature of the firm's assets. The easier it is to sell off assets and thus to pay off debts, the more appropriate it is to use large amounts of short-term debt.

DEFINITIONAL QUESTIONS

1. The ________ ________ is the price paid for borrowed capital.

2. The supply of investment capital depends on consumers' time preferences for ________ versus __________ consumption.

3. The ________ ________ - ________ ________ of ________ is the interest rate that would exist on a riskless security if no inflation were expected.

4. The __________ rate of interest is the real risk-free rate of interest plus premiums to compensate investors for inflation and various types of risk.

5. The risk that a borrower will not pay the interest or principal on a loan is ____________ risk.

6. ___ ___ ___________ bonds have zero default risk.

7. A(n) ___________ premium is added to the real risk-free rate to protect investors against loss of purchasing power.

8. The nominal rate of interest is determined by adding a(n) __________ premium plus a(n) __________ risk premium plus a(n) __________ premium plus a(n) __________ risk premium to the real risk-free rate of return.

9. The relationship between short-term and long-term interest rates is called the __________ __________ of interest rates, while the resulting plotted curve is called the ______ curve.

10. The "normal" yield curve has a(n) ______ slope.

11. Three theories proposed to explain the term structure of interest rates are the market __________ theory, the __________ preference theory and the __________ theory.

12. Because interest rates fluctuate, a sound financial policy calls for using a mix of _______- and _______-_______ debt, and _______.

13. The __________ _____ ___ _______ is that rate which is required to induce savers to invest and, simultaneously, it is the rate which borrowers are willing to pay.

14. A security which can be sold and quickly converted into cash at a "fair market value" is said to be _________.

15. ________ ____ _____ is the risk of incurring capital losses on a fixed-rate debt instrument due to changing interest rates over time.

16. While long-term bonds are subject to interest rate risk, short-term bonds are subject to ___________ _____ _____.

17. A(n) __________, or __________-__________, yield curve signifies that investors expect inflation to decrease.

18. The __________ __________ theory states that the yield curve tends to be upward sloping because investors prefer to hold short-term securities and borrowers prefer long-term debt.

19. When the federal government spends more than it takes in from tax revenues, it runs a(n) _______, which must be covered either by borrowing or printing money.

20. Businesses and individuals in the U.S. buy from and sell to people and firms in other countries. If we buy more than we sell, we are said to be running a(n) _________ _______ _________.

CONCEPTUAL QUESTIONS

21. If management is sure that the economy is at the peak of a boom and is about to enter a recession, a firm which needs to borrow money should probably use short-term rather than long-term debt.

    a. True b. False

22. Long-term interest rates reflect expectations about future inflation. Inflation has varied greatly from year to year over the last 10 years, and, as a result, long-term rates have fluctuated more than short-term rates.

    a. True b. False

23. Suppose the Fed takes actions which lowers expectations for inflation this year by 1 percentage point, but these same actions raise expectations for inflation in Years 2, and thereafter, by 2 percentage points. Other things held constant, the yield curve becomes steeper.

    a. True b. False

24. Assume interest rates on 30-year government and corporate bonds were as follows: T-bond = 6.2%; AAA = 7.4%; A = 7.9%; and BBB = 8.2%. The differences in rates among these issues are caused primarily by:

    a. Tax effects.
    b. Default risk differences.
    c. Maturity risk differences.
    d. Inflation differences.
    e. Both statements b and d.

25. Which of the following statements is most *correct*?

    a. Suppose financial institutions, such as savings and loans, were required by law to make long-term, fixed interest rate mortgages, but, at the same time, they were largely restricted, in terms of their capital sources, to taking deposits that could be withdrawn on demand. Under these conditions, these financial institutions should prefer a "normal" yield curve to an "inverted" yield curve.
    b. You are considering establishing a new firm, the University Assistance Company (UAC). UAC would obtain funds in the short-term money market and write long-term mortgage loans to students so that they might buy condominiums rather than rent. A downward sloping yield curve, if it persisted over time, would be best for UAC.
    c. The yield curve is upward sloping, or normal, if short-term rates are higher than long-term rates.
    d. All of the above statements are correct.
    e. Only statements a and b are correct.

PROBLEMS

26. You have determined the following data:

Real risk-free rate (k*) = 2%
Inflation premium = 4%
Default risk premium = 2%
Liquidity premium = 1%
Maturity risk premium = 1%

Assume that the rate of inflation is expected to be constant and a liquid market exists *only* for very short-term Treasury securities. What is the nominal risk-free rate?

a. 5%
b. 6%
c. 7%
d. 8%
e. 9%

27. Refer to Problem 26. What is the interest rate on long-term Treasury securities, or T-bonds? (Hint: Remember that a liquid market exists *only* for very short-term Treasury securities.)

a. 5%
b. 6%
c. 7%
d. 8%
e. 9%

28. Assume that a 3-year Treasury note has no maturity risk premium or liquidity premium and that the real risk-free rate of interest is 2 percent. A 3-year T-note carries a yield to maturity of 8 percent. If the expected inflation rate is 4 percent next year and 6 percent the year after, what is the implied expected inflation rate for the third year?

a. 5%
b. 7%
c. 8%
d. 9%
e. 10%

29. Assume that the real risk-free rate is 3 percent, that the expected inflation rate during Year 2 is 4 percent, and that 2-year T-bonds yield 6.5 percent. If the maturity risk premium is zero, what is the inflation during Year 1?

a. 3.0%
b. 5.0%
c. 3.5%
d. 4.0%
e. 2.5%

30. Refer to Problem 29. Given the same information, what is the rate of return on 1-year T-bonds?

a. 5.5%
b. 6.0%
c. 5.0%
d. 6.5%
e. 4.5%

ANSWERS AND SOLUTIONS

1. interest rate
2. current; future
3. real risk-free rate; interest
4. nominal
5. default
6. U.S. Treasury
7. inflation
8. inflation; default; liquidity; maturity
9. term structure; yield
10. upward
11. segmentation; liquidity; expectations
12. short; long-term; equity
13. equilibrium rate of return
14. liquid
15. interest rate risk
16. reinvestment rate risk
17. inverted; downward-sloping
18. liquidity preference
19. deficit
20. foreign trade deficit

21. a. The firm should borrow short-term until interest rates drop due to the recession, then go long-term. Predicting interest rates is extremely difficult, for managers can rarely be sure about what is going to happen to the economy.

22. b. Fluctuations in long-term rates are smaller because the long-term inflation premium is an average of inflation expectations over many years.

23. a. The yield curve does indeed become steeper. Although interest rates in Year 1 decrease by 1 percent, interest rates in the following years increase by 2 percent, making the yield curve steeper.

24. b. $k = k^* + IP + DRP + LP + MRP$. Since each of these bonds has a 30-year maturity, the MRP and IP would all be equal. Thus, the differences in

the interest rates among these issues are the default risk and liquidity premiums.

25. a. Statement b is incorrect. If a downward-sloping yield curve existed, long-term interest rates would be lower than short-term rates. This would be very serious for UAC: UAC receives as income the interest it charges on its long-term mortgage loans, but it has to pay out interest for obtaining funds in the short-term money market. Therefore, UAC would be receiving low interest income, but it would be paying out even higher interest. Statement c is incorrect. An upward-sloping yield curve would indicate higher interest rates for long-term securities than for short-term securities.

26. b. $k_{RF} = k^* + IP = 2\% + 4\% = 6\%$.

27. d. $k = k^* + IP + DRP + LP + MRP$
$= 2\% + 4\% + 0\% + 1\% + 1\%$
$= 8\%$.

There is virtually no risk of default on a U.S. Treasury security.

28. c. $k_3 = k^* + IP + DRP + LP + MRP$
$8\% = 2\% + IP + 0\% + 0\% + 0\%$
$IP = 6\%$,

the average expected inflation rate over the next three years.

The implied expected inflation rate for the third year can be found by solving the equation that sets the average of the two known plus the one unknown expected inflation rates equal to 6%:

$$\frac{4\% + 6\% + IP_3}{3} = 6\%$$

$$IP_3 = 8\%.$$

29. a.

Year	k^*	Inflation	Average Inflation	k_t
1	3%	?	I_1 = ?	?
2	3	4%	$(I_1 + 4\%)/2$	6.5%

$k_2 = 3\% + (I_1 + 4\%)/2 = 6.5\%$.

Solving for I_1, we find I_1 = Year 1 inflation = 3%.

30. b. $I_1 = IP = 3\%$. $k_1 = k^* + IP = 3\% + 3\% = 6\%$.

CHAPTER 5
EXAMINING A FIRM'S FINANCIAL DATA

OVERVIEW

This chapter describes the basic financial statements. Those statements, which are included in every firm's annual report, are the income statement, the balance sheet, the statement of retained earnings, and the statement of cash flows. These financial statements are designed to provide information about the firm's financial status. Financial managers need this information to evaluate the firm's past performance and to map future plans. Financial analysts and investors need this information to estimate both future cash flows from the firm and the riskiness of these flows. In following chapters, we discuss the techniques of financial analysis used to evaluate financial data in an effort to determine the firm's relative riskiness, its profit potential, and its general managerial competence.

OUTLINE

I. **The annual report is by far the most important of the various reports corporations issue to their stockholders.**

A. A firm's annual report to shareholders presents two important types of information. The first is a *verbal statement* of the company's recent operations and its expectations for the coming year. The second is a *set of financial statements* which report what actually happened, and gives an accounting picture of the firm's operations and financial position.

B. Information contained in the annual report is used by investors to form expectations about future earnings and dividends, and about the riskiness of these expected cash flows.

II. **The income statement reports the results of operations for the past year. In this statement, a firm's revenues and expenses over an accounting period are summarized.**

A. At the top of the income statement are *net sales* (net of returns and discounts).

B. Operating costs and expenses include all costs required to obtain and convert raw materials into finished products, the costs of selling, and the costs associated with overseeing operations.

1. *Cost of goods sold* represents costs associated with raw materials acquisition and direct production costs.
2. Expenses attributable to assets employed in the business must be accounted for through *depreciation* or, if the firm leases assets, through *lease payments*.

C. *Earnings before interest and taxes*, or *operating profit*, are obtained by reducing net sales by cost of goods sold and operating expenses.

D. Income taxes and interest payments on debt are the remaining disbursements which reduce a firm's operating profits to arrive at net income available to common stockholders.
   1. If a firm uses preferred stock in its long-term financing mix, preferred dividends would be paid *after* taxes, which would further reduce net income available to common stockholders.

E. Net income, or the "bottom line," is the result of all the items on the income statement and is considered the most important single item on this statement.
   1. Net income is either paid to the shareholders in the form of *dividends* or *retained* by the firm to support its growth.
      a. EPS = Net income/Shares outstanding.
      b. DPS = Dividends paid/Shares outstanding.

III. The balance sheet shows the firm's assets and the claims on those assets at a specific point in time.

A. *Assets*, shown on the left hand side, are listed in the order of their liquidity, or the length of time it typically takes to convert them to cash.
   1. *Current assets*, also known as *working capital*, consist of assets that are normally converted into cash within one year, and include cash, marketable securities, inventories, and accounts receivable.
   2. *Fixed assets* are those assets with a useful life of more than one year, and include plant, equipment, and other assets which are used in the production process.
      a. Depreciation was at one time supposed to reflect the decline in an asset's useful productive value, but today the actual relationship between an asset's productive value and its book value is low.

B. *Liabilities* are claims on the assets of the firm, and are listed on the right hand side of the balance sheet in the order in which they mature and must be repaid.
   1. *Current liabilities* are those debts that mature within one year, and include accounts payable, notes payable, accruals, accrued wages, and accrued federal income taxes.
   2. *Long-term liabilities* are debt obligations with more than one year remaining until maturity, and may come from many sources, such as financial intermediaries or the public through the sale of bonds.

C. *Stockholders' equity,* or *net worth,* represents the owners' claims on the assets of the firm. It differs from liabilities, which are claims from nonowners, because the claims do not mature and never need to be paid.

1. Stockholders' equity is not a set amount, but rather a *residual:* Assets - Liabilities = Stockholders' equity.
2. The equity section of the balance sheet is divided into three accounts: *common stock, paid-in capital,* and *retained earnings.*
    a. Common stock and paid-in capital arise from the sale of stock by the firm, and thus are *external sources of equity funds.*
    b. Retained earnings are *built up over time by the firm "saving" a part of its net income* rather than paying all of its earnings out as dividends.
3. Common equity is that part of the total net worth belonging to the common stockholders.
4. *Preferred stock* appears on the balance sheet after long-term debt but before common equity.
    a. Preferred stock is considered equity but not *common* equity; these investors receive *preferential treatment* both in the payment of dividends and in the event of bankruptcy and liquidation of the firm.

IV. **The statement of retained earnings reports changes in the equity accounts between balance sheet dates.**

A. The balance sheet account "retained earnings" represents a *claim on assets,* not assets per se.

B. Retained earnings *do not represent cash,* and the amount reported in this balance sheet account is not available for the payment of dividends or anything else. Firms retain earnings primarily to expand the business by investing in plant and equipment, inventories, and so on.

1. A positive number in the retained earnings account indicates only that in the past the firm has earned an income, and its total dividends have been less than its reported income over the same period.

C. *In any given year* dividends per share (DPS) may exceed earnings per share (EPS), but *in the long run* dividends are paid from earnings, so DPS is normally smaller than EPS.

1. The ratio of DPS to EPS is called the *dividend payout ratio.*

V. **A firm's cash flow is the actual net cash, as opposed to accounting net income, that flows into or out of the firm during a specified period.**

A. Time lags are implicit in the cash flow cycle of a firm, since firms expecting an increase in sales will normally expend considerable cash before any new sales occur.

B. Even profitable firms can experience a cash shortage if growth is rapid. Thus, additional cash may have to be obtained through bank loans or by selling stocks or bonds.

VI. **The statement of cash flows is designed to show how the firm's operations have affected its liquidity, as measured by its cash flows, and to show the relationships among cash flows from operating, investing, and financing activities.**

A. Depreciation is a *noncash charge* against income; it is a very rough estimate of the dollar cost of fixed assets used in the production process.
   1. Depreciation's primary importance is its effect on cash flows. Depreciation shields income from taxation; the larger the depreciation charge, the lower the taxable income, and the lower the taxes paid. The value of depreciation is the tax shelter it provides: reducing taxes increases after-tax, spendable cash flows.
   2. Cash flows = Net income + Depreciation (and other noncash expenses).

B. The statement of cash flows answers three questions: (1) What were the firm's sources of funds during the year? (2) How did the firm use its available funds? (3) Did operations during the year tend to increase or decrease the firm's liquidity as measured by its cash and marketable securities balances?

C. A first step in preparing a statement of cash flows is to identify which balance sheet items provided cash and which used cash during the year. This is done on a sources and uses of funds statement.
   1. Sources of funds are an *increase in claims* (for example, borrowing from a bank) or a *decrease in assets* (for example, reducing inventories).
   2. Uses of funds are a *decrease in claims* (for example, paying a loan) or an *increase in assets* (for example, buying fixed assets).
   3. Depreciation does not physically provide funds and should be considered a source of funds *only so long as there are actual sales revenues against which the depreciation charges can be made.*

D. Data from the sources and uses of funds statement are used to prepare the formal statement of cash flows, which is divided into "cash flows from operations," "cash flows associated with long-term investments," and "cash flows associated with financing activities." The final entry shows the net increase or decrease in the firm's cash and marketable securities accounts as a result of its sources and uses of funds over the specified period of time.

E. The statement of cash flows treats all sources of financing as equal, but, in fact, there is a dramatic difference between obtaining a short-term bank loan which has to be paid back in one year and obtaining equity funds through the sale of new common stock or by being profitable and paying out less than 100 percent in dividends. Equity additions are lasting, permanent sources of funds, while short-term borrowing is not.

DEFINITIONAL QUESTIONS

1. Of all its communications with shareholders, a firm's _______ _______ is generally the most important.

2. The ________ statement reports the results of operations during the past year, the most important single item on this statement being ________ ________.

3. The _______ _______ lists the firm's assets as well as _______ on those assets at a specific point in time.

4. Typically, assets are listed in order of their __________, while ___________ are listed in the order in which they mature and must be repaid.

5. Assets - Liabilities = ______ worth, or _____________ equity.

6. The three accounts which normally make up the common equity section of the balance sheet are _______ stock, _______-______ capital, and _________ _________.

7. ________ ________ as reported on the balance sheet represent income earned by the firm in past years that has not been paid out as __________.

8. Retained earnings are generally reinvested in operating assets and are not held in the form of _______.

9. A(n) ________ in a claim against assets or a decrease in a(n) ________ account is a source of funds.

10. A decrease in a(n) _________ account or a(n) _________ in an asset account is a use of funds.

11. Expenses attributable to assets employed in the business must be accounted for through ______________.

12. ______ ___ _______ ______ represents costs associated with raw materials acquisition and direct production costs.

13. Net income is either paid to the shareholders in the form of __________ or _________ by the firm to support its growth.

14. _______ ______, also known as _______ _______, consist of assets that are normally converted into cash within one year.

15. __________ ______, or ____ ______, represents the owners' claims on the assets of the firm. It differs from __________, which are claims from nonowners, because the claims do not mature and never need to be paid.

16. Common stock and paid-in capital arise from the sale of stock by the firm, and thus are __________ sources of equity funds.

17. The ratio of DPS to EPS is called the __________ ________ _______.

18. A firm's ______ ______ is the actual net cash, as opposed to accounting _____ ________, that flows into or out of the firm during a specified period.

19. The __________ ___ ______ ______ is designed to show how the firm's operations have affected its liquidity, as measured by its cash flows, and to show the relationships among cash flows from operating, investing, and financing activities.

20. Depreciation is a _________ ________ against income.

CONCEPTUAL QUESTIONS

21. Retained earnings, kept in the form of cash, are built up from undistributed earnings.

    a. True　　　　b. False

22. A firm's annual report to shareholders contains only quantitative information which report what actually happened, and gives an accounting picture of the firm's operations and financial position.

    a. True　　　　b. False

23. If a firm uses preferred stock in its long-term financing mix, preferred dividends would be paid *after* taxes, which reduces net income available to common stockholders.

    a. True　　　　b. False

24. Preferred stock appears on the balance sheet after long-term debt, so it is considered common equity.

    a. True　　　　b. False

25. Which of the following account changes qualifies as a *use* of funds?

    a. An increase in accounts payable.
    b. A decrease in cash.
    c. A decrease in accounts receivable.
    d. An increase in retained earnings.
    e. A decrease in mortgage bonds.

26. Which of the following account changes qualifies as a *source* of funds?

a. An increase in inventories.
b. A decrease in accounts payable.
c. A decrease in net fixed assets.
d. A decrease in retained earnings.
e. An increase in cash.

27. Which of the following statements is most *correct*?

a. Depreciation does not physically provide funds and should be considered a source of funds only so long as there are actual sales revenues against which the depreciation charges can be made.
b. The larger the depreciation charge, the higher the taxable income, and the higher the taxes paid.
c. In any given year dividends per share may exceed earnings per share, but in the long run dividends are paid from earnings, so DPS is normally smaller than EPS.
d. Both statements a and c are true.
e. All of the above statements are false.

PROBLEMS

(The following balance sheets apply to the next five problems.)

American Products Corporation
Balance Sheets
(Dollars in Millions)

	December 31, 1993	December 31, 1992
Cash	$ 21	$ 45
Marketable securities	0	33
Net receivables	90	66
Inventories	225	159
Total current assets	$336	$303
Gross fixed assets	450	225
Less accumulated depreciation	(123)	(78)
Net fixed assets	$327	$147
Total assets	$663	$450
Accounts payable	$ 54	$ 45
Notes payable	9	45
Other current liabilities	45	21
Long-term debt	78	24
Common stock	192	114
Retained earnings	285	201
Total liabilities and equity	$663	$450

During 1993, the company earned $114 million after taxes, of which $30 million were paid out as dividends.

28. Looking only at the balance sheet accounts, what are the total sources of funds (which must equal the total uses of funds) for 1993?

a. $213 million
b. $286 million
c. $351 million
d. $428 million
e. $531 million

29. What are the net cash flows from operations for 1993?

a. -$123 million
b. $102 million
c. $123 million
d. -$57 million
e. -$102 million

30. What are the cash flows associated with long-term investments for 1993?

a. $225 million
b. $180 million
c. -$270 million
d. -$180 million
e. -$225 million

31. What are the net cash flows from financing for 1993?

a. $96 million
b. $66 million
c. $75 million
d. $85 million
e. $60 million

32. What change has occurred in the cash and marketable securities accounts during 1993?

a. $57 million
b. $24 million
c. $33 million
d. -$57 million
e. -$24 million

ANSWERS AND SOLUTIONS

1. annual report
2. income; net income
3. balance sheet; claims
4. liquidity; liabilities
5. Net; Stockholders'
6. common; paid-in; retained earnings
7. Retained earnings; dividends
8. cash
9. increase; asset
10. liability; increase
11. depreciation
12. Cost of goods sold
13. dividends; retained
14. Current assets; working capital
15. Stockholders' equity; net worth; liabilities
16. external
17. dividend payout ratio
18. cash flow; net income
19. statement of cash flows
20. noncash charge

21. b. Retained earnings are not kept in the form of cash. They are normally reinvested in various types of operating assets.

22. b. A firm's annual report contains a verbal statement of the company's recent operations and its expectations for the coming year in addition to the quantitative financial statements.

23. a. This statement is correct.

24. b. Preferred stock is considered equity but not common equity; preferred stockholders receive preferential treatment both in the payment of dividends and in the event of bankruptcy and liquidation of the firm.

25. e. A use of funds is a decrease in a liability or equity account, or an increase in an asset account. Therefore, a decrease in mortgage bonds qualifies as a use of funds.

26. c. A source of funds is an increase in a liability or equity account, or a decrease in an asset account. Therefore, a decrease in net fixed assets qualifies as a source of funds.

27. d. Statement a is correct. Statement b is incorrect; the higher the depreciation charge, the lower the taxable income, and the lower the taxes paid. (Depreciation provides a tax shelter.) Statement c is correct; therefore, statement d is the best choice.

28. c.

	Sources	Uses
Cash	$ 24	
Marketable securities	33	
Net receivables		$ 24
Inventories		66
Gross fixed assets		225
Accumulated depreciation	45	
Accounts payable	9	
Notes payable		36
Other current liabilities	24	
Long-term debt	54	
Common stock	78	
Retained earnings	84	
	$351	$351

Note that accumulated depreciation is a contra-asset account, and an increase in accumulated depreciation is a source of funds. Also note that no total lines such as total current assets are used to determine sources and uses since to do so would be to "double count."

29. b. Net cash flows from operations (in millions of dollars):

Net income	$114
Additions (sources of cash):	
Depreciation	45
Increase in accounts payable	9
Increase in other current liabilities	24
Subtractions (uses of cash):	
Increase in accounts receivable	(24)
Increase in inventories	(66)
Net cash flows from operations	$102

30. e. A review of the balance sheets indicates that the acquisition of fixed assets totaled $225 million--a use of funds. Note that the increase in accumulated depreciation was accounted for in the operations section of the cash flow statement, the increase in gross fixed assets is accounted for here.

31. b. Net cash flows (in millions of dollars) associated with financing activities:

Increase in long-term debt	$54
Increase in common stock	78
Repayment of notes payable	(36)
Common dividends paid	(30)
Net cash flows from financing	$66

32. d. From the answers to the previous three problems we have (in millions of dollars):

Net cash flows from operations	$102
Acquisition of fixed assets	(225)
Net cash flows from financing	66
Net reduction in cash & mkt. sec.	($ 57)

CHAPTER 6
INTERPRETING FINANCIAL STATEMENTS

OVERVIEW

Financial analysis is designed to determine the relative strengths and weaknesses of a company. While Chapter 5 described the basic financial statements, this chapter discusses the techniques of financial analysis, specifically ratio analysis, by which interested parties can appraise the relative riskiness, credit worthiness, profit potential, and general managerial competence of firms. Financial analysis concentrates on financial statement analysis, which highlights the key aspects of a firm's operations. Financial statement analysis involves a study of the relationships between income statement and balance sheet accounts, how these relationships change over time (or trend analysis), and how a particular firm compares with other firms in its industry (comparative ratio analysis). Although financial analysis has limitations, when used with care and judgment, it can provide some very useful insights into a company's operations.

OUTLINE

I. **Financial statements are important to investors, who are interested in past events primarily as an aid in predicting future success or failure, and to management, who analyzes the data in order to anticipate future events and to help identify actions which will influence the firm's future course of events.**

A. Common-size financial statements are a tool frequently used by financial analysts.
1. *Common-size balance sheets* are formed by dividing each asset, liability, and equity item by total assets and expressing the result as a percentage.
2. *Common-size income statements* are formed by dividing each income statement item by sales and expressing the result as a percentage.
3. Common-size financial statements can be compared with common-size statements of larger or smaller firms or with those of the same firm over time.

II. **Ratio analysis shows relationships among financial statement accounts.**

A. A single ratio is relatively useless in making relevant evaluations of a firm's health. Besides taking care to select similar firms of corresponding size and industry type to insure appropriate comparison of financial data, other types of comparisons should be noted:

1. The ratio should be compared with several ratios in a network, such as the Du Pont system, or other logical grouping.
2. The ratio should be compared with trends of the firm's own ratios.
3. The ratio should be compared with management's goals for key ratios.
4. The ratio should be compared with selected ratios of other firms in the same industry.

B. Analysts who use financial ratios extensively may be characterized as belonging to three main groups: (1) managers, (2) credit analysts, and (3) security analysts.

1. *Managers* use ratios to help analyze, control, and thus improve the firm's operations.
2. *Credit analysts,* such as bank loan officers or credit managers for industrial companies, analyze ratios to help ascertain a company's ability to pay its debts.
3. *Security analysts,* including both stock and bond analysts, use ratios to determine a company's efficiency and growth prospects, a company's ability to pay interest on its bonds, and the availability of assets to bondholders if the company goes bankrupt.

C. Financial ratios are categorized into five groups: liquidity, asset management, debt management, profitability, and market value ratios.

D. *Liquidity ratios* provide a quick and easy-to-use measure of a firm's ability to meet its current obligations as they come due.

1. The *current ratio* is the most commonly used measure of short-term solvency because it provides an indicator of the extent to which the claims of short-term creditors are covered by assets that are expected to be converted to cash in a period roughly corresponding to the maturity of the claims. It is determined by dividing current assets by current liabilities.
2. The *quick, or acid test, ratio* is calculated by deducting inventories from current assets and then dividing the remainder by current liabilities. Inventories are excluded because it may be difficult to liquidate them at their full book value.

E. *Asset management ratios* measure how effectively a firm is managing its assets, and whether or not the level of those assets is properly related to the level of operations.

1. The *inventory turnover ratio,* or *inventory utilization ratio,* is defined as sales divided by inventories.
   a. It is often necessary to use an average inventory figure rather than a year-end figure, especially for seasonal business.
   b. Because inventories are carried at cost, it may be more appropriate to use cost of goods sold in the numerator rather than sales. However, compilers of financial ratio statistics use the ratio of sales to inventories carried at cost; therefore, sales should be used in the numerator.

2. The *days sales outstanding (DSO)*, also called *average collection period (ACP)*, is the average length of time that a firm must wait after making a sale before receiving cash. Annual sales are divided by 360 to obtain average daily sales, which are then divided into accounts receivable to find the average number of days' sales tied up in receivables.
3. The *fixed assets turnover*, or *fixed assets utilization, ratio* is the ratio of sales to net fixed assets. It measures how effectively the firm utilizes its plant and equipment.
   a. One potential problem when comparisons are made: All assets except cash and accounts receivable reflect historical cost, and inflation has caused the value of many assets purchased in the past to be understated. Older firms would report higher turnover ratios than newer firms.
4. The *total assets turnover*, or *total assets utilization, ratio* is calculated by dividing sales by total assets. It measures the utilization of all the firm's assets.

F. *Debt management ratios* measure the extent to which a firm is using debt, or financial leverage, and the degree of safety afforded to creditors.
1. The extent to which a firm uses *financial leverage* has three important implications.
   a. By raising funds through debt, owners can maintain control of the firm with a limited investment.
   b. Creditors look to the equity to provide a margin of safety.
   c. If the firm earns more on investments financed with borrowed funds than it pays in interest, the return on the owners' capital is magnified, resulting in "favorable leverage."
2. The *debt ratio*, or *ratio of total debt to total assets*, measures the percentage of total funds provided by creditors. Debt includes both current liabilities and long-term debt. The lower the ratio, the greater the protection afforded creditors in the event of liquidation.
3. The *times-interest-earned (TIE) ratio* is calculated by dividing earnings before interest and taxes (EBIT) by interest charges. The TIE ratio shows the degree to which operating income can decline before the firm is unable to meet its annual interest costs.
4. The *fixed charge coverage ratio* is similar to the times-interest-earned ratio, but it recognizes long-term obligations under lease contracts and sinking funds, which are similar to interest payments, that must be made in a timely manner to avoid possible bankruptcy. It is calculated by adding lease payments to both the numerator and denominator of the TIE ratio equation, and by adding sinking fund payments divided by (1 - Tax rate) to the denominator.

G. *Profitability ratios* show the combined effects of liquidity, asset management, and debt management on operating income and net income.

1. The *profit margin on sales* is calculated by dividing net income by sales, which gives the profit per dollar of sales.
2. The *basic earning power ratio* is calculated by dividing the earnings before interest and taxes (EBIT) by total assets.
3. The *return on total assets (ROA)*, or *return on investment (ROI) ratio*, is the ratio of net income to total assets, after interest and taxes.
4. The *return on common equity (ROE)* measures the *rate of return on the stockholders' investment*. It is equal to net income divided by common equity.

H. *Market value ratios* relate the firm's stock price to its earnings and book value per share, and give management an indication of what investors think of the company's past performance and future prospects.

1. The *price/earnings (P/E) ratio*, or price per share divided by earnings per share, shows how much investors are willing to pay per dollar of reported profits. The P/E ratio is *positively related* to a firm's growth prospects, and *inversely related* to its risk.
2. The *market/book ratio* is defined as market value per share divided by book value per share. Book value per share is computed by dividing stockholders' equity by shares outstanding. Higher ratios are generally associated with firms that have relatively high rates of return on equity.

III. It is important to analyze trends in ratios as well as their absolute levels, for trends give clues as to whether the financial situation is improving or deteriorating.

A. A *modified Du Pont chart* shows the relationships among return on total assets, total assets turnover, the profit margin, and financial leverage.

1. The *Du Pont equation* is equal to the profit margin times the total assets turnover, and it gives the rate of return on assets (ROA): ROA = Profit margin x Total assets turnover.
2. The rate of return on assets times the *equity multiplier* (total assets divided by common equity) yields the return on equity (ROE): ROE = Profit margin x Total assets turnover x Equity multiplier.
   a. An alternative method to calculating ROE is: ROE = ROA x 1/(1 - Debt ratio).
3. Management can use the modified Du Pont chart to analyze ways of improving the firm's performance.

IV. Comparative ratio analysis among firms in the same industry can be performed using information from financial sources such as Dun & Bradstreet, Robert Morris Associates, and the U.S. Department of Commerce.

A. When you select a comparative data source, you should either be sure that your emphasis is similar to that of the agency whose ratios you use or recognize the limitations of its ratios for your purposes.

B. There are often definitional differences in the ratios presented by different sources, so before using a source, be sure to verify the exact definitions of the ratios to ensure consistency.

V. There are a number of limitations to ratio analysis.

A. Ratios are often not useful for analyzing the operations of large firms which operate in many different industries, because for them comparative ratios are not meaningful.

B. The use of industry averages may not provide a very challenging target for high-level performance.

C. Inflation affects depreciation charges, inventory costs, and therefore the value of both balance sheet items and net income. For this reason, the analysis of a firm over time, or a comparative analysis of firms of different ages, can be misleading.

D. Ratios may be distorted by seasonal factors, or manipulated by management to give the impression of a sound financial condition.

E. Firms can employ *"window dressing" techniques* to make their financial statements look better to credit analysts.

F. Different accounting practices, such as inventory valuation and depreciation methods, may have an impact on financial ratios.

G. It is difficult to generalize about whether a particular ratio is "good" or "bad," since there can be many favorable and unfavorable factors contributing to a given ratio figure.

H. A firm may have some ratios which look "good" and others which look "bad," making it difficult to tell whether the company is, on balance, in a strong or a weak position. However, statistical procedures can be used to analyze the net effects of a set of ratios.

DEFINITIONAL QUESTIONS

1. The current and acid test ratios are examples of ______________ ratios. They measure a firm's ability to meet its __________________ obligations.

2. Days sales outstanding (DSO) is found by dividing ________ ________ by ______, and then dividing average sales per day into accounts ______________. The DSO is the length of time that a firm must wait after making a sale before it receives ________.

3. Debt management ratios are used to evaluate a firm's use of financial _________.

4. The debt ratio, which is the ratio of _____ _____ to _____ _____, measures the proportion of funds supplied by __________.

5. The _________-_________-__________ ratio is calculated by dividing earnings before interest and taxes by the amount of _____ charges.

6. The combined effects of liquidity, asset management, and debt management are measured by ______________ ratios.

7. Dividing net income by sales gives the ________ _______ on sales.

8. The _____/_________ ratio measures how much investors are willing to pay for each dollar of a firm's current income.

9. Firms with higher rates of return on stockholders' equity tend to sell at relatively high ratios of _______ _______ to _______ ________.

10. Individual ratios are of little value in analyzing a company's financial condition. More important are the _________ of a ratio over time and the comparison of the company's ratios to ____________ _________ ratios.

11. A modified _____ ________ chart shows the relationships among return on total assets, debt, total assets turnover, and profit margin, and how they combine to produce return on ___________.

12. Return on assets is a function of two variables, the profit _______ and _______ _________ turnover.

13. The _____ of a particular ratio over time or a _____________ ratio analysis among firms in the same industry gives a good indication of a firm's actual financial situation with regard to that ratio.

14. _______-_____ ________ _______ are formed by dividing each asset, liability, and equity item by total assets and expressing the result as a percentage.

15. Analysts who use financial ratios extensively may be characterized as belonging to three main groups: _________, _______ _________, and _________ _________.

16. ______ __________ ratios measure how effectively a firm is managing its assets, and whether or not the level of those assets is properly related to the level of operations.

17. The ______ _______ ________ ratio measures how effectively the firm utilizes its plant and equipment.

18. The _______ _______ _________ ratio is similar to the times-interest-earned ratio, but it recognizes long-term obligations under lease contracts and sinking funds that must be made in a timely manner to avoid possible bankruptcy.

19. ________ _______ ratios relate the firm's stock price to its earnings and book value per share, and give management an indication of what investors think of the company's past performance and future prospects.

20. The ______ __________ is calculated as total assets divided by common equity.

CONCEPTUAL QUESTIONS

21. The equity multiplier can be expressed as 1 - (Debt/Assets).

a. True b. False

22. A high quick ratio is *always* a good indication of a well-managed liquidity position.

a. True b. False

23. Midwest Appliances Inc. has a current ratio of 0.5. Which of the following actions would improve (increase) this ratio?

a. Use cash to pay off current liabilities.
b. Collect some of the current accounts receivable.
c. Use cash to pay off some long-term debt.
d. Purchase additional inventory on credit (accounts payable).
e. Sell some of the existing inventory at cost.

24. Refer back to Question 23. Assume that Midwest Appliances has a current ratio of 1.4. Now, which of the following actions would improve (increase) this ratio?

a. Use cash to pay off current liabilities.
b. Collect some of the current accounts receivable.
c. Use cash to pay off some long-term debt.
d. Purchase additional inventory on credit (accounts payable).
e. Use cash to pay for some fixed assets.

25. Examining the ratios of a particular firm against the same measures for a group of firms from the same industry, at a point in time, is an example of

a. Trend analysis.
b. Comparative ratio analysis.
c. Du Pont analysis.
d. Simple ratio analysis.
e. Industry analysis.

26. Which of the following statements is most *correct*?

a. Having a high current ratio and a high quick ratio is always a good indication that a firm is managing its liquidity position well.
b. A decline in the inventory turnover ratio suggests that the firm's liquidity position is improving.
c. If a firm's times-interest-earned ratio is relatively high, then this is one indication that the firm should be able to meet its debt obligations.
d. Since ROA measures the firm's effective utilization of assets (without considering how these assets are financed), two firms with the same EBIT must have the same ROA.
e. All of the above statements are false.

PROBLEMS

(The following financial statements apply to the next six problems.)

Roberts Manufacturing
Balance Sheet
December 31, 1993
(Dollars in Thousands)

Cash	$ 200	Accounts payable	$ 205
Receivables	245	Notes payable	425
Inventory	625	Other current liabilities	115
Total current assets	$1,070	Total current liabilities	$ 745
Net fixed assets	1,200	Long-term debt	420
		Common equity	1,105
Total assets	$2,270	Total liabilities & equity	$2,270

Roberts Manufacturing
Income Statement for Year Ended December 31, 1993
(Dollars in Thousands)

Sales		$2,400
Cost of goods sold:		
Materials	$1,000	
Labor	600	
Heat, light and power	89	
Indirect labor	65	
Depreciation	80	1,834
Gross profit		$ 566
Selling expenses		(175)
General and administrative expenses		(216)
Earnings before interest and taxes (EBIT)		$ 175
Less interest expense		(35)
Earnings before taxes (EBT)		$ 140
Less taxes (40%)		(56)
Net income		$ 84

27. Calculate the liquidity ratios, that is, the current ratio and the quick ratio.

a. 1.20; 0.60
b. 1.20; 0.80
c. 1.44; 0.60
d. 1.44; 0.80
e. 1.60; 0.60

28. Calculate the asset management ratios, that is, the inventory turnover ratio, fixed assets turnover, total assets turnover, and days sales outstanding.

a. 3.84; 2.00; 1.06; 36.75 days
b. 3.84; 2.00; 1.06; 35.25 days
c. 3.84; 2.00; 1.06; 34.10 days
d. 3.84; 2.00; 1.24; 34.10 days
e. 3.84; 2.20; 1.48; 34.10 days

29. Calculate the debt management ratios, that is, the debt ratio and times-interest-earned ratio.

a. 0.39; 3.16
b. 0.39; 5.00
c. 0.51; 3.16
d. 0.51; 5.00
e. 0.73; 3.16

30. Calculate the profitability ratios, that is, the profit margin on sales, return on total assets, return on common equity, and basic earning power of assets.

a. 3.50%; 4.25%; 7.60%; 8.00%
b. 3.50%; 3.70%; 7.60%; 7.71%
c. 3.70%; 3.50%; 7.60%; 7.71%
d. 3.70%; 3.50%; 8.00%; 8.00%
e. 4.25%; 3.70%; 7.60%; 8.00%

31. Calculate the market value ratios, that is, the price/earnings ratio and the market/book value ratio. Roberts had an average of 10,000 shares outstanding during 1993, and the stock price on December 31, 1993, was $40.00.

a. 4.21; 0.36
b. 3.20; 1.54
c. 3.20; 0.36
d. 4.76; 1.54
e. 4.76; 0.36

32. Use the Du Pont equation with the equity multiplier to determine Roberts' return on equity.

a. 6.90%
b. 7.24%
c. 7.47%
d. 7.60%
e. 8.41%

33. Lewis Inc. has sales of $2 million per year, all of which are credit sales. Its days sales outstanding is 42 days. What is its average accounts receivable balance?

a. $233,333
b. $266,667
c. $333,333
d. $350,000
e. $366,667

34. A firm has total interest charges of $20,000 per year, sales of $2 million, a tax rate of 40 percent, and a profit margin of 6 percent. What is the firm's times-interest-earned ratio?

a. 10
b. 11
c. 12
d. 13
e. 14

35. A fire has destroyed many of the financial records at Anderson Associates. You are assigned to piece together information to prepare a financial report. You have found the return on equity to be 12 percent, and the debt ratio was 0.40. What was the return on assets?

a. 4.90%
b. 5.35%
c. 6.60%
d. 7.20%
e. 8.40%

36. Rowe and Company has a debt ratio of 0.50, a total assets turnover of 0.25, and a profit margin of 10 percent. The president is unhappy with the current return on equity, and he thinks it could be doubled. This could be accomplished (1) by increasing the profit margin to 14 percent and (2) by increasing debt utilization. Total assets turnover will not change. What new debt ratio, along with the 14 percent profit margin, is required to double the return on equity?

a. 0.55
b. 0.60
c. 0.65
d. 0.70
e. 0.75

37. TipTop Jewelers Inc. sells only on credit. Its days sales outstanding is 60 days, and its average accounts receivable balance is $500,000. What are its sales for the year?

a. $1,500,000
b. $3,000,000
c. $2,000,000
d. $2,750,000
e. $3,225,000

38. The Clarke Corporation has $1,000,000 of debt outstanding, and it pays an interest rate of 12 percent annually. Clarke's annual sales are $4 million, its federal-plus-state tax rate is 25 percent, and its net profit margin on sales is 10 percent. If the company does not maintain a TIE ratio of at least 5 times, its bank will refuse to renew the loan, and bankruptcy will result. What is Clarke's TIE ratio?

a. 2.50
b. 3.33
c. 4.00
d. 5.25
e. 5.44

39. The Stanton Corporation had sales last year of $1.2 million and total assets of $660,0000. Current liabilities were $225,000 on December 31st. The firm's current ratio was 2.0 and its quick ratio was 1.5. What was Stanton's investment in inventory?

a. $112,500
b. $125,000
c. $137,500
d. $150,000
e. $175,000

40. The liabilities and equity section of Barak Inc.'s end-of-year balance sheet is as follows:

Long-term debt	$15,000,000
Common stock	6,000,000
Paid-in-capital	9,375,000
Retained earnings	21,443,182

If sales for the year were $135 million and the profit margin was 6 percent, what was Barak's return on equity (ROE)?

a. 16%
b. 18%
c. 20%
d. 22%
e. 25%

ANSWERS AND SOLUTIONS

1. liquidity; current
2. annual sales; 360; receivable; cash
3. leverage
4. total debt; total assets; creditors
5. times-interest-earned (TIE); interest
6. profitability
7. profit margin
8. price/earnings
9. market price; book value
10. trend; industry average
11. Du Pont; equity
12. margin; total assets
13. trend; comparative
14. Common-size balance sheets
15. managers; credit analysts; security analysts
16. Asset management
17. fixed assets turnover (utilization)
18. fixed charge coverage
19. Market value
20. equity multiplier

21. b. The equity multiplier is Total assets/Common equity.

22. b. Excess cash resulting from poor management could produce a high quick ratio. Similarly, if accounts receivable are not collected promptly, this could also lead to a high quick ratio.

23. d. This question is best analyzed using numbers. For example, assume current assets = \$50 and current liabilities = \$100; thus, the current ratio = 0.5. For Answer a, assume \$5 in cash is used to pay off \$5 in current liabilities. The new current ratio would be \$45/\$95 = 0.47. For Answer d, assume a \$10 purchase of inventory on credit (accounts payable). The new current ratio would be \$60/\$110 = 0.55, which is an increase over the old current ratio of 0.5.

24. a. Again, this question is best analyzed using numbers. For example, assume current assets equal \$140 and current liabilities equal \$100; thus, the current ratio equals 1.4. For answer a, assume \$5 in cash is used to pay off \$5 in current liabilities. The new current ratio would be \$135/\$95 = 1.42, which is an increase over the old current ratio of 1.4. For answer d, assume a \$10 purchase of inventory on credit (accounts payable). The new current ratio would be \$150/\$110 = 1.36, which is a decrease over the old current ratio of 1.4.

25. b. The correct answer is comparative ratio analysis. A trend analysis compares the firm's ratios over time, while a Du Pont analysis shows the relationships among return on investment, assets turnover, profit margin, and leverage.

26. c. Excess cash resulting from poor management could produce high current and quick ratios; thus statement a is false. A decline in the inventory turnover ratio suggests that either sales have decreased or inventory has increased--which suggests that the firm's liquidity position is *not* improving; thus statement b is false. Statement c is correct; the TIE ratio is used to measure whether the firm can meet its debt obligation, and a high TIE ratio would indicate this is so. Statement d is false. ROA = Net income/Total assets, and EBIT does not equal net income. Two firms with the same EBIT could have different financing and different taxes resulting in different net incomes. Also, two firms with the same EBIT do not necessarily have the same total assets. Obviously, statement e is incorrect because statement c is true.

27. c. $\text{Current ratio} = \dfrac{\text{Current assets}}{\text{Current liabilities}} = \dfrac{\$1,070}{\$745} = 1.44\text{x}.$

$\text{Quick ratio} = \dfrac{\text{Current assets - Inventory}}{\text{Current liabilities}} = \dfrac{\$1,070 - \$625}{\$745} = 0.60\text{x}.$

28. a. $\text{Inventory turnover} = \dfrac{\text{Sales}}{\text{Inventories}} = \dfrac{\$2,400}{\$625} = 3.84\text{x}.$

$\text{Fixed assets turnover} = \dfrac{\text{Sales}}{\text{Net fixed assets}} = \dfrac{\$2,400}{\$1,200} = 2.00\text{x}.$

$$\text{Total assets turnover} = \frac{\text{Sales}}{\text{Total assets}} = \frac{\$2,400}{\$2,270} = 1.06\text{x}.$$

$$\text{Days sales outstanding} = \frac{\text{Receivables}}{\text{Sales/360}} = \frac{\$245}{\$2,400/360} = 36.75 \text{ days}.$$

29. d. $$\text{Debt ratio} = \frac{\text{Total debt}}{\text{Total assets}} = \frac{\$1,165}{\$2,270} = 0.51.$$

$$\text{TIE ratio} = \frac{\text{EBIT}}{\text{I}} = \frac{\$175}{\$35} = 5.00.$$

30. b. $$\text{Profit margin} = \frac{\text{Net income}}{\text{Sales}} = \frac{\$84}{\$2,400} = 0.0350 = 3.50\%.$$

$$\text{ROA} = \frac{\text{Net income}}{\text{Total assets}} = \frac{\$84}{\$2,270} = 0.0370 = 3.70\%.$$

$$\text{ROE} = \frac{\text{Net income}}{\text{Common equity}} = \frac{\$84}{\$1,105} = 0.0760 = 7.60\%.$$

$$\text{BEP} = \frac{\text{EBIT}}{\text{Total assets}} = \frac{\$175}{\$2,270} = 0.0771 = 7.71\%.$$

31. e. $$\text{EPS} = \frac{\text{Net income}}{\text{Number of shares outstanding}} = \frac{\$84,000}{10,000} = \$8.40.$$

$$\text{P/E ratio} = \frac{\text{Price}}{\text{EPS}} = \frac{\$40.00}{\$8.40} = 4.76.$$

$$\text{Market/book value} = \frac{\text{Market value}}{\text{Book value}} = \frac{\$40(10,000)}{\$1,105,000} = 0.36.$$

32. d. $$\text{ROE} = \begin{matrix}\text{Profit}\\ \text{margin}\end{matrix} \times \begin{matrix}\text{Total assets}\\ \text{turnover}\end{matrix} \times \begin{matrix}\text{Equity}\\ \text{multiplier}\end{matrix}$$

$$= \frac{\$84}{\$2,400} \times \frac{\$2,400}{\$2,270} \times \frac{\$2,270}{\$1,105}$$

$$= (0.035)(1.057)(2.054) = 0.0760 = 7.60\%.$$

33. a. $$\text{DSO} = \frac{\text{Receivables}}{\text{Sales/360}}$$

$$42 \text{ days} = \frac{\text{Receivables}}{\$2,000,000/360}$$

Receivables = $233,333.

34. b. Net income = $2,000,000(0.06) = $120,000.
Earnings before taxes = $120,000/0.6 = $200,000.
EBIT = $200,000 + $20,000 = $220,000.
TIE = EBIT/I = $220,000/$20,000 = 11.

35. d. If Total debt/Total assets = 0.40, then Total equity/Total assets = 0.60, and the equity multiplier (Assets/Equity) = 1/0.60 = 1.667.

$$ROE = \frac{NI}{S} \times \frac{S}{A} \times \frac{A}{E}.$$

ROE = (ROA)(EM)
12% = (ROA)(1.667)
ROA = 7.20%.

36. c. If Total debt/Total assets = 0.50, then Total equity/Total assets = 0.50, and the equity multiplier (Assets/Equity) = 1/0.50 = 2.0.

$$ROE = \frac{NI}{S} \times \frac{S}{A} \times \frac{A}{E} = (PM)(\text{Total assets turnover})(EM).$$

Before: ROE = (10%)(0.25)(2.00) = 5.00%.

After: 10.00% = (14%)(0.25)(EM)
EM = 2.86.

$$\text{Equity multiplier} = \frac{\text{Assets}}{\text{Equity}}$$

$$2.86 = \frac{1}{\text{Equity}}$$

Equity = 0.35.

Debt = Assets - Equity = 1 - 35% = 65%.

37. b. DSO = Accounts receivable/(Sales/360)
60 days = $500,000/(Sales/360)
60(Sales/360) = $500,000
Sales = $3,000,000.

38. e. TIE = EBIT/Interest, so find EBIT and Interest.
Interest = $1,000,000(0.12) = $120,000.
Net Income = $4,000,000(0.10) = $400,000.
Pretax income = $400,000/(1-T) = $400,000(0.75) = $533,333.
EBIT = $533,333 + $120,000 = $653,333.
TIE = $653,333/$120,000 = 5.44x.

39. a. Current assets/$225,000 = 2.0; Current assets = $450,000.

(Current assets - Inventory)/Current liabilities = 1.5
($450,000 - Inventory)/$225,000 = 1.5
$450,000 - Inventory = $337,500
Inventory = $112,500.

40. d. Net income = 0.06($135,000,000) = $8,100,000.

ROE = $8,100,000/($6,000,000 + $9,375,000 + $21,443,182) = 22%.

CHAPTER 7
DETERMINING FUTURE FINANCIAL NEEDS

OVERVIEW

Managers are vitally concerned with future financial statements and with the effects of alternative assumptions and policies on these projected, or pro forma, financial statements. The construction of pro forma statements begins with a sales (demand) forecast. On the basis of the sales forecast, the amount of assets necessary to support this sales level is determined. Although some liabilities will increase spontaneously with increased sales, if the sales growth rate is rapid, then external capital will be required to support the growth in sales. Pro forma statements are important for two reasons. First, if projected operating results look poor, management can reformulate its plans for the coming year. Second, it is desirable to plan the acquisition of funds well in advance to insure that funds will be available when they are needed.

OUTLINE

I. **Both managers and investors are concerned about the impact of future operations and alternative financial plans on the future financial condition of the firm. Pro forma, or projected, financial statements are useful in forecasting the results of different courses of action.**

- **A.** The most important element in financial planning is the *sales (demand) forecast*.
  - *1.* Sales forecasts involve the entire management team and are often the product of a specialized planning group or committee.
  - *2.* Companies must project the state of the national economy, economic conditions within their own geographic areas, and conditions in the product markets they serve.

- **B.** Several methods are used to develop forecasted financial statements. We concentrate on the *percentage of sales method*.

II. **The percentage of sales method is a simple but practical method of forecasting financial statement variables. The procedure is based on the assumptions that most balance sheet items are tied directly to sales and that current levels of all assets are optimal for the current sales level.**

- **A.** Identify those balance sheet items that vary directly and proportionately with sales.
  - *1.* Assets that vary directly and proportionately with sales are called *spontaneous assets*. If the firm has been operating at full capacity,

each asset item must increase if the higher sales level is to be attained.

2. Likewise, liabilities and equity must rise to match the increase in assets because the balance sheet must balance.
3. *Spontaneously generated funds* come from such sources as accounts payable and accruals, which increase spontaneously with sales.
4. Other sources of financing, such as notes payable, mortgage bonds, and common stock, will not increase spontaneously with sales, since *their levels depend on formal actions by the financial manager*.

B. The first approximation pro forma balance sheet and income statement are constructed as follows:

1. Multiply each of the balance sheet items that vary directly with sales by one plus the growth rate to arrive at the new pro forma balances.
2. Carry over the remaining liability and equity figures from the prior year (except for retained earnings), since these are the nonspontaneous funds.
3. Multiply the income statement items by one plus the growth rate to arrive at pro forma figures. By doing this, we are assuming *constant returns to scale*.
4. Determine the addition to retained earnings by calculating net income and then subtracting dividends paid from this amount.
5. Add up the projected assets and subtract the liabilities and equity. The difference equals the *additional funds needed (AFN)*.
   a. To make up for this shortfall in funds, the firm could use short-term bank loans (notes payable), mortgage bonds, common stock, or a combination of these funds.
   b. Restrictions on additional debt, additional current liabilities, and common equity requirements will determine the exact amounts obtained from each of these financing sources.

C. Financial managers can use the pro forma financial statements to analyze the ratios implied by these statements and to construct a projected statement of cash flows.

III. The forecast of capital requirements is normally made by constructing pro forma financial statements. However, a simple forecasting formula provides a shortcut to projecting additional funds needed (AFN) and can be used to clarify the relationship between sales growth and financial requirements.

A. The formula is as follows: Additional funds needed = Required increase in assets - Spontaneous increase in liabilities - Increase in retained earnings; or $AFN = A^*/S(\Delta S) - L^*/S(\Delta S) - MS_1(1 - d)$.

B. The terms of the equations are defined as follows:

1. A^*/S = assets that increase spontaneously with sales as a percentage of sales, or required dollar increase in assets per $1 increase in sales.

2. L^*/S = liabilities that increase spontaneously with sales as a percentage of sales, or spontaneously generated financing per $1 increase in sales.
3. S_1 = total sales projected for next year. (Note that S_0 = last year's sales.)
4. ΔS = change in sales = $S_1 - S_0$.
5. M = profit margin, or rate of profit per $1 of sales.
6. d = percentage of earnings paid out in dividends, or the dividend payout ratio. Notice that 1 - d is the percentage of earnings the firm retains, often called the *retention rate*.

C. Because no *excess capacity* exists and ratios are assumed constant, values can be inserted into the formula to find the additional funds needed.

D. The faster a firm's growth rate in sales, the greater is its need for additional, external financing.
1. At very low growth rates, a firm may need no external financing. However, at high growth rates, management may have to seek capital from outside sources, or else reconsider the feasibility of expansion plans.

E. Dividend policy also affects external capital requirements as reflected in the payout ratio. Thus, *the higher the payout ratio*, the smaller the addition to retained earnings, and hence *the greater the requirements for external capital*. Therefore, the firm might want to consider a reduction in the dividend payout ratio if it is having difficulties in raising capital.

F. The *capital intensity ratio* is the amount of assets required per dollar of sales, or A^*/S. If the capital intensity ratio is low, then sales can grow rapidly without much outside capital. However, if a firm is capital intensive, even a small growth in output will require a great deal of outside capital.
1. The capital intensity ratio is the *reciprocal of the total assets turnover ratio* only if all assets grow proportionately with sales.

G. An increase in spontaneous liabilities provides capital; however, there is usually not much a firm can do to raise the portion of L^*/S that is due to accrued wages and taxes. Suppliers can sometimes be persuaded to give customers longer to pay.

H. Profit margin, M, also has an effect on capital requirements. The higher the profit margin, the lower the external funds requirement, other things held constant. Because of the relationship between profit margin and external capital requirements, some very rapidly growing firms do not need much external capital.

IV. **The percentage of sales method assumes that spontaneous asset and liability items increase at the same rate as sales, in other words, that the**

Assets/Sales and Liabilities/Sales ratios remain constant over time. There are times, however, when this assumption is incorrect.

A. *Economies of scale* are present in the use of many kinds of assets, and where these economies occur, ratios are likely to change over time as the size of the firm increases.

B. *Lumpy assets* are those fixed assets which, because of technological considerations, increase only in large, discrete units. Thus, even a small increase in sales may require a doubling of fixed assets, thus creating large financial requirements.
   1. An alternative approach to dealing with lumpy assets would be to determine whether the firm is at full capacity, include in the spontaneous assets only those assets that realistically increase in proportion to sales, and add into the AFN formula a new term, FA, representing those lumpy, fixed assets.
   2. FA would not be stated as a percentage, but simply as the estimated dollar amount of lumpy, fixed assets needed for the year in question.

C. *Cyclical/Seasonal changes* can affect excess operating capacity and influence the stability of other ratios.

D. To determine the future optimal level of an asset not currently being used to full capacity, a modification of the forecast of additional funds needed is required.
   1. Determine *full capacity sales* by dividing current sales by the percentage at which fixed assets were operated.
   2. Then use this figure to determine the *target fixed assets to sales ratio* (by dividing the current level of fixed assets by full capacity sales) in the calculation of additional financing requirements.

V. **Larger, well-managed firms have computerized financial planning models. These models automatically generate pro forma statements based on a set of assumptions and input parameters.**

DEFINITIONAL QUESTIONS

1. The most important element in financial planning is the _______ __________.

2. Those asset items that typically increase proportionately with higher sales are ______, ___________, and ________________. _______ assets are frequently not used to full capacity and hence would not increase in proportion to sales.

3. If various asset categories increase, _____________ and/or ______ must also increase if the balance sheet is to balance.

4. Typically, certain liabilities will rise _________________ with sales. These include accounts __________ and _________.

5. __________ _______ and _______ ________ are examples of liability accounts that do not increase automatically with higher levels of sales, since their levels depend on formal action by the financial manager.

6. As the dividend ____________ ______ is increased, the amount of earnings available to finance new assets is ____________.

7. Retained earnings depend not only on next year's sales level and dividend payout ratio but also on the _________ _________.

8. The amount of assets required per dollar of sales, A*/S, is often called the _________ ____________ ______.

9. A capital intensive industry will require large amounts of __________ capital to finance increased growth.

10. The percentage of sales method assumes that the ______ of balance sheet items to ______ is ___________ at all levels of sales.

11. The assumption of constant percentage of sales ratios may not be accurate when assets must be added in discrete amounts, called _____________ assets, or when ____________ of scale are considered.

12. The ____________ ____ _______ ________ is based on the assumptions that most balance sheet items are tied directly to sales and that current levels of all assets are optimal for the current sales level.

13. Assets that vary directly and proportionately with sales are called ____________ assets.

14. _______________ ___________ _______ come from such sources as accounts payable and accruals.

15. The difference between projected assets and the liabilities and equity of the pro forma balance sheet is the ____________ _______ ________.

16. The term 1 - d in the AFN formula is the percentage of earnings the firm retains, which is often called the ___________ ______.

17. If all assets grow proportionately with sales, the capital intensity ratio is the reciprocal of the _______ ________ __________ _______.

18. ______ __________ _______ is calculated by dividing current sales by the percentage at which fixed assets were operated.

19. The ________ _______ ________ ____ _______ ratio is calculated by dividing the current level of fixed assets by full capacity sales.

CONCEPTUAL QUESTIONS

20. An increase in a firm's inventories will call for additional financing unless the increase is offset by an equal or larger decrease in some other asset account.

a. True b. False

21. If the capital intensity ratio of a firm actually decreases as sales increase, use of the percentage of sales method will typically *overstate* the amount of additional funds required, other things held constant.

a. True b. False

22. If the dividend payout ratio is 100 percent, all ratios are held constant, and the firm is operating at full capacity, then any increase in sales will require additional financing.

a. True b. False

23. One of the first steps in the percentage of sales method is to identify those asset and liability accounts which increase spontaneously with retained earnings.

a. True b. False

24. Which of the following would *reduce* the additional funds needed if all other things are held constant?

a. An increase in the dividend payout ratio.
b. A decrease in the profit margin.
c. An increase in the capital intensity ratio.
d. An increase in the expected sales growth rate.
e. A decrease in the firm's tax rate.

PROBLEMS

25. United Products Inc. has the following balance sheet:

Current assets	$5,000	Accounts payable	$1,000
Net fixed assets	5,000	Notes payable	1,000
		Long-term debt	4,000
		Common equity	4,000
Total assets	$10,000	Total liabilities & equity	$10,000

Business has been slow; therefore, fixed assets are vastly underutilized. Management believes it can double sales next year with the introduction of a new product. No new fixed assets will be required, and management expects that there will be no earnings retained next year. What is the firm's additional funding requirement for next year?

a. $0
b. $4,000
c. $6,000
d. $13,000
e. $19,000

26. The 1993 balance sheet for American Pulp and Paper is shown below (millions of dollars):

Cash	$ 3.0	Accounts payable	$ 2.0
Accounts receivable	3.0	Notes payable	1.5
Inventory	5.0	Long-term debt	3.0
Current assets	$11.0	Common equity	7.5
Fixed assets	3.0		
Total assets	$14.0	Total liabilities & equity	$14.0

In 1993, sales were $60 million. In 1994, management believes that sales will increase by 20 percent to a total of $72 million. The profit margin is expected to be 5 percent, and the dividend payout ratio is targeted at 40 percent. The firm has excess capacity and no increase in fixed assets will be required. What additional funds are needed for 1994?

a. $0.36 million
b. $0.24 million
c. $0 million
d. -$0.24 million
e. -$0.36 million

27. Refer to Problem 26. Assume no excess capacity exists. How much can sales grow above the 1993 level of $60 million without requiring any additional funds?

a. 12.28%
b. 14.63%
c. 15.75%
d. 17.65%
e. 18.14%

28. Smith Machines Inc. has net income this year of $500 on sales of $2,000 and is operating its fixed assets at full capacity. Management expects sales to increase by 25 percent next year and is forecasting a dividend payout ratio of 30 percent. The profit margin is not expected to change. If spontaneous liabilities are $500 this year, and no excess funds are expected next year, what is Smith's total assets this year?

a. $1,000
b. $1,500
c. $2,250
d. $3,000
e. $3,500

29. A firm has the following balance sheet and other data (in thousands of dollars):

Cash	$ 80	Accounts payable	$ 80
Accounts receivable	80	Notes payable	160
Inventories	80	Long-term debt	320
Net fixed assets	720	Common stock	320
		Retained earnings	80
Total assets	$960	Total liab. & equity	$960

Fixed assets are being used at 80 percent of capacity; sales for the year just ended were $1,600,000; sales will increase $800,000 next year; the profit margin is 5 percent; and the dividend payout ratio is 60 percent. What is the firm's additional financing requirements for next year?

a. $176,000
b. $200,000
c. $225,000
d. $250,000
e. $275,000

(The following data applies to the next five problems.)

Whitney Inc. has been growing at a rapid rate lately. As a result, Ms. Whitney has been unable to devote proper attention to the management of the firm's assets. Expected sales for next year are $5.4 million with a net profit margin of 3 percent. The expected beginning of the year retained earnings are $980,000 and current liabilities are $475,000. Long-term debt of $850,000 and common stock equal to $500,000 have remained constant for some time. In addition, the firm wishes to maintain a cash balance of $120,000. Whitney anticipates no dividend payout next year and any additional financing needed (AFN) will be raised through notes payable. Ms. Whitney computed the following financial ratios:

Days sales outstanding = 35 days,
Inventory turnover = 5 times,
Fixed assets turnover = 4 times.

30. Including the expected increase in cumulative retained earnings, how much will Whitney have to raise to support the expected level of sales?

a. $108,000
b. $162,000
c. $208,775
d. $270,000
e. $298,475

31. How much of the total will be generated internally (equity) and externally (debt)?

a. $60,000; $48,000
b. $100,000; $62,000
c. $162,000; $46,775
d. $162,000; $108,000
e. $162,000; $136,475

32. What is Whitney's debt ratio?

a. 42.3%
b. 46.6%
c. 48.9%
d. 51.3%
e. 54.5%

33. What is Whitney's current ratio?

a. 1.58
b. 1.75
c. 2.06
d. 2.45
e. 2.96

34. What is the firm's return on assets?

a. 3.33%
b. 5.27%
c. 7.75%
d. 9.00%
e. 10.75%

(The following data applies to the next four problems.)

Midland Manufacturing Company has estimated that the following balance sheet accounts from this year should equal the same percentages of next year's sales:

Cash	$135,000	(8%)	Accounts payable	$421,875	(25%)
Receivables	506,250	(30%)	Accruals	270,000	(16%)
Inventory	759,375	(45%)			

The forecasted sales level for next year represents a $675,000 increase over this year's sales. In keeping with past dividend policy, management plans to pay out $165,375 in dividends next year and retain $70,875. The firm has excess capacity and therefore does not need new fixed assets.

35. How much additional external financing does Midland need next year?

a. $212,625
b. $225,825
c. $246,898
d. $255,037
e. $278,091

36. If Midland has to maintain a current ratio of at least 1.8, how much of the projected external financing can be short-term bank loans? (Assume that the firm has no short-term debt at this time other than payables and accruals.)

a. $ 54,398
b. $ 76,134
c. $101,456
d. $112,875
e. $120,750

37. What is the expected profit margin and dividend payout ratio for next year?

a. 10%; 25%
b. 10%; 30%
c. 10%; 70%
d. 12%; 70%
e. 15%; 70%

38. Now assume that one of Midland's competitors has just gone out of business. This creates an opportunity for Midland to increase its sales dramatically next year to $3 million by purchasing the other firm's building and land for $575,000. There will still be some excess capacity at the original plant, but that cannot be helped. If the profit margin, the dividend payout ratio, A^*/S, and L^*/S remain unchanged, what is Midland's AFN for next year if it goes ahead with the purchase and realizes $4 million in combined sales? (Hint: Treat this as a lumpy fixed asset and modify the AFN equation.)

a. $ 989,175
b. $1,036,250
c. $1,088,136
d. $1,112,798
e. $1,153,333

ANSWERS AND SOLUTIONS

1. sales (demand) forecast
2. cash; receivables; inventories; Fixed
3. liabilities; equity
4. spontaneously; payable; accruals
5. Mortgage bonds; notes payable
6. payout ratio; decreased
7. profit margin
8. capital intensity ratio
9. external
10. ratio; sales; constant
11. lumpy; economies
12. percentage of sales method
13. spontaneous
14. Spontaneously generated funds
15. additional funds needed (AFN)
16. retention rate
17. total assets turnover ratio
18. Full capacity sales
19. target fixed assets to sales

20. a. When an increase in one asset account is not offset by an equivalent decrease in another asset account, then financing is needed to reestablish equilibrium on the balance sheet. Note, though, that this additional financing may come from a spontaneous increase in accounts payable or from retained earnings.

21. a. A decreasing capital intensity ratio, A*/S, means that less assets are required, proportionately, as sales increase. Thus, the external funding requirement is overstated. Always keep in mind that the percentage of sales method assumes that the asset/sales ratios are constant regardless of the level of sales.

22. a. With a 100% payout ratio, there will be no retained earnings. When the firm is operating at full capacity, all assets are spontaneous, but all liabilities cannot be spontaneous since a firm must have common equity. Thus, the growth in assets cannot be matched by a growth in spontaneous liabilities, so additional financing will be required in order to keep the financial ratios (the debt ratio in particular) constant.

23. b. The first step is to identify those accounts which increase spontaneously with sales.

24. e. Answers a through d would increase the additional funds required, but a decrease in the tax rate would raise the profit margin and thus increase the amount of available retained earnings.

25. b. Look at next year's balance sheet:

Current assets	\$10,000	Accounts payable	\$2,000
Net fixed assets	5,000	Notes payable	1,000
		Long-term debt	4,000
		Common equity	4,000
Total assets	\$15,000	Total claims	\$11,000

With no retained earnings next year, the common equity account remains at \$4,000. Thus, the additional financing requirement is \$15,000 - \$11,000 = \$4,000.

26. e. Since fixed assets are sufficient to absorb the increase in sales, this item is not included in the computation. Therefore, only \$11 million of the \$14 million in total assets will increase spontaneously with sales. None of the items on the right side of the balance sheet rises spontaneously with sales except accounts payable. Therefore,

$$AFN = (A^*/S)(\Delta S) - (L^*/S)(\Delta S) - MS_1(1 - d)$$

$$= (\$11/\$60)(\$12) - (\$2/\$60)(\$12) - 0.05(\$72)(0.6)$$

$$= \$2.2 - \$0.4 - \$2.16 = -\$0.36 \text{ million.}$$

This means that the increased profits and spontaneously generated liabilities are sufficient to support the additional assets required. Thus, no additional funds will be required. In fact, there will be an internally generated surplus of funds of \$360,000.

27. d. Note that g = sales growth = $(S_1 - S_0)/S_0$, and $S_1 = S_0(1 + g)$. Then,

$$AFN = A^*g - L^*g - M[(S_0)(1 + g)](1 - d) = 0$$

$$0 = \$14g - \$2g - 0.05[(\$60)(1 + g)](0.6)$$

$$0 = \$12g - 1(\$3 + \$3g)(0.60)$$

$$0 = \$12g - \$1.8 - \$1.8g$$

$$\$10.20g = \$1.80$$

$$g = 0.1765 = 17.65\%.$$

28. c. $\$0 = (A^*/S)(\Delta S) - (L^*/S)(\Delta S) - MS_1(1 - d)$

$\$0 = (A^*/\$2,000)(\$500) - (\$500/\$2,000)(\$500) - (\$500/\$2,000)(\$2,500)(1 - 0.3)$

$\$0 = (\$500A^*/\$2,000) - \$125 - \$437.50$

$\$0 = (\$500A^*/\$2,000) - \$562.50$

$\$562.50 = 0.25A^*$

$A^* = \$2,250.$

29. a. Full capacity sales = \$1,600,000/0.80 = \$2,000,000.

Target FA to Sales = \$720,000/\$2,000,000 = 0.36.

Target FA level = 0.36(\$1,600,000 + \$800,000) = \$864,000, but already have \$720,000 in fixed assets.

Fixed assets needed = \$864,000 - \$720,000 = \$144,000.

AFN calculation (in thousands of dollars):

$$\begin{aligned} AFN &= A^*/S(\Delta S) + FA - L^*/S(\Delta S) - MS_1(1 - d) \\ &= \$240/\$1,600(\$800) + FA - \$80/\$1,600(\$800) - 0.05(\$2,400)(0.4) \\ &= \$120 + \$144 - \$40 - \$48 \\ &= \$176. \end{aligned}$$

30. d.

Cash	\$ 120,000[1]	Curr. Liab.	\$ 475,000[1]
Receivables	525,000[2]	Notes Payable	108,000[8]
Inventory	1,080,000[3]		
Tot. Curr. Assets	\$1,725,000	Tot. Curr. Liab.	\$ 583,000[7]
Net FA	1,350,000[4]	LT Debt	850,000[1]
		Common Stock	500,000[1]
		Ret. Earnings	\$1,142,000[6]
Total Assets	\$3,075,000[5]	Total Liab. & Eq.	\$3,075,000[5]

[1] Given.

[2] Receivables/(Sales/360) = 35; Receivables/(\$5,400,000/360) = 35; Receivables = \$15,000(35) = \$525,000.

[3] Sales/Inventory = 5; \$5,400,000/Inventory = 5; Inventory = \$5,400,000/5 = \$1,080,000.

[4] Sales/NFA = 4; \$5,400,000/NFA = 4; Net FA = \$5,400,000/4 = \$1,350,000.

[5] Total Assets = Cash + Receivables + Inventory + Fixed Assets

Total Assets = \$120,000 + \$525,000 + \$1,080,000 + \$1,350,000
Total Assets = Total Liab. & Equity = \$3,075,000.

[6] Retained Earnings = Beg. R/E + Net Income - Dividends
= \$980,000 + 0.03(\$5,400,000)- \$0
= \$980,000 + \$162,000 = \$1,142,000.

[7] Total Curr. Liab. = \$3,075,000 - \$1,142,000 - \$500,000 - \$850,000
= \$583,000.

[8] Notes Payable = \$583,000 - \$475,000 = \$108,000.

Total Funds to be Raised = Debt + Equity = \$108,000 + \$162,000 = \$270,000.

31. d. See answer to Problem 30.

32. b. Debt Ratio = Total Debt/Total Assets
= (\$583,000 + \$850,000)/\$3,075,000 = 46.6%.

33. e. Current Ratio = Current Assets/Current Liabilities
= \$1,725,000/\$583,000 = 2.96.

34. b. ROA = Net Income/Total Assets = \$162,000/\$3,075,000 = 5.27%.

35. a. ΔS = \$675,000 (given).
S_0 = \$1,687,500. (Any of the sales percentages given can be used to determine S_0.)

S_1 = \$1,687,500 + \$675,000 = \$2,362,500.

Net Income = Dividends + Addition to R/E
= \$165,375 + \$70,875 = \$236,250.

Profit Margin = \$236,250/\$2,362,500 = 10%.

Dividend Payout = \$165,375/\$236,250 = 70%.

$AFN = A^*/S(\Delta S) - L^*/S(\Delta S) - MS_1(1 - d)$
$= \$1,400,625/\$1,687,500(\$675,000) - \$691,875/\$1,687,500(\$675,000)$
$- 0.1(\$2,362,500)(1 - 0.7)$
$= \$560,250 - \$276,750 - \$70,875 = \$212,625.$

36. e. Current Assets = (0.08 + 0.30 + 0.45)(\$2,362,500) = \$1,960,875.

Current Assets/Current Liabilities = 1.8.
Current Liabilities = \$1,960,875/1.8 = \$1,089,375.
Spontaneous Liabilities = (0.25 + 0.16)(\$2,362,500) = \$968,625.
Additional Debt Possible = \$1,089,375 - \$968,625 = \$120,750.

37. c. See answer to Problem 35.

38. b. ΔS = \$3,000,000 - \$1,687,500 = \$1,312,500.

$$AFN = A^*/S(\Delta S) + FA - L^*/S(\Delta S) - MS_1(1 - d).$$
$$= \$1{,}400{,}625/\$1{,}687{,}500(\$1{,}312{,}500) + \$575{,}000$$
$$- \$691{,}875/\$1{,}687{,}500(\$1{,}312{,}500) - 0.1(\$3{,}000{,}000)(1 - 0.7)$$
$$= \$1{,}089{,}375 + \$575{,}000 - \$538{,}125 - \$90{,}000 = \$1{,}036{,}250.$$

CHAPTER 8
WORKING CAPITAL POLICY AND MANAGEMENT

OVERVIEW

Working capital policy involves decisions relating to current assets, including decisions about financing them. Since about 40 percent of the typical firm's capital is invested in current assets, working capital policy and management are important to the firm and its shareholders. Decisions made about working capital will have an impact on both the risk and the expected return of the firm, and due to the level of investment in working capital the impact on the firm is significant. In addition, about 60 percent of a financial manager's time is devoted to working capital policy and management, and many finance students' first assignment on the job will involve working capital policy.

OUTLINE

I. **Working capital policy is concerned with current assets, including decisions about how these assets will be financed. Financial managers spend more of their daily time and energy on working capital matters than on any other single function discussed in the text. In contrast, the choice of business projects and the associated fixed asset commitment occurs, for most firms, perhaps once or twice a year.**

A. *Working capital,* sometimes called *gross working capital,* is defined as total current assets, while *net working capital* is defined as current assets minus current liabilities. Net working capital is, therefore, the current assets financed by long-term sources of funds.

B. *Working capital ratios,* such as the *current ratio* and the *quick ratio,* provide an indication of the firm's liquidity, or its ability to meet obligations that will come due within a year.

1. These ratios, however, provide an incomplete picture of a firm's liquidity position, since they do not include cash flows from operations.

2. They provide only a starting point in analyzing a firm's financial position. The best and most comprehensive picture of a firm's liquidity position is obtained by examining its *cash budget,* which forecasts cash inflows and outflows.

3. Another tool used by managers in trying to estimate the firm's liquidity and its need for financing is the *cash conversion cycle.*

C. *Working capital management* involves the administration, within policy guidelines, of current assets and current liabilities.

1. Important elements include cash management, credit and collections, inventory management, and short-term borrowings.
2. Working capital management primarily concerns day-to-day operations.

II. **The working capital cash flow cycle, frequently referred to as the cash conversion cycle, is the process of converting cash into inventory which is sold--often on credit, in which case receivables result--and ultimately cash is again available and may be reinvested into current assets. Profits generated through this cycle increase equity.**

A. The essence of the *working capital cash flow cycle* is that the longer the cycle and the greater the investment in working capital per cycle, the greater the need for external financing.

B. The *cash conversion cycle model* utilizes three time periods which measure the average length of time to convert operating events into cash flows.

1. The *inventory conversion period* is the average length of time required to convert raw materials into finished goods and then to sell these goods.
   a. It can be calculated as 360/Inventory turnover ratio.
2. The *receivables conversion period* is the average length of time required to convert the firm's receivables into cash, that is, to collect cash from a sale.
   a. It is also called days sales outstanding (DSO).
3. The *payables deferral period* is the average length of time between the purchase of raw materials and labor and the cash payments for them.

C. The cash conversion cycle combines the three periods defined above to measure the average length of time the firm has funds tied up in current assets, in other words, from the day labor and suppliers are paid to the day receivables are collected.

D. The cash conversion cycle is measured by the following equation:

$$\begin{array}{c}\text{Inventory} \\ \text{conversion} \\ \text{period}\end{array} + \begin{array}{c}\text{Receivables} \\ \text{conversion} \\ \text{period}\end{array} - \begin{array}{c}\text{Payables} \\ \text{deferral} \\ \text{period}\end{array} = \begin{array}{c}\text{Cash} \\ \text{conversion.} \\ \text{cycle}\end{array}$$

1. The first two periods are the delay in the receipt of cash, while the third period is the payment delay. The result is the net delay in the receipt of cash.

E. The firm's goal should be to shorten the cash conversion cycle as much as possible without hurting operations, thus freeing up cash for the firm's use.

1. Actions such as reducing the inventory conversion period (by processing and selling goods more quickly), reducing the receivables conversion period (by speeding up collections), and extending the

payables deferral period (by slowing down the firm's payments) all combine to shorten the cash conversion cycle.

2. One must be cautious as to the adverse effects such actions can have on costs and/or sales.

III. Working capital policy involves two basic questions. An examination of alternative working capital investment policies deals with the first question, the level of investment in current assets.

A. The decision regarding the level of current assets involves a risk-return tradeoff. In general, the *greater* the proportion of current assets to fixed assets at any given level of output, the *less risky* the firm's working capital investment policy.

B. A *conservative working capital investment policy* means that the firm invests in larger amounts of cash or marketable securities, accounts receivable, and inventory than its level of sales seems to require.

C. An *aggressive working capital investment policy* is one under which levels of cash or marketable securities, inventories, and receivables are reduced to the minimum possible amount at a given level of operations.

D. A *moderate working capital investment policy* is between these two extremes.

E. An overly conservative working capital policy misallocates resources, which lowers the overall earning power of the firm. Just as lower returns are the price for the safety of a conservative working capital policy, there is a price associated with the higher potential returns in the aggressive policy--higher risk.

1. The preferred working capital investment policy lies somewhere between the two extremes.
2. A general guideline is that the level of current assets should be reduced as long as the marginal return from such an action is greater than or equal to the expected marginal cost.

IV. The second working capital policy decision involves how the firm's current asset investment is financed.

A. A firm's current asset requirements rise and fall with both business cycles and seasonal trends. However, even when a business is at its cyclical or seasonal low, its current assets do not drop to zero.

1. *Permanent current assets* make up the minimum working capital held throughout a firm's business cycle.
2. *Temporary current assets* are those that rise and fall with business activity for seasonal or cyclical reasons.

B. The manner in which the permanent and temporary current assets are financed constitutes the firm's *working capital financing policy.*

C. The *maturity matching approach* calls for the use of permanent financing (long-term debt and equity) to finance fixed assets and permanent current assets, and the use of short-term financing to cover temporary current assets.
   1. This strategy reduces the risk that the firm will be unable to pay off its maturing obligations.

D. The *aggressive approach* calls for the use of short-term financing to cover a portion of its permanent current assets, as well as all of its temporary current assets. Here, short-term debt is used because it is flexible and generally cheaper than long-term debt; however, it is a riskier source of debt.

E. The *conservative approach* calls for the use of long-term debt and equity capital to finance its fixed assets and all permanent current assets as well as a portion of temporary current assets, and then to hold temporary surplus funds as marketable securities at the cyclical lows. This is a safe approach to current asset financing, but one that potentially generates lower profits.

F. The aggressive financing policy calls for the greatest amount of short-term debt, the conservative financing policy uses the lowest amount, and the maturity matching approach falls in between.

G. The primary advantages of short-term credit are speed, flexibility, and lower cost.
   1. Since a short-term loan can be obtained much more quickly than a long-term loan, speed is important for a firm that needs funds in a hurry.
   2. For firms whose needs for funds are cyclical, short-term debt offers the advantage of flexibility. Long-term loan agreements are almost always restrictive and can have associated costs, for example when a firm decides to prepay a loan.
   3. Since short-term interest rates are normally lower than long-term rates, cost is an advantage to financing with short-term debt.

H. The primary disadvantage of short-term debt is that it is generally more risky than long-term debt.
   1. Short-term interest rates can fluctuate widely, so if a company finances with short-term debt, its interest expenses will also fluctuate. With long-term debt, interests costs will be fixed.
   2. Since short-term debt comes due in a shorter period, a firm may not have generated the cash to repay the debt. Thus, if its business is temporarily depressed, then it may be unable to refinance the loan, and it may be forced into bankruptcy.
   3. The lender may choose not to renew the loan, for reasons that have little to do with the potential borrower's financial position.
      a. In the 1990-1992 credit crunch, many smaller firms found themselves unable to renew short-term loans, which they could have obtained easily only a few years before.

b. Bankers had become more cautious because of the S&L crisis, declining real estate values, and the recession, and stricter banking regulations contributed to their suddenly very conservative lending practices.

DEFINITIONAL QUESTIONS

1. _______ working capital is defined as ____________ assets minus current __________.

2. The _______ _____________ ________ measures the average length of time to convert operating events into cash flows.

3. __________ ______ ________ is concerned with current assets, including decisions about how these assets will be financed.

4. In the maturity matching approach to current asset financing, permanent current assets should be financed with ________-______ capital, while __________ current assets should be financed with short-term credit.

5. __________ __________ __________ involves the administration, within policy guidelines, of current assets and current liabilities.

6. The primary advantages of short-term credit are _______, ____________, and ________ ______.

7. Short-term debt will be less expensive than long-term debt if the yield curve is __________ sloping.

8. Short-term interest rates fluctuate _________ than long-term rates.

9. _________ _________, sometimes referred to as _______ _________ _________, is defined as total current assets.

10. Net working capital is the current assets financed by ______-______ sources of funds.

11. Working capital ratios, such as the current ratio and the quick ratio, provide an indication of the firm's __________, or its ability to meet obligations that will come due within a year.

12. The essence of the working capital cash flow cycle is that the longer the cycle and the greater the investment in working capital per cycle, the _________ the need for __________ financing.

13. The __________ ____________ ________ is the average length of time required to convert raw materials into finished goods and then to sell these goods.

14. The ____________ ____________ ________ is the average length of time required to convert the firm's receivables into cash, that is, to collect cash from a sale.

15. The __________ __________ ________ is the average length of time between the purchase of raw materials and labor and the cash payments for them.

16. The firm's goal should be to _________ the cash conversion cycle as much as possible without hurting operations, thus freeing up cash for the firm's use.

17. The decision regarding the level of current assets involves a ______-________ tradeoff.

18. A(n) ______________ working capital investment policy means that the firm invests in larger amounts of cash or marketable securities, accounts receivable, and inventory than its level of sales seems to require.

19. A(n) ____________ working capital investment policy is one under which levels of cash or marketable securities, inventories, and receivables are reduced to the minimum possible amount at a given level of operations.

20. ___________ current assets make up the minimum working capital held throughout a firm's business cycle, while ___________ current assets are those that rise and fall with business activity for seasonal or cyclical reasons.

CONCEPTUAL QUESTIONS

21. The matching of asset and liability maturities is considered desirable because this strategy minimizes interest rate risk.

    a. True b. False

22. Other things held constant, an increase in the payables deferral period will lead to a reduction in the need for nonspontaneous financing.

    a. True b. False

23. Generally, a firm should use short-term debt, rather than long-term financing, to minimize its interest expense.

    a. True b. False

PROBLEMS

24. Schnell Industries Inc. has an inventory conversion period of 60 days, a receivables conversion period of 35 days, and a payables deferral period of 28 days. What is the length of the firm's cash conversion cycle?

a. 67 days
b. 82 days
c. 95 days
d. 104 days
e. 117 days

25. Refer to Problem 24. If Schnell's sales are $972,000 annually, what is the firm's investment in accounts receivables?

a. $72,450
b. $79,600
c. $85,300
d. $94,500
e. $100,000

26. On average, a firm sells $1 million in merchandise a month. It keeps inventory equal to its monthly sales on hand at all times. If the firm analyzes its accounts using a 360-day year, what is the firm's inventory conversion period?

a. 360 days
b. 180 days
c. 60 days
d. 30 days
e. 15 days

27. A company has a quick ratio of 1.5x and a current ratio of 2.25x. Total current assets are $1.8 million. What is the firm's net working capital?

a. $750,000
b. $1,000,000
c. $1,225,000
d. $1,250,000
e. $1,450,000

(The following data applies to the next four problems.)

Gapenski & Associates has $6 million in credit sales for the year, inventory of $975,000, and net fixed assets of $3.125 million. The firm has $200,000 in cash and marketable securities combined, and its total assets turnover ratio is 1.2x.

28. What is Gapenski's investment in accounts receivable?

a. $600,000
b. $650,000
c. $700,000
d. $750,000
e. $825,000

29. What is the firm's days sales outstanding (DSO)?

a. 36.0 days
b. 38.5 days
c. 42.0 days
d. 45.0 days
e. 49.5 days

30. What is the firm's inventory turnover ratio?

a. 4.72
b. 5.15
c. 5.38
d. 5.76
e. 6.15

31. If the payables deferral period is 30 days, what is Gapenski's cash conversion cycle?

a. 60.0 days
b. 62.5 days
c. 67.5 days
d. 70.5 days
e. 75.0 days

(The following data applies to the next two problems.)

Parker & Associates has sales of $6 million, earnings before interest and taxes of $700,000, and total assets of $2.5 million. Assets have been financed with $1,250,000 of 8 percent debt, the balance by common equity. The firm's average federal-plus-state tax rate is 40 percent.

32. What is the firm's return on equity?

a. 22.2%
b. 25.6%
c. 27.5%
d. 28.8%
e. 30.0%

33. If half of the firm's debt were short-term bank borrowing and short-term rates rise to 14 percent because of an inverted yield curve, and the cost of long-term debt remains 8 percent, what would be the firm's new ROE?

a. 21.0%
b. 24.2%
c. 26.4%
d. 27.0%
e. 28.5%

ANSWERS AND SOLUTIONS

1. Net; current; liabilities
2. cash conversion cycle
3. Working capital policy
4. long-term; temporary
5. Working capital management
6. speed; flexibility; lower cost
7. upward
8. more
9. Working capital; gross working capital
10. long-term
11. liquidity
12. greater; external
13. inventory conversion period
14. receivables conversion period
15. payables deferral period
16. shorten
17. risk-return
18. conservative
19. aggressive
20. Permanent; temporary

21. b. The matching of maturities lowers default risk, or the risk that the firm will be unable to pay off its maturing obligations.

22. a. An increase in the payables deferral period results in decreasing the length of the cash conversion cycle, thus reducing the need for nonspontaneous financing.

23. a. Generally, the yield curve slopes up, making the statement true. Even when the curve slopes down, this suggests that rates are likely to fall, in which case interest expense will fall if the firm uses short-term debt, but rates will be locked in (at a high level) if it uses long-term debt. Of course, if interest rates rise, the firm which financed with short-term debt may end up paying far more interest than a firm which obtained long-term funds when rates were lower.

24. a.

$$\begin{matrix}\text{Cash} & & \text{Inventory} & & \text{Receivables} & & \text{Payables}\\ \text{conversion} & = & \text{conversion} & + & \text{conversion} & - & \text{deferral}\\ \text{cycle} & & \text{period} & & \text{period} & & \text{period}\end{matrix}$$

= 60 days + 35 days - 28 days = 67 days.

25. d. Average sales per day = $972,000/360 = $2,700.

Average investment in receivables = $2,700(35) = $94,500.

26. d. Inventory conversion period = Inventory/(Sales/360).

Annual sales = $1 million x 12 = $12 million. Inventory = $1 million.

Inventory conversion period = 360/($12/$1) = 30 days.

27. b. Current assets/Current liabilities = 2.25
$1,800,000/Current liabilities = 2.25
2.25(Current liabilities) = $1,800,000
Current liabilities = $1,800,000/2.25 = $800,000.

NWC = CA - CL = $1,800,000 - $800,000 = $1,000,000.

28. c. Sales/Total assets = 1.2
$6,000,000/TA = 1.2
TA = $5,000,000.

Cash + A/R + INV + NFA = TA
$200,000 + A/R + $975,000 + $3,125,000 = $5,000,000
A/R = $5,000,000 - ($200,000 + $975,000 + $3,125,000)
= $700,000.

29. c. DSO = Accounts receivable/(Sales/360)
= $700,000/($6,000,000/360) = 42 days.

30. e. Inventory turnover = Sales/Inventory
= $6,000,000/$975,000 = 6.15x.

31. d. Cash conversion cycle = Inventory conversion period + Receivables conversion period - Payables deferral period

= 360/($6,000,000/$975,000) + 42 - 30 = 70.5 days.

32. d. TA = $2,500,000; 50% TA financed with debt ($1,250,000) and 50% financed with equity ($1,250,000).

EBIT	$700,000	
INT	100,000	($1,250,000 × 0.08)
EBT	$600,000	
Taxes (40%)	240,000	
NI	$360,000	

ROE = NI/E = $360,000/$1,250,000 = 28.8%.

33. d. INT = $625,000 × 0.14 + $625,000 × 0.08 = $137,500.

EBIT	$700,000
INT	137,500
EBT	$562,500
Taxes	225,000
NI	$337,500

ROE = NI/E = $337,500/$1,250,000 = 27.0%.

CHAPTER 9
MANAGING CASH AND MARKETABLE SECURITIES

OVERVIEW

This chapter begins with an overview of cash management, and then goes on to discuss the cash budget, cash management techniques, and matching the costs and benefits of cash management procedures. In addition, various types of marketable securities in which firms can invest temporary cash surpluses are discussed. Many factors contribute to good cash management. For example, it is possible to influence the timing of cash inflows and outflows by speeding up the collection of checks received and slowing down the payment of checks written. Excess cash is generally held as marketable securities. Here, safety is the watchword, and rarely will a financial manager sacrifice safety for higher yields.

OUTLINE

I. **Cash is defined as the total of demand deposits plus currency. Also, near-cash, short-term marketable securities are often reported on corporate financial statements. Cash balances vary widely both across industries and among firms within a given industry, depending on specific conditions and on their owners' and managers' aversion to risk.**

A. Firms hold cash for four primary reasons:
1. *Transactions balances* are held to provide the cash needed to conduct routine business operations.
2. *Compensating balances* are often required by banks to offset the costs of providing loans and services.
3. *Precautionary balances* are held in reserve for unpredictable fluctuations in cash inflows and outflows.
4. *Speculative balances* are held to enable the firm to take advantage of bargain purchases.

B. Most firms do not segregate funds for each of these motives, but they do consider them in setting their overall cash positions.

C. Because cash is a nonearning asset, excessive cash balances reduce the total assets turnover, thereby reducing both the firm's rate of return on equity and the value of its stock.
1. The higher the level of short-term interest rates, the greater the *opportunity cost* associated with holding excess cash.

II. **A cash budget shows the firm's projected cash inflows and outflows over some specified period of time.**

A. The *target cash balance* is the amount of cash that a firm plans to maintain in order to conduct business. Any firm's target cash balance is normally set as the larger of (1) its transactions balances plus precautionary (safety stock) balances or (2) its required compensating balances as determined by its agreements with banks.

B. Firms generally construct a monthly *cash budget* forecasted over the next 6 to 12 months for general planning purposes, plus a more detailed daily or weekly cash budget for the coming month for actual cash control.

1. Cash budgets may need to be prepared on a daily basis if a firm's cash inflows and outflows are not uniform during the month.
2. Because depreciation is a noncash expense, it does not appear on the cash budget.
3. Because the cash budget represents a forecast, all the values in the table are *expected values*. The financial manager must constantly monitor the cash budget in order to modify it as actual sales and purchases differ from forecasted levels.
4. Computerized spreadsheet programs are particularly helpful for constructing and analyzing cash budgets, and can answer many "what-if" questions about different levels of forecasted cash flows.
5. Methods have been developed for setting and controlling a firm's cash balance, based on such variables as the fixed costs of obtaining a loan or of liquidating marketable securities and the opportunity cost of holding cash.
6. The target cash balance probably will be adjusted over time, rising and falling with seasonal patterns and with long-term changes in the scale of the firm's operations.

III. **Although a carefully prepared cash budget is a necessary starting point for managing the firm's cash, there are other elements of a good cash management program. The financial manager is responsible for the effectiveness of the cash management program.**

A. New techniques, particularly computerized electronic funds transfer mechanisms, have made improved cash management possible.

B. *Synchronizing cash inflows and outflows* increases the certainty of the firm's cash budget forecasts, and thus reduces its cash balances, decreases its required bank loans, lowers interest expenses, and boosts profits.

C. *Speeding up collections* permits a firm to operate with smaller cash balances. Although cash collection is the financial manager's responsibility, the speed with which checks are cleared is dependent on the banking system. Several techniques are used both to speed collection and to get the funds where they are needed.

1. The use of a *lockbox plan*, which is one of the oldest cash management tools, can substantially reduce the time required to process checks and thus to receive payments.

a. In a lockbox system, customers mail checks to a post office box in a specified city. A local bank then collects the checks, deposits them, starts the clearing process, and notifies the selling firm that payment has been received.
b. Processing time is further reduced because it takes less time for banks to collect local checks.
c. To determine whether a lockbox system is advantageous, the firm must compare the banks' fees with the savings from freeing up funds.
d. Higher annual savings will be realized by firms from a lockbox plan when their volume of sales is high, the reduction in collection time is significant, and the opportunity cost is high (what can be earned on freed-up funds by investing in marketable securities or paying down short-term debt).

2. *Pre-authorized debits* allow funds to be automatically transferred from a customer's account to the firm's account on specified dates. These transactions are also called "checkless" or "paperless" transactions because they are accomplished without using traditional paper checks. The transfer of funds is accelerated because mail and check-clearing times are totally eliminated.
3. The primary purpose of *concentration banking* is to mobilize funds from decentralized receiving locations into one or more central cash pools. Concentration accounts allow firms to take maximum advantage of economies of scale in cash management and investment.
4. At any given time, a firm has a number of checks that it has written but that have not been deducted by the bank from its account (*disbursement float*) as well as a number of checks that it has received but that have not yet been credited to its account (*collections float*). This difference is called *net float*:

Net float = Disbursement float - Collections float.

a. Net float can also be defined as the difference between a firm's checkbook balance and the balance shown on the bank's books.
b. In general, it is good to operate with positive net float.
c. The size of a firm's net float is a function of its ability to speed up collections on checks received and to slow down collections on checks written.

D. *Controlling and slowing disbursements* permits a firm to operate with smaller cash balances.

1. A widely used procedure for delaying payments is the use of *drafts*. A draft must be transmitted to the issuer for approval, and then the issuer must deposit the funds to cover the draft, after which it can be collected.
2. No single action controls cash outflows more effectively than *payables centralization*, which permits the financial manager to evaluate the payments coming due for the entire firm and to schedule cash transfers to meet these needs on a company-wide basis.

3. In an *overdraft system* a firm writes checks in excess of its actual balance, and its bank automatically extends loans to cover the shortage.
4. *Zero-balance accounts (ZBAs)* are special disbursement accounts on which checks are written. They are typically established at concentration banks and have a zero-dollar balance. ZBAs simplify the control of disbursements and cash balances, hence reduce the amount of idle cash.
5. *Controlled disbursement accounts* can be set up at any bank and are not funded until the day's checks are presented against the account.

E. Cash management techniques and procedures must be extended when applied to large, national or multinational firms. A sound cash management program for a *multidivisional firm* necessarily includes provisions for keeping strict control over the level of funds in each account and for shifting funds among accounts to minimize the total corporate cash balance.

F. Though firms can make direct fee payments for bank services, they often find it more convenient to maintain compensating balances to avoid paying cash service charges to the bank. These cash balances provide the bank with enough income to compensate for the costs associated with the firm's business.

1. Compensating balances also are required by some bank loan agreements.
2. Compensating balances may be established as an *absolute minimum* or as a *minimum average balance* over some time period, generally a month.

IV. **A firm should incur expenses for cash management programs as long as marginal returns exceed or equal marginal expenses.**

A. Larger firms with larger cash balances can better afford to hire the personnel necessary to maintain tight control over their cash positions. Cash management is one element of business operations in which *economies of scale* are present.

B. The value of careful cash management depends greatly on the costs of funds invested in cash, which in turn depend on the current interest rate.

V. **Marketable securities typically provide much lower yields than a firm's operating assets, yet they are often held in sizable amounts.**

A. Firms hold marketable securities as a *substitute for larger cash balances*, and then sell some securities when cash is needed.

1. Marketable securities could be a substitute for transactions, precautionary, or speculative balances, or all three.
2. In most cases the securities are held primarily for precautionary balances. Most firms prefer to rely on bank credit to meet temporary transactions or speculative needs.

B. Marketable securities are often held as a *temporary investment*.
   1. Seasonal or cyclical operations may generate surplus cash at some times and deficits at other times. Marketable securities may be used to smooth out these cash fluctuations.
   2. Marketable securities may be used to accumulate funds for a known financial requirement such as a bond redemption or a major tax payment.
   3. Proceeds from a major stock or bond issue may be temporarily invested in marketable securities until they are needed for permanent investment in operating assets.

C. A firm's marketable securities policy is an integral part of its overall working capital policy.

D. A wide variety of securities are available, and they differ in terms of inflation risk, default risk, liquidity risk, interest rate risk, and expected rate of return (yield).
   1. *Inflation risk* is the risk that inflation will reduce the purchasing power of a given sum of money.
      a. It is usually somewhat easier to assess what inflation will be over the next 3 months to a year than to estimate inflation over 30 years. It is, therefore, more likely that the inflation premium built into the nominal interest rate of short-term securities is close to actual inflation, than when the inflation premium is incorporated into the nominal rate of a 30-year bond.
   2. *Default risk* is the risk that an issuer will not be able to make promised interest payments or to repay principal amounts on schedule.
   3. *Liquidity risk* refers to whether an asset can be sold on short notice for its *fair market value*.
   4. *Interest rate risk* involves the changes in security prices that occur with changes in interest rates.
   5. Most firms emphasize safety in their marketable securities portfolios even though such an investment policy requires a sacrifice in terms of the rates of return (yields) earned on the portfolios.

E. The *marketable securities portfolio* is generally composed of highly liquid short-term securities issued either by the U.S. government or by the very strongest corporations.

F. Many types of securities are available for investment of surplus cash.
   1. Government securities are issued by the U.S. Treasury and other federal agencies and provide a wide variety of securities with different maturities.
      a. *Treasury bills* have maturities that run from 91 days to one year.
      b. *Treasury notes* offer longer maturities of 2 to 10 years, while *Treasury bonds* offer maturities of up to 30 years. Because of their longer maturities, these securities may be poor choices for *near-cash reserves*.

c. U.S. federal agencies also issue notes and bonds that are riskier than Treasury issues because they are not backed by the U.S. Treasury.

2. A *banker's acceptance* is a promissory note of a business debtor resulting from a business transaction, in which the bank has endorsed it and assumed obligation of payment at the due date.
   a. It is widely used, has a low degree of risk if guaranteed by a strong bank, and there is a ready market for it.
   b. It is sold at a discount below face value and then paid off at face value when it matures, so the discount amounts to interest on the acceptance.
   c. The effective yield on a strong banker's acceptance is generally a little above the Treasury bill rate.
3. *Commercial paper* are short-term unsecured promissory notes issued by the largest, most financially secure U.S. corporations.
   a. Commercial paper is highly liquid, and can be sold to raise cash in a matter of hours.
   b. Maturities generally vary from one to nine months, with an average of five months. Its rates are relatively low compared to other securities due to its low default risk.
4. Major banks issue *negotiable certificates of deposit* as marketable receipts for large time deposits, which usually mature within 12 months after issuance.
   a. The interest paid on these instruments is negotiated and is paid at maturity.
5. *Money market mutual funds* are a popular source of liquidity for both businesses and individuals, and hold only short-term securities such as Treasury bills, CDs, and commercial paper.
   a. They are a popular temporary investment alternative for small firms because of low initial investment requirements.
6. *Eurodollar bank time deposits* are interest-bearing time deposits, denominated in U.S. dollars and placed in banks outside the U.S.
   a. In some ways, Eurodollars are an international counterpart to the negotiable certificate of deposit because interest and maturities are negotiated.

DEFINITIONAL QUESTIONS

1. The funds needed to carry on the everyday business activities of the firm are referred to as __________ balances.

2. __________ balances are maintained in order to allow for random, unforeseen fluctuations in cash __________ and __________.

3. Cash balances held to enable the firm to take advantage of bargain purchases are known as __________ balances.

4. ____________ balances are maintained to pay banks for services they perform.

5. A(n) __________ ___________ shows the firm's projected cash inflows and outflows over some specified time period.

6. Efficient cash management is often concerned with speeding up the __________ of checks received and slowing down the _________ of checks written.

7. One method for improving the collection process is the use of a(n) ___________ system, which is one of the oldest cash management tools.

8. Many firms delay the actual payment of bills by the use of ______, which must be submitted to the issuer for approval, rather than checks.

9. The difference between a firm's balance on its own books and its balance as carried on the bank's books is known as _____ _________.

10. As a general rule, a firm should invest in cash management operations so long as the marginal ______ on the cash saved exceed the marginal ______ of freeing this cash.

11. Compensating balances may be determined as an absolute ______ amount or as a minimum ______ balance over some period of time, generally a month.

12. A procedure whereby a bank automatically extends a loan to cover checks in excess of the actual balance in an account is known as a(n) ___________ system.

13. Business firms subject to ______ or cyclical patterns of cash flows may invest ______ funds in marketable securities and then liquidate them when cash ______ occur.

14. ___________ risk refers to an issuer's inability to make interest payments and to repay the ___________ at maturity.

15. The higher the level of short-term interest rates, the greater the ______________ ______ associated with holding excess cash.

16. The _________ _______ __________ is the amount of cash that a firm plans to maintain in order to conduct business.

17. ________________ cash inflows and outflows increases the certainty of the firm's cash budget forecasts, and thus reduces its cash balances, decreases its required bank loans, lowers interest expenses, and boosts profits.

18. _____-_______________ _________ allow funds to be automatically transferred from a customer's account to the firm's account on specified dates.

19. The primary purpose of ________________ ___________ is to mobilize funds from decentralized receiving locations into one or more central cash pools.

20. Firms hold marketable securities as a ___________ for larger cash balances and as a __________ ___________.

CONCEPTUAL QUESTIONS

21. Money market mutual funds are suitable vehicles for investment of surplus cash, especially for small firms.

    a. True   b. False

22. The term "interest rate risk" refers to the probability that a firm will be unable to continue making interest payments on its debt.

    a. True   b. False

23. Which of the following actions would not be consistent with good cash management?

    a. Increasing the synchronization of cash flows.
    b. Using ZBA accounts in disbursing funds.
    c. Using lockboxes in funds collection.
    d. Maintaining an average cash balance equal to that required as a compensating balance or that which minimizes total cost.
    e. Minimizing the use of float.

24. Which of the following investments is not likely to be a proper investment for temporarily idle cash?

    a. Commercial paper.
    b. Treasury bills.
    c. Recently issued long-term AAA corporate bonds.
    d. Treasury bonds due within one year.
    e. AAA corporate bonds due within one year.

PROBLEMS

25. The Mill Company has a daily average collection of checks of $250,000. It takes the company 4 days to convert the checks to cash. Assume a lockbox system could be employed which would reduce the cash conversion period to 3 days. The lockbox system would have a net cost of $25,000 per year, but any additional funds made available could be invested to net 8 percent per year. Should Mill adopt the lockbox system?

a. Yes; the system would free $250,000 in funds.
b. Yes; the benefits of the lockbox system exceed the costs.
c. No; the benefit is only $10,000.
d. No; the firm would lose $5,000 per year if the system were used.
e. The benefits and costs are equal; hence the firm is indifferent toward the system.

26. Nesca Corporation has a daily average collection of checks equal to $300,000. It takes the firm approximately 5 days to convert the funds into cash. Assume a lockbox system could be employed which would reduce the cash conversion procedure to 3 days and the firm could invest any additional cash received at 5% (after tax). The maximum Nesca should pay for the lockbox system is:

a. $24,000
b. $27,000
c. $29,000
d. $30,000
e. $32,000

27. Matthew and Sarah Weisner recently leased space in the Plaza Shopping Center and opened a new business, Weisner's Ice Cream Shop. Business has been good but the Weisners frequently run out of cash. This has necessitated late payment on certain ice cream orders, which in turn is beginning to cause a problem with suppliers. The Weisners plan to borrow from a bank to have cash ready as needed, but first they need to forecast how much cash will be needed. Therefore, they have decided to prepare a cash budget for June, July, and August to determine their cash needs. Ice cream sales are made on a cash basis only. The Weisners must pay for their ice cream orders 1 month after the purchase. Rent is $1,000 per month, and they pay themselves a combined salary of $2,400 per month. In addition, they must make a tax payment of $6,000 in June. The current cash on hand (June 1) is $200, but the Weisners have decided to maintain a target cash balance of $3,000. Estimated ice cream sales and purchases for June, July, and August are given below. May purchases amounted to $70,000.

	Sales	Purchases
June	$80,000	$20,000
July	20,000	20,000
August	30,000	20,000

What amount of money will the Weisners need to borrow or have in surplus in each of the months in the budget period (June, July, and August)?

a. $2,200; $5,600; ($1,000)*
b. $2,700; $5,600; ($1,000)*
c. $2,200; $9,400; ($1,000)*
d. ($1,000)*; $4,700; $500
e. $2,200; $5,600; $2,000

*The firm projects a cash surplus in this month.

ANSWERS AND SOLUTIONS

1. transactions
2. Precautionary; inflows; outflows
3. speculative
4. Compensating
5. cash budget
6. collection; payment
7. lockbox
8. drafts
9. net float
10. returns; costs
11. minimum; average
12. overdraft
13. seasonal; surplus; shortages
14. Default; principal
15. opportunity cost
16. target cash balance
17. Synchronizing
18. Pre-authorized debits
19. concentration banking
20. substitute; temporary investment

21. a. They offer safety and liquidity, the two most important factors in choosing marketable securities.

22. b. Interest rate risk stems from a security's loss of value if interest rates rise. Default risk refers to the probability of missing interest payments.

23. e. Management should try to maximize float.

24. c. Long-term bonds have too much interest rate risk for the firm's liquid asset portfolio.

25. d. Currently, Mill has 4($250,000) = $1,000,000 in unavailable collections. If lockboxes were used, this could be reduced to $750,000. Thus, $250,000 would be available to invest at 8 percent, resulting in an annual return of 0.08($250,000) = $20,000. If the system costs $25,000, Mill would lose $5,000 per year by adopting the system.

26. d. Proceeds = $300,000(2)(0.05) = $30,000. If Nesca paid more than $30,000, they would be losing money on the lockbox system.

27. a.

Worksheet	June	July	August
Sales	$80,000	$20,000	$30,000
Purchases	20,000	20,000	20,000
Payments for purchases	70,000	20,000	20,000
Cash budget			
Receipts from sales	$80,000	$20,000	$30,000
Payments:			
Purchases	$70,000	$20,000	$20,000
Salaries	2,400	2,400	2,400
Rent	1,000	1,000	1,000
Taxes	6,000		
Total payments	$79,400	$23,400	$23,400
Net cash gain (loss)	$ 600	($ 3,400)	$ 6,600
Cash at start of month	200	800	(2,600)
Cumulative cash	$ 800	($ 2,600)	$ 4,000
Less: Target cash bal.	3,000	3,000	3,000
Surplus cash or total loans to maintain $3,000 target cash balance	($ 2,200)	($ 5,600)	$ 1,000

CHAPTER 10
ACCOUNTS RECEIVABLE AND INVENTORIES

OVERVIEW

The average firm has about 25 percent of its assets in receivables and another 25 percent in inventories. Effective management of these two accounts is therefore vital to the firm's profitability. If receivables and inventories are allowed to build up to excessive levels, the firm's total assets turnover ratio and its return on total assets (ROA) will decline. In addition, because some portion of these current assets is typically financed through debt, the resulting higher interest payment will reduce the firm's net income, and consequently, its profit margin, which reduces the firm's ROA even further.

In general, firms would rather sell for cash than on credit, but granting credit normally stimulates sales. The investment in receivables is dependent on the firm's credit policy, which reflects four variables: (1) the credit period if no discount is taken, (2) cash discounts offered, (3) credit standards, and (4) collection policy. Easier credit stimulates sales, but it also has some costs, and the optimal credit policy involves a tradeoff between these benefits and costs.

Inventory management focuses on three basic questions: (1) How many units of each inventory item should the firm hold in stock? (2) How many units should be ordered (or produced) at a given time? (3) At what point should inventory be ordered (or produced)? Since inventories must be acquired prior to sales, accurate sales forecasts are essential if these questions are to be answered correctly. It should be noted that inventory models center around the balancing of a set of costs that decline with larger holdings, and another set of costs that increase with larger holdings. The economic ordering quantity (EOQ) model is a formal model which balances these two sets of costs and minimizes the total costs of ordering and carrying inventories.

OUTLINE

I. **Accounts receivable are created when goods and services are sold on credit rather than on a cash basis. Carrying receivables is costly, but the costs involved can be offset by the fact that granting credit benefits the firm by increasing its sales. The optimal credit policy is the one at which the marginal benefits of increased sales are exactly offset by the marginal costs of granting credit.**

   A. The total amount of a firm's accounts receivable outstanding at any given time is determined by two factors:
   1. The volume of credit sales.
   2. The average length of time between sales and collections (DSO).

B. Both the volume of credit sales and DSO are functions of economic conditions that are not controllable by management, and credit policy variables which, subject to such considerations as industry practice, are factors that management can change, if such change appears to offer benefits that at least match the costs involved.

II. A firm's credit policy, a major controllable variable which can contribute to the level of sales for a firm, consists of four elements.

A. *Credit period* is the length of time a company gives its customers to pay.

1. The actual credit period depends on terms offered by competitors and the relationship to the normal inventory holding period.
2. The credit period and the discount allowed, when combined, are called the *credit terms*.
3. The bottom line in establishing a credit period is determining the point at which marginal profits on increased sales just offset the marginal costs.

B. *Cash discounts* to encourage early payment can be analyzed by balancing the costs and benefits of different discount terms.

1. Cash discounts should attract new customers who consider discounts a type of price reduction.
2. Cash discounts should reduce days sales outstanding (DSO) because some old customers will pay more promptly to take advantage of the discount.
3. If sales are seasonal, a firm may use *seasonal dating* on discounts, terms to induce customers to buy early by not requiring payment until the customers' selling season, regardless of when the merchandise is shipped.

C. *Credit standards* refer to the strength and creditworthiness a customer must exhibit in order to qualify for credit. If the firm extended credit sales to only the strongest of customers, it would never have bad debt losses. However, it would probably be losing some sales.

1. Setting credit standards implicitly requires a measurement of *credit quality*, which is defined in terms of the probability of a customer's default. To measure credit quality, credit managers consider the five Cs of credit.
   a. *Character* refers to the likelihood that customers will try to honor their obligations.
   b. *Capacity* is a subjective judgment of customers' ability to pay.
   c. *Capital* is measured by the general financial condition of firms as indicated by an analysis of their financial statements, with special emphasis on the risk ratios.
   d. *Collateral* refers to any assets the customers may offer as security to obtain credit.
   e. *Conditions* refers both to general economic trends and to special developments in certain geographic regions or sectors of the economy that may affect customers' ability to meet their obligations.

2. Two major sources of external credit information are *credit associations*, which are local groups that meet frequently and correspond with one another to exchange information on credit customers, and *credit-reporting agencies*, which collect credit information and sell it for a fee, such as Dun & Bradstreet.
3. Although most credit decisions are subjective, many firms now use a sophisticated statistical *credit scoring system* method called *multiple discriminant analysis (MDA)* to assess credit quality.
    a. One major advantage of MDA is that a customer's credit quality is expressed in a single numerical value rather than as a subjective assessment of various factors.
4. Modern credit managers often practice *management by exception*, where statistical procedures are used to classify customers into five or six categories according to degree of risk, and the credit manager then concentrates time and attention on the customers judged most likely to cause problems.

D. *Collection policy* refers to the procedures used to collect receivables. The collection process can be expensive in terms of both direct costs and lost goodwill, but some firmness is needed to prevent an undue lengthening of the collection period and to minimize outright losses.

1. Changes in collection policy influence the sales level, the collection period, the bad debt loss percentage, and the percentage of customers who take discounts.

III. In addition to the four basic policy variables previously discussed, there are three other considerations influencing credit policy: the profit potential in carrying receivables, the use of receivables in obtaining short-term credit, and legal considerations.

A. It is possible sometimes to sell on credit and assess a carrying charge (interest) on the receivables that are outstanding, making credit sales more profitable than cash sales.

B. Having receivables often means that a firm has access to short-term financing it otherwise might not have obtained. This financing takes two forms:

1. *Pledging of receivables* as collateral for short-term borrowing.
2. *Factoring of receivables*, where a third party, such as a bank or a financing company, purchases the receivables outright.

C. It is illegal to offer more favorable credit terms to one customer or class of customers than to another, unless the differences are cost justified.

IV. Two tools are useful in monitoring the effectiveness of a firm's credit policy.

A. The *days sales outstanding (DSO)* can be compared to the firm's credit terms. If the DSO is greater than the length of time permitted by the firm's credit terms, then, on average, its customers are not paying their bills on time.

B. An *aging schedule* provides a better view of the situation by breaking down a firm's receivables according to how long they have been outstanding.

C. Management should constantly monitor the firm's DSO and aging schedule to detect trends, to see how the firm's collection experience compares with its credit terms, and to see how effectively the credit department is operating in comparison with other firms in the industry.

D. Although a change in the DSO or the aging schedule should be a signal to the firm to investigate its credit policy, a deterioration in either of these measures does not necessarily indicate that the firm's credit policy has weakened.
   1. If a firm experiences sharp seasonal variations, or if its sales have been growing or declining rapidly, then both the aging schedule and the DSO will be distorted.

V. **Easing the credit policy normally stimulates sales. However, as sales rise, costs also rise because more labor and materials will be required to produce the additional goods, receivables outstanding will increase, which will raise carrying costs, and bad debt or discount expenses may also rise.**

A. The key question when considering a credit policy change is whether sales revenues will rise more than costs. The way to answer this question is to compare projected income statements which reflect the incremental changes in expected sales revenues and costs that would result from proposed changes in the credit policy.

B. Once the estimated increase in net sales has been determined by factoring in expected changes in gross sales, discounts, and production costs, changes in credit-related costs must be determined.
   1. The *cost of carrying receivables* is the product of the days sales outstanding, sales per day, the variable cost ratio, and the cost of funds used to carry receivables.
      a. *Only variable costs are considered* because only this portion needs to be financed as a result of a change in the credit policy.
   2. Credit analysis and collection expenses will likely *decrease* with a change toward a more relaxed credit policy.
   3. Bad debt losses, however, will likely *increase* with a more relaxed policy.

C. The combined effects of all the estimated changes in credit policy are summarized in the change in net income. While an increase in net income could indicate that the change in the credit policy is a favorable one, financial managers must be cautious of the uncertainty in credit policy analysis.

1. For example, the projected increase in sales may not occur at all if the firm's competitors match the credit policy changes.
2. In the final analysis, the decision to make the credit policy change will be based on judgment, but the quantitative analysis set forth above is essential to a good judgmental decision.

VI. **Inventories, which include raw materials, work-in-process, and finished goods (or merchandise for a retailer), are an essential part of most business operations.**

A. Inventories are greatly influenced by the level of sales, and since inventories must be acquired before sales can take place, an accurate sales forecast is critical to effective inventory management.

B. Managers must maintain inventories at levels which balance the benefits of reducing the level of investment against the costs associated with lowering inventories.

C. Inventory management focuses on three basic questions:
1. How many units of each inventory item should the firm hold in stock?
2. How many units should be ordered (or produced) at a given time?
3. At what point should inventory be ordered (or produced)?

VII. **The goal of inventory management is to provide the level of inventory necessary for efficient operations at the minimum cost. The first step in developing an inventory model is to identify the costs associated with ordering and carrying inventories.**

A. *Carrying costs* generally rise in direct proportion to the average amount of inventory held. These costs include cost of the capital tied up in inventories, storage costs, insurance, property taxes, and depreciation and obsolescence.

B. *Ordering costs* decline with large orders, because the costs of placing orders, setting up production runs, and handling shipments will decline if the firm orders infrequently and thus holds larger quantities.

C. *Stock-out costs* are those costs associated with running short of inventory.

VIII. **The economic ordering quantity (EOQ) model is a commonly used approach to determine the optimal inventory level for a firm. The EOQ model is based on the premise that some costs rise with larger inventories while other costs decline, and that there is an optimal order size which minimizes total costs associated with inventories.**

A. The *EOQ model*, which is derived by minimizing the total inventory cost function, is

$$EOQ = \sqrt{\frac{2(F)(S)}{(C)(P)}}.$$

EOQ = the optimal quantity to order each time an order is placed.
F = fixed costs of placing and receiving an order.
S = annual sales in units.
C = carrying cost expressed as a percentage of inventory value.
P = purchase price the firm must pay per unit of inventory.

B. The assumptions of the model include the following:

1. Sales can be forecast perfectly.
2. Sales are evenly distributed throughout the year.
3. Orders are received with no delays.
4. F,C, and P are all fixed and independent of the ordering procedures.

C. The *reorder point* is the inventory level at which an order should be placed and is calculated as follows:

Reorder point = Lead time x Usage rate - Goods in transit.

1. *Lead time* is the time lag between the order and delivery of goods.
2. *Usage rate* is the number of units of inventory sold in a given time period.
3. *Goods in transit* are items which have been ordered but have not been received yet.

D. *Safety stocks* are additional inventories carried by firms to guard against uncertainty in sales rates and the potential for production and shipping delays.

1. The optimal level of safety stock increases with the uncertainty in sales forecasts, the costs associated from inventory shortages, and the probability of delays in receiving shipments.
2. The optimal level of safety stock decreases with the increased cost of carrying extra inventory.

IX. In addition to the EOQ model, plus the safety stock analysis, inventory ordering and control systems are used by firms to establish the proper inventory level. There are several methods available to determine when the reorder point is reached.

A. The *red-line method* is a simple control procedure in which a red line is drawn around the inside of the bin at the level of the reorder point. When the red line shows, an order is placed.

B. The *two-bin method* has inventory items stocked in two bins. When the working bin is empty, an order is placed and inventory is drawn from the second bin.

C. Companies are increasingly employing *computerized inventory control systems* which automatically monitor changes in inventory levels and then place orders when the inventory level of an items falls to a specified amount.

   1. A good inventory control system is dynamic, not static.

D. Inventory management should focus on those items which are most critical to the firm. The *ABC system* analyzes and classifies each inventory item on the basis of its cost, frequency of usage, seriousness of a stock-out, order lead time, and other criteria related to the item's importance. Thus, Category A items, are those that are expensive, are frequently used, and have long order lead times. Category B items are somewhat less important items, and Category C are relatively unimportant items.

X. **Two other inventory control practices are worth noting.**

A. The *just-in-time (JIT) system* is used by a manufacturer to coordinate production with suppliers so that raw materials and components arrive from suppliers just as they are needed in the production process. This increased coordination between suppliers and users reduces total inventory requirements as well as total production costs.

B. *Out-sourcing* is the practice of purchasing components rather than making them in-house. Because of its own labor costs, a firm may find it can purchase components at a lower cost outside the firm than within the firm, thus reducing total inventory costs.

C. There is a relationship between production scheduling and inventory levels. If a firm established a level production schedule, its inventories would rise sharply during periods when sales were low and then decline during peak sales periods, but the average inventory held would be substantially higher than if production were geared to rise and fall with sales.

D. Just-in-time systems, out-sourcing, and production scheduling all point out the necessity of coordinating inventory policy with manufacturing and procurement policies.

DEFINITIONAL QUESTIONS

1. __________ ______________ are created when goods are sold or services are performed on credit.

2. A firm's outstanding accounts receivable will be determined by the __________ of credit sales and the length of time between ______ and ______________.

3. Sales volume and the collection period will be affected by a firm's ________ _________.

4. Extremely strict credit standards will result in lost ________.

5. Effective credit standards require a balance between the ___________ costs of credit and the marginal ________ on increased sales.

6. The five Cs of credit refer to ____________, ___________, __________, ___________, and _____________.

7. Credit terms generally specify the _________ for which credit is granted and any ______ ___________ that are offered for early payment.

8. The optimal credit terms involve a tradeoff between increased ______ and the cost of carrying additional __________ _____________.

9. ______________ policy refers to the manner in which a firm tries to obtain payment from past-due accounts.

10. Credit sales may be especially profitable if __________ is charged on outstanding accounts receivable.

11. _______ _____________ are local groups which meet to exchange credit information.

12. Inventories include ______ ______________, ________- _____-_________ and ___________ ________.

13. The ___________ classification method is used to focus managerial resources on those inventory items deemed most critical.

14. Storage costs, obsolescence, and other costs that ___________ with larger inventories are known as ___________ costs.

15. Ordering and receiving costs are ________ related to average inventory size.

16. The __________ __________ quantity minimizes the total costs of ordering and holding inventories.

17. When the level of inventories reaches the _________ _________, the EOQ amount should be ordered.

18. A(n) _________ _________ must be maintained in order to allow for shipping delays and changes in the _________ rate.

19. _________ ____________ refer to the strength and creditworthiness a customer must exhibit in order to qualify for credit.

20. Although most credit decisions are subjective, many firms now use a sophisticated statistical _________ __________ _________ method called multiple discriminant analysis (MDA) to assess credit quality.

21. A(n) _________ ___________ breaks down a firm's receivables according to how long they have been outstanding.

22. The ______ ____ ___________ ______________ is the product of the days sales outstanding, sales per day, the variable cost ratio, and the cost of funds used to carry receivables.

23. ________ __________ and _____________ __________ will likely decrease with a change toward a more relaxed credit policy, while _____ ______ ________ will likely increase with a more relaxed policy.

24. _______-_____ _______ are those costs associated with running short of inventory.

25. _______ ___ _________ are items which have been ordered but have not been received yet.

CONCEPTUAL QUESTIONS

26. A firm changes its credit policy from 2/10, net 30, to 3/10, net 30. The change is to meet competition, so no increase in sales is expected. The firm's average investment in accounts receivable will probably increase as a result of the change.

    a. True   b. False

27. If a credit policy change increases accounts receivable, the entire amount of the increase must be financed by some external source of funds.

    a. True   b. False

28. The economic ordering quantity (EOQ) is the order quantity that provides the minimum total cost; that is, both the ordering and carrying cost components are minimized.

    a. True   b. False

29. An aging schedule is constructed by a firm to keep track of when its accounts payable are due.

    a. True   b. False

30. The goal of credit policy is to

    a. Minimize bad debt losses.
    b. Minimize the DSO.
    c. Maximize sales.
    d. Minimize collection expenses.
    e. Extend credit to the point where marginal profits equal marginal costs.

31. The addition of a safety stock to the EOQ model

a. Increases the EOQ proportionately.
b. Raises the reorder point.
c. Lowers the reorder point.
d. Does not change the total inventory costs.
e. Results in greater variability in the time required to receive deliveries.

32. The costs of a stock-out do *not* include

a. Disruption of production schedules.
b. Loss of customer goodwill.
c. Depreciation and obsolescence.
d. Loss of sales.
e. Both statements c and d above.

PROBLEMS

(The following data apply to the next three problems.)

Simmons Brick Company sells on terms of 3/10, net 30. Gross sales for the year are $1,200,000 and the collections department estimates that 30 percent of the customers pay on the tenth day and take discounts; 40 percent pay on the thirtieth day; and the remaining 30 percent pay, on average, 40 days after the purchase. Assume 360 days per year.

33. What is the days sales outstanding (DSO)?

a. 10 days
b. 13 days
c. 20 days
d. 27 days
e. 40 days

34. What is the current receivables balance?

a. $60,000
b. $70,000
c. $75,000
d. $80,000
e. $90,000

35. What would be the new receivables balance if Simmons toughened up on its collection policy, with the result that all nondiscount customers paid on the thirtieth day?

a. $60,000
b. $70,000
c. $75,000
d. $80,000
e. $90,000

(The following data apply to the next three problems.)

Furston Inc., a retail firm, currently has sales of $1 million. Its credit period and DSO are both 30 days, and 1 percent of its sales end up as bad debts. Furston's credit manager estimates that if the firm extends its credit period to 45 days, sales will increase by $100,000, but its bad debt losses on the incremental sales would be 3 percent. Variable costs are 40 percent, and the cost of carrying receivables, k, is 15 percent. Assume a tax rate of 40 percent and 360 days per year.

36. What would be the *incremental* investment in receivables if the change were made?

a. $3,250
b. $12,352
c. $21,667
d. $33,891
e. $41,667

37. What would be the incremental cost of carrying receivables?

a. $0
b. $3,250
c. $5,000
d. $8,250
e. $10,000

38. What would be the incremental change in profits?

a. $15,875
b. $26,875
c. $29,250
d. $32,250
e. $41,857

(The following data apply to the next four problems.)

The Magnuson Company is trying to determine its optimal inventory policy. The following relationships and conditions exist for the firm:

1. Annual sales are 120,000 units.
2. The purchase price per unit is $500.
3. The carrying cost is 20 percent of inventory value.
4. The fixed costs per order are $600.
5. The optimal safety stock is 500 units, which are already on hand.
6. Assume 360 days per year.

39. What is the economic ordering quantity (EOQ)?

a. 600 units
b. 800 units
c. 1,000 units
d. 1,200 units
e. 1,400 units

40. What is the maximum inventory the company will hold?

a. 1,300 units
b. 1,400 units
c. 1,500 units
d. 1,600 units
e. 1,700 units

41. What is the average inventory the company will hold?

a. 600 units
b. 850 units
c. 1,100 units
d. 1,200 units
e. 1,700 units

42. How often will the company order?

a. Every 2.0 days
b. Every 3.60 days
c. Every 5.25 days
d. Every 2 weeks
e. Continually

43. Eileen Barak, credit manager of Household Gadgets Inc., uses multiple discriminant analysis in assessing its customers' risk. The firm has an extensive data base of historical information on its customers and Barak has developed the following discriminant function:

Score = 3.5(TIE) + 8.0(Quick ratio) - 31.0(Debt/Assets)
+ 1.9(Years in business).

Household Gadgets considers a score above 40 indicative of a good credit risk. One of the firm's customers, Kitchen Wizard, has asked for credit, and Barak must decide whether to grant the request. Kitchen Wizard has the following ratios:

TIE = 2.70
Quick ratio = 1.50
Debt/Assets = 0.45
Years in business = 12

What is Kitchen Wizard's credit score, and should Barak grant the customer credit?

a. Kitchen Wizard's credit score is 30.30; consequently, Barak should not grant the firm credit because its credit score is below 40.
b. Kitchen Wizard's credit score is 34.65; consequently, Barak should not grant the firm credit because its credit score is below 40.
c. Kitchen Wizard's credit score is 41.24; consequently, Barak should grant the firm credit because its credit score is above 40.
d. Kitchen Wizard's credit score is 45.91; consequently, Barak should grant the firm credit because its credit score is above 40.
e. Kitchen Wizard's credit score is 48.00; consequently, Barak should grant the firm credit because its credit score is above 40.

ANSWERS AND SOLUTIONS

1. Accounts receivable
2. volume; sales; collections
3. credit policy
4. sales
5. marginal; profits
6. character; capacity; capital; collateral; conditions
7. period; cash discounts
8. sales; accounts receivable
9. Collection
10. interest
11. Credit associations
12. raw materials; work-in-process; finished goods
13. ABC
14. increase; carrying
15. inversely
16. economic ordering
17. reorder point
18. safety stock; usage
19. Credit standards
20. credit scoring system
21. aging schedule
22. cost of carrying receivables
23. Credit analysis; collection expenses; bad debt losses
24. Stock-out costs
25. Goods in transit

26. b. No new customers are being generated. The current customers pay either on Day 10 or Day 30. The increase in trade discount will induce some customers who are now paying on Day 30 to pay on Day 10. Thus, the days sales outstanding will be shortened, and this will cause a decline in accounts receivable.

27. b. Receivables are based on the sales price, which generally includes a profit, but only the actual cash outlays associated with receivables must be financed. The remainder, or profit, appears on the balance sheet as an increase in retained earnings.

28. b. The total cost, or the sum of the ordering and carrying costs, is minimized, but neither of these component costs is minimized. For example, to minimize carrying costs, no inventory would be kept on hand at all, but then ordering costs would be very large.

29. b. The aging schedule breaks down accounts receivable according to how long they have been outstanding.

30. e. The goal of credit policy is to maximize overall profits. This is achieved when marginal profits equal marginal costs.

31. b. The addition of a safety stock increases the reorder point by the amount of the safety stock.

32. c. Depreciation and obsolescence are inventory carrying costs.

33. d. 0.3(10 days) + 0.4(30 days) + 0.3(40 days) = 27 days.

34. e. Receivables = (DSO)(Sales/360) = 27($1,200,000/360) = $90,000.

35. d. New days sales outstanding = 0.3(10) + 0.7(30) = 24 days.
Sales per day = $1,200,000/360 = $3,333.33.
Receivables = $3,333.33(24 days) = $80,000.00.

Thus, the average receivables would drop from $90,000 to $80,000. Furthermore, sales may decline as a result of the tighter credit and reduce receivables even more. Also, some additional customers may now take discounts, which would further reduce receivables.

36. c. The incremental receivable investment is calculated as follows:

Old credit policy: (DSO)(Sales per day)(Variable cost ratio)

$$(30)\left(\frac{\$1,000,000}{360}\right)(0.4) = \$33,333.$$

New credit policy: (DSO)(Sales per day)(Variable cost ratio)

$$(45)\left(\frac{\$1,100,000}{360}\right)(0.4) = \$55,000.$$

The incremental investment in receivables is $55,000 - $33,333 = $21,667.

37. b. The incremental cost of carrying receivables is calculated as follows:

Old credit policy:

(DSO)(Sales per day)(Variable cost ratio)(Cost of funds)

$$(30)\left(\frac{\$1,000,000}{360}\right)(0.4)(0.15) = \$5,000.$$

New credit policy:

(DSO)(Sales per day)(Variable cost ratio)(Cost of funds)

$$(45)\left(\frac{\$1,100,000}{360}\right)(0.4)(0.15) = \$8,250.$$

Thus, the incremental cost is \$8,250 - \$5,000 = \$3,250.

38. d.

	Income Statement Under Current Policy	Effect of Change	Income Statement Under New Policy
Sales	\$1,000,000	\$100,000	\$1,100,000
Less discounts			
Net sales			
Variable costs	400,000	40,000	440,000
Profit before credit costs	\$ 600,000	\$ 60,000	\$ 660,000
Credit related costs:			
Cost of carrying receivables	5,000	3,250	8,250
Collection expenses	0	0	0
Bad debt losses	10,000	3,000	13,000
Earnings before taxes	\$ 585,000	\$ 53,750	\$ 638,750
Taxes (40%)	234,000	21,500	255,500
Net income	\$ 351,000	\$ 32,250	\$ 383,250

39. d.

$$EOQ = \sqrt{\frac{2(F)(S)}{(C)(P)}} = \sqrt{\frac{2(\$600)(120{,}000)}{0.20(\$500)}} = \sqrt{\frac{\$144{,}000{,}000}{\$100}} = 1{,}200 \text{ units.}$$

40. e. Maximum inventory = EOQ + Safety stock = 1,200 + 500 = 1,700 units.

41. c. Average inventory = EOQ/2 + Safety stock = 600 + 500 = 1,100 units.

42. b. 120,000 units per year/1,200 units per order = 100 orders per year.

360 days per year/100 orders per year = 3.60 days.

The firm must place one order every 3.60 days.

43. a. Kitchen Wizard's credit score is calculated as follows:

$$\begin{aligned} \text{Score} &= 3.5(\text{TIE}) + 8.0(\text{Quick}) - 31.0(\text{D/A}) + 1.9(\text{Yrs.}) \\ &= 3.5(2.7) + 8.0(1.5) - 31.0(0.45) + 1.9(12) \\ &= 30.3. \end{aligned}$$

Because Kitchen Wizard's credit score is below 40, Barak should not grant them credit.

CHAPTER 11
SHORT-TERM FINANCING

OVERVIEW

Working capital management involves decisions relating to current assets, including decisions about how these assets are to be financed. Any statement about the flexibility, cost, and riskiness of short-term versus long-term credit depends to a large extent on the nature of the short-term credit that is actually used. The choice of the short-term credit instrument will affect both the firm's riskiness and its expected rate of return, and, hence the market value of its stock. This chapter examines the sources and characteristics of the major types of short-term credit available to the firm.

Short-term credit is defined as any liability originally scheduled for payment within one year. There are four major types of short-term credit: (1) accruals such as accrued wages and taxes, (2) accounts payable (trade credit), (3) loans from commercial banks and finance companies (notes payable), and (4) commercial paper. Companies use accruals on a regular basis, but this usage is not discretionary. Trade credit, bank loans, and commercial paper are controllable, at least within limits. In many situations, lenders require security when furnishing short-term credit, and this security is often in the form of accounts receivable and inventories.

OUTLINE

I. **Accrued wages and taxes increase automatically as a firm's operations expand.**

A. This type of debt is "free" in the sense that no explicit interest is paid on funds raised through accruals.

B. A firm cannot ordinarily control its accruals: the timing of wage payments is set by economic forces and industry custom, while tax payment dates are established by law. Thus, firms use all the accruals they can, but they have little control over the level of these accounts.

II. **Accounts payable (trade credit), is the largest single category of short-term debt, representing about 40 percent of the current liabilities of the average nonfinancial corporation.**

A. *Trade credit* is a spontaneous source of financing in the sense that it arises from ordinary business transactions. Most firms make purchases on credit, recording the debt as an *account payable*.

B. Lengthening the credit period, as well as expanding sales and purchases, generates additional financing.

C. The cost of trade credit is based on discounts lost by not paying invoices within the discount period.
   1. For example, if credit terms are 2/10, net 30, the cost of 20 additional days of credit is 2 percent of the dollar value of the purchases made.
   2. The following equation may be used to calculate the *approximate percentage cost,* on an annual basis, of not taking discounts:

$$\text{Approximate percentage cost} = \frac{\text{Discount percent}}{100 - \begin{pmatrix}\text{Discount}\\ \text{percent}\end{pmatrix}} \times \frac{360}{\begin{pmatrix}\text{Days credit is}\\ \text{outstanding}\end{pmatrix} - \begin{pmatrix}\text{Discount}\\ \text{period}\end{pmatrix}}.$$

   3. The first term in the equation is the *periodic cost* of the trade credit and the second term shows how many times each year the cost is incurred.

D. Competitive conditions may permit firms to lower the cost of trade credit by taking discounts beyond the discount period or by paying late. Such practices, called *stretching accounts payable,* reduce the cost of trade credit, but they also result in poor relationships with suppliers.

E. Trade credit can be divided into two components.
   1. *Free trade credit* is that credit received during the discount period.
   2. *Costly trade credit,* which involves credit in excess of the free trade credit, has an implicit cost equal to the forgone discounts. This costly component should be used only when it is less expensive than the cost of funds obtained from other sources.

III. **Bank loans, which appear on a firm's balance sheet as notes payable, represent another important source of short-term financing.**

A. Bank loans are not generated spontaneously but must be negotiated and renewed on a regular basis, and consequently, banks' influence is actually greater than it appears from the dollar amounts they lend.

B. Choosing a bank involves an analysis of the following variables:
   1. Policies toward risk. Some banks are quite conservative, while others are more willing to make risky loans.
   2. Advice and counsel. A bank's ability to provide advice and counsel is particularly important to firms in their formative years.
   3. Degree of loyalty. Banks differ in the extent to which they will support the activities of their borrowers during bad economic times.
   4. Degree of loan specialization. Firms should seek out a bank which specializes in making loans for their particular type of business.
   5. Size of the bank. This is a consideration for large companies when establishing a borrowing relationship because most banks cannot lend

to a single customer more than 15 percent of the total amount of the bank's capital accounts.

6. Ability to provide merchant banking services. The term merchant bank was originally applied to banks which not only loaned depositors' money, but also provided customers with equity capital and financial advice. Currently, the larger banks, often through holding companies, are being permitted to get back into merchant banking, at least to a limited extent.
7. Other services. The availability of services such as lockbox systems and assistance with electronic funds transfers should also be taken into account when selecting a bank.

C. The main features of bank loans include the following:

1. The majority of a bank's loans are short-term loans; two thirds of all bank loans mature in a year or less.
2. When a bank loan is approved, the agreement is executed by the signing of a *promissory note* which specifies the following:
   a. The amount borrowed;
   b. The percentage interest rate;
   c. The repayment schedule;
   d. Any collateral offered as security; and
   e. Any other terms of the loan, such as guarantees by third parties, limitations on additional debt, and the like.
3. Banks normally require regular borrowers to maintain *compensating balances* equal to 10 to 20 percent of the face value of loans. Such required balances increase the loan's *effective interest rate*.
4. A *line of credit* is an agreement between the bank and the borrower indicating the maximum amount of credit the bank will extend to the borrower.
5. A *revolving credit agreement* is a formal line-of-credit arrangement often used by large firms. Normally, the borrower will pay the bank a *commitment fee* to compensate the bank for guaranteeing that the funds will be available. This fee is paid in addition to the regular interest charge on funds actually borrowed.
   a. The bank has a legal obligation to honor a revolving credit agreement, while no legal obligation exists under the line-of-credit agreement.

D. The cost of bank loans varies for different types of borrowers at a given point in time, and for all borrowers over time. Rates charged vary depending on economic conditions, Federal Reserve policy, the risk of the borrower, and the size of the loan.

1. If a firm can qualify as a "prime risk" because of its size and financial strength, it can borrow at the *prime rate*, which has traditionally been the lowest rate banks charge.

E. Interest rates on bank loans are calculated in several ways:

1. *Regular, or simple, interest*. For a loan with simple interest, the borrower receives the entire amount of the loan's face value and then

repays both interest and principal at maturity. In this case, *the nominal, or stated, rate of interest is also the effective rate.*

$$\text{Effective annual rate}_{\text{Simple}} = \frac{\text{Interest}}{\text{Amount received}}.$$

2. *Discount interest.* Under this method, the bank deducts interest from the approved loan amount before the borrower receives the proceeds of the loan. Discounting the loan, therefore, increases the effective rate of interest.

$$\text{Effective annual rate}_{\text{Discount}} = \frac{\text{Interest}}{\text{Amount received}} = \frac{\text{Interest}}{\text{Face value} - \text{Interest}}.$$

3. *Installment loans: add-on interest.* Interest charges are calculated and then added on to the funds received to determine the face value of the note, which is paid off in equal installments. The borrower has use of the full amount of the funds received only until the first installment is paid. The approximate effective annual rate is double the stated rate, because the average amount of the loan outstanding is only about half the face amount borrowed.

$$\begin{array}{c}\text{Approximate}\\ \text{effective annual rate}_{\text{Add-on}}\end{array} = \frac{\text{Interest}}{(\text{Amount received})/2}.$$

4. *Compensating balances* tend to raise the effective interest rate on bank loans.
   a. Firms will be required to borrow more than they actually need in order to maintain the compensating balance. The total amount is calculated as follows:

$$\text{Face amount of loan} = \frac{\text{Funds needed}}{1.0 - \text{CB (decimal)}}.$$

   b. In general, this formula is used to find the effective interest rate when compensating balances apply and interest is paid at the end of the period:

$$\text{Effective annual rate}_{\text{Simple/CB}} = \frac{\text{Nominal interest rate (\%)}}{1.0 - \text{CB (decimal)}}.$$

   c. The analysis can be extended to the case where compensating balances are required and the loan is based on discount interest:

$$\text{Effective annual rate}_{\text{Discount/CB}} = \frac{\text{Nominal interest rate (\%)}}{1.0 - \begin{array}{c}\text{Nominal}\\ \text{rate (decimal)}\end{array} - \begin{array}{c}\text{CB}\\ \text{(decimal)}\end{array}}.$$

   d. It should be noted that when compensating balances or discount interest or both apply, the borrower must borrow a face amount *significantly greater* than the funds actually received. For a *discount loan with a compensating balance,* the face amount is calculated as follows:

$$\text{Face amount of loan} = \frac{\text{Funds needed}}{1.0 - \text{Nominal rate (decimal)} - \text{CB (decimal)}}.$$

IV. **Commercial paper, another source of short-term credit, is unsecured promissory notes of large, strong firms, which are sold primarily to other business firms, to insurance companies, to pension funds, to banks, and to money market funds in denominations of $100,000 or more.**

A. Maturities of commercial paper vary from one to nine months from the original date of issue.

B. Interest rates on prime commercial paper generally range from two to three percentage points below the stated prime rate and only slightly above the T-bill rate. However, rates fluctuate daily in the marketplace, and since no compensating balance is required, the effective cost differential versus the prime rate is still wider.

C. One potential problem with commercial paper is that a debtor who is in temporary financial difficulty may receive little help, because commercial paper dealings are generally less personal than banking relationships. On the other hand, using commercial paper permits a corporation to tap a wide range of credit sources, and this can reduce interest costs.

D. Like bonds, commercial paper is *rated*, and the quality of the commercial paper is reflected in the rating.

V. **For a strong firm, borrowing on an unsecured basis is generally cheaper and simpler than on a secured loan basis because of the administrative costs associated with the use of security. However, lenders will refuse credit without some form of collateral if a borrower's credit standing is questionable.**

A. Most secured short-term business loans involve the pledge of short-term assets such as accounts receivable or inventories as collateral.

B. The legal procedures for establishing loan security have been standardized and simplified in the *Uniform Commercial Code*.
   1. The heart of the Uniform Commercial Code is the *Security Agreement*, a standardized document or form on which the specific pledged assets are listed.

VI. **In Appendix 11A, accounts receivable and inventory financing are discussed. Particular items discussed are the pledging and factoring of accounts receivable and the use of inventory blanket liens, trust receipts, and warehouse receipt financing for inventory.**

DEFINITIONAL QUESTIONS

1. __________ wages and taxes are a common source of short-term credit. However, most firms have little control over the ______ of these accounts.

2. Accounts payable, or __________ __________, is the largest single source of short-term credit for most businesses.

3. Trade credit is a(n) __________ source of funds in the sense that it automatically increases when sales increase.

4. Trade credit can be divided into two components: ______ trade credit and ______ trade credit.

5. ______ trade credit is that credit received during the discount period.

6. ______ trade credit should only be used when the cost of the trade credit is less than the cost of funds from other sources.

7. The instrument signed when bank credit is obtained is called a(n) __________ ______.

8. Most banks require borrowers to keep __________ ________ on deposit with the bank equal to 10 or 20 percent of the face value of the loan which increase the loan's effective interest rate.

9. Maturities on commercial paper generally range from ______ to ______ months, with interest rates set two to three percentage points below the ______ rate.

10. A(n) __________ loan is one for which collateral such as __________ or __________ has been pledged in support of the loan.

11. A(n) ______ ____ ______ is an agreement between a bank and a borrower indicating the maximum amount of credit the bank will extend to the borrower. No legal obligation exists under this type of agreement.

12. The fee paid to a bank to institute a revolving credit agreement is known as a(n) __________ fee.

13. Commercial paper can only be issued by ______, __________ ______ firms.

14. If interest charges are deducted in advance, this is known as __________ interest, and the effective rate is higher than the __________ interest rate.

15. With a(n) __________ loan, the average amount of the usable funds during the loan period is equal to approximately ______ - ______ of the face amount of the loan.

16. Most firms make purchases on credit, recording the debt as a(n) __________ __________.

17. ____________ __________ tend to raise the effective interest rate on bank loans.

18. The legal procedures for establishing loan security have been standardized and simplified in the ________ ___________ ______.

19. The _________ __________ is a standardized document or form on which specific pledged assets are listed.

20. _______-_______ ________ is defined as any liability originally scheduled for payment within one year.

CONCEPTUAL QUESTIONS

21. Accruals are "free" in the sense that no interest must be paid on these funds.

    a. True b. False

22. The effect of compensating balances is to decrease the effective interest rate of a loan.

    a. True b. False

23. Which of the following statements concerning commercial paper is correct?

    a. Commercial paper is secured debt of large, financially strong firms.
    b. Commercial paper is sold primarily to individual investors.
    c. Maturities of commercial paper generally exceed nine months.
    d. Commercial paper interest rates are typically 1.25 to 1.50 percentage points above the stated prime rate.
    e. None of the above statements is correct.

PROBLEMS

24. A firm buys on terms of 2/10, net 30, but generally does not pay until 40 days after the invoice date. Its gross purchases total $1,080,000 per year. How much "non-free" trade credit does the firm use on average each year?

    a. $117,600
    b. $ 88,200
    c. $ 58,200
    d. $ 29,400
    e. $ 18,200

25. Refer to Problem 24. What is the *approximate* cost of the "non-free" trade credit?

a. 16.2%
b. 19.4%
c. 21.9%
d. 24.5%
e. 27.4%

26. Lawton Pipelines Inc. has developed plans for a new pump that will allow more economical operation of the company's oil pipelines. Management estimates that $2,400,000 will be required to put this new pump into operation. Funds can be obtained from a bank at 10 percent discount interest, or the company can finance the expansion by delaying payment to its suppliers. Presently, Lawton purchases under terms of 2/10, net 40, but management believes payment could be delayed 30 additional days without penalty; that is, payment could be made in 70 days. Which means of financing should Lawton use? (Use the *approximate* cost of trade credit.)

a. Trade credit, since the cost is about 12.24 percent.
b. Trade credit, since the cost is about 3.13 percentage points less than the bank loan.
c. Bank loan, since the cost is about 1.13 percentage points less than trade credit.
d. Bank loan, since the cost is about 3.13 percentage points less than trade credit.
e. The firm could use either since the costs are the same.

(The following data apply to the next four problems.)

You plan to borrow $10,000 from your bank, which offers to lend you the money at a 10 percent nominal, or stated, rate on a 1-year loan.

27. What is the *effective* interest rate if the loan is a discount loan?

a. 11.1%
b. 13.3%
c. 15.0%
d. 17.5%
e. 20.0%

28. What is the *approximate* effective interest rate if the loan is an add-on interest loan with 12 monthly payments?

a. 11.1%
b. 13.3%
c. 15.0%
d. 17.5%
e. 20.0%

29. What is the *effective* interest rate if the loan is a discount loan with a 15 percent compensating balance?

a. 11.1%
b. 13.3%
c. 15.0%
d. 17.5%
e. 20.0%

30. Under the terms of Problem 29, how much would you have to borrow to have the use of $10,000?

a. $10,000
b. $11,111
c. $12,000
d. $13,333
e. $15,000

ANSWERS AND SOLUTIONS

1. Accrued; size
2. trade credit
3. spontaneous
4. free; costly
5. Free
6. Costly
7. promissory note
8. compensating balances
9. one; nine; prime
10. secured; receivables; inventories
11. line of credit
12. commitment
13. large; financially strong
14. discount; simple (or nominal or stated)
15. installment; one-half
16. account payable
17. Compensating balances
18. Uniform Commercial Code
19. Security Agreement
20. Short-term credit

21. a. Neither workers nor the IRS require interest payments on wages and taxes that are not paid as soon as they are earned.

22. b. Compensating balances increase the effective rate.

23. e. Commercial paper is the unsecured debt of strong firms. It generally has a maturity of less than 9 months and is sold primarily to other corporations and financial institutions. Rates on commercial paper are typically below the prime rate.

24. b. $1,080,000(0.98)/360 = $2,940 in net purchases per day. Typically, there will be $2,940(40) = $117,600 of accounts payable on the books at any given time. Of this, $2,940(10) is "free" credit, while $2,940(30) = $88,200 is "non-free" credit.

25. d.

$$\text{Approx. cost} = \frac{\text{Discount \%}}{100 - \text{Discount \%}} \times \frac{360}{\text{Days credit is outstanding} - \text{Discount period}}$$

$$= \frac{2\%}{100\% - 2\%} \times \frac{360}{40 - 10} = 24.5\%.$$

26. c. Credit terms are 2/10, net 40, but delaying payments 30 additional days is the equivalent of 2/10, net 70. Assuming no penalty, the approximate cost is as follows:

$$\text{Approx. cost} = \frac{\text{Discount \%}}{100 - \text{Discount \%}} \times \frac{360}{\text{Days credit is outstanding} - \text{Discount period}}$$

$$= \frac{2\%}{100\% - 2\%} \times \frac{360}{70 - 10} = 0.0204(6) = 12.24\%.$$

$$\text{Effective rate}_{\text{Discount}} = \frac{\text{Interest}}{\text{Face value - Interest}}$$

$$= \frac{(\$2,400,000)(0.10)}{\$2,400,000 - (\$2,400,000)(0.10)}$$

$$= \frac{\$240,000}{\$2,160,000} = 0.1111 = 11.11\%.$$

Therefore, the loan cost is 1.13 percentage points less than trade credit.

27. a.

$$\text{Effective rate} = \frac{\$10,000(0.10)}{\$10,000-\$10,000(0.10)} = \frac{\$1,000}{\$9,000} = 11.1\%.$$

28. e. Approximate effective rate = \$1,000/\$5,000 = 20.0%.

29. b. Effective rate = 10%/(1 - 0.15 - 0.10) = 13.3%.

30. d. \$10,000/(1 - 0.15 - 0.10) = \$13,333, since 0.15(\$13,333) = \$2,000 is required for the compensating balance, and 0.10(\$13,333) = \$1,333 is required for the immediate interest payment.

CHAPTER 12
RISK AND RETURN

OVERVIEW

Risk is an important concept in financial analysis, especially in terms of how it affects security prices and rates of return. Risk and return are relevant considerations not only for lenders but for investors in general, whether they are individuals investing in stocks or corporations investing in physical assets and other long-term projects. All types of investments involve cash flows. The riskiness of these cash flows can be considered on a stand-alone basis or in a portfolio context, where the investment is combined with other assets and where risk may be reduced through diversification.

Investment risk is associated with the probability of low or negative future returns. There are two types of risk pertinent to investors: company-specific risk and market risk. Company-specific risk is the risk that is associated with the events that are unique to a particular firm, and it can be eliminated through diversification. Market risk is the risk associated with general movements of the stock market, and it cannot be further reduced or eliminated by diversification. Since most investors are rational, they eliminate company-specific risk through diversification. Therefore, the relevant risk to investors is market risk.

An attempt has been made to quantify market risk with a measure called beta. Beta is a measurement of how a particular firm's stock returns move relative to overall movements of stock market returns. The Capital Asset Pricing Model (CAPM), using the concept of beta and investors' aversion to risk, quantifies the relationship between market risk and the required rate of return. This relationship can be visualized graphically with the Security Market Line (SML). The slope of the SML can change, or the line can shift upward or downward, in response to changes in risk or required rates of return.

OUTLINE

I. Risk refers to the possibility that some unfavorable event will occur. Investment risk is related to the probability of earning a return less than the expected return.

A. The relationship between risk and return is such that no investment will be made unless the expected rate of return is high enough to compensate the investor for the perceived risk of the investment.

B. An event's *probability* is defined as the chance that the event will occur. The *probability distribution* for an event is the listing of all the possible outcomes for the event, with mathematical probabilities assigned to each outcome. The sum of the probabilities for a particular event must equal 1.0.

C. The *expected rate of return* ($\hat{k}$) is the sum of the products of each possible outcome times its associated probability--it is a *weighted average* of the various possible outcomes, with the weights being their probabilities of occurrence:

$$\hat{k} = \sum_{i=1}^{n} P_i k_i .$$

D. *Continuous probability distributions* are used in determining the expected rate of return of the event when the number of possible outcomes is virtually unlimited.

E. One measure for determining the tightness of a distribution is the *standard deviation,* σ:

$$\sigma = \sqrt{\sum_{i=1}^{n} (k_i - \hat{k})^2 P_i} .$$

1. The smaller the standard deviation, the tighter the distribution and the lower the risk associated with the event.
2. Another useful measure of risk is the *coefficient of variation, CV,* which is the standard deviation divided by the expected return. The coefficient of variation shows the risk per unit of return, and it provides a more meaningful comparison when the expected returns on two alternatives are not the same.

F. Most investors are *risk averse.* This means that for two alternatives with the same expected rate of return, investors will choose the one with the lower risk. Therefore, in market equilibrium, riskier securities must have higher expected returns than less risky ones to compensate for the additional risk.

G. The additional amount of return required on a risky security versus a riskless security with the same expected life is called the *risk premium, RP.* It represents the compensation investors require for assuming additional risk.

II. **Most institutions and individual investors hold portfolios of securities rather than one stock. Thus, the performance of any one security is less important than the performance of the portfolio as a whole. The Capital Asset Pricing Model (CAPM) is a generalized framework for analyzing the relationship between risk and rates of return.**

A. The *expected return on a portfolio* is the weighted average of the expected returns of the individual stocks in the portfolio, with the weights being the fraction of the total portfolio invested in each stock.

B. The *riskiness of a portfolio*, σ_p, is not the weighted average of the standard deviations of the individual stocks in the portfolio. The riskiness (standard deviation) of a portfolio depends not only on the standard deviations of the individual stocks, but also on the correlation between the stocks.

1. The tendency of two variables to move together is called *correlation*, and the *correlation coefficient*, *r*, measures this tendency.
2. Two *perfectly positively correlated* stocks move up and down together, while two *perfectly negatively correlated* stocks move countercyclically to each other.

C. *Diversification* can lower a portfolio's risk without changing its overall expected rate of return.

1. This may be accomplished by selecting stocks whose returns do not move together. Such stocks are not perfectly positively correlated.
2. As a rule, as the number of securities in the portfolio increases, the standard deviation of the expected returns decreases, and, hence, portfolio risk decreases.

D. *Total risk* can be separated into two parts, company-specific risk and market risk.

1. *Company-specific*, or *diversifiable (unsystematic)*, *risk* is caused by events that are unique to a particular firm. It can be eliminated by proper diversification of securities.
2. *Market*, or *nondiversifiable (systematic)*, *risk* is present in a portfolio due to general economic conditions and stock market forces. It cannot be eliminated by further diversification.

E. The *relevant risk* of an individual stock is its contribution to the riskiness of a well-diversified portfolio. Different stocks will affect a portfolio differently; thus, they have different degrees of relevant risk.

III. The beta coefficient, b, is a measure of the tendency of the returns of a stock to move with the market. In other words, it is a measure of the stock's volatility relative to that of an average stock.

A. An *average-risk stock* is one that tends to move up and down in step with the general market, and by definition has a *beta coefficient* of 1.0.

B. A stock that is twice as volatile as the market will have a beta of 2.0, while a stock that is half as volatile as the market will have a beta coefficient of 0.5.

C. Because a stock's beta measures its contribution to the riskiness of any portfolio, beta is the appropriate measure of the stock's riskiness.

1. A stock's market risk is measured by its beta coefficient, and so we use the terms "market risk" and "beta risk" interchangeably.

D. The *beta of a portfolio*, b_p, is the weighted average of the betas of the specific securities in that portfolio.

IV. **The Security Market Line (SML) quantifies the relationship between risk and rates of return within the CAPM framework, and is given by this equation:**

$$k_i = k_{RF} + (k_M - k_{RF})b_i.$$

Here k_i is the required rate of return on the stock, k_{RF} is the rate of interest on risk-free securities, b_i is the stock's beta, and k_M is the return on the market or, alternatively, on an average stock.

A. The term, $k_M - k_{RF}$, is the market risk premium, RP_M. This is a measure of the additional return over the risk-free rate that is required to compensate investors for assuming an average amount of risk. It is dependent upon the degree of aversion that investors in the aggregate have to risk--the higher investors' risk aversion, the larger RP_M.

1. In the CAPM the market risk premium, $k_M - k_{RF}$, is multiplied by the stock's beta to determine the additional premium over the risk-free rate that is required to compensate investors for the risk inherent in a particular stock.
2. This premium may be larger or smaller than the premium required on an average stock, depending on the riskiness of that stock in relation to the overall market as measured by the stock's beta.

B. The risk premium calculated by $(k_M - k_{RF})b_i$ is added to the risk-free rate, k_{RF} (the rate on Treasury securities), to determine the total rate of return required by investors on a particular stock.

C. A graph of the SML equation can be used to visualize the relationship between risk and rate of return.

1. k_{RF} is the vertical axis intercept.
2. The slope of the SML reflects the degree of risk aversion in the economy; the greater the average investors' aversion to risk, the *steeper* the slope of the line, the *greater* the risk premium for any stock, and the *higher* the required rate of return on stocks.

V. **Both the Security Market Line and a company's position on it change over time because of changes in interest rates, investors risk aversion, and individual companies' betas.**

A. The risk-free rate of interest is called the *nominal rate*, and it consists of two parts: (1) a real inflation-free rate of return, k^*, and (2) an inflation premium, IP, equal to the anticipated rate of inflation.

1. The real rate on long-term Treasury bonds has, historically, ranged from 2 to 4 percent.
2. As inflation increases, a higher premium must be added to the real risk-free rate of return to compensate for the loss of purchasing power.

3. An increase in the risk-free rate will cause an *upward parallel shift* in the SML. (A downward parallel shift will occur with a decrease in the risk-free rate.)

B. The *slope of the SML* reflects the extent to which investors are averse to risk--the steeper the slope of the line, the greater the average investor's aversion to risk.

1. If investor risk aversion increases, then the SML pivots upward with the risk-free rate acting as an anchor, since it is not influenced by changes in investor risk aversion. (A downward pivoting of the SML occurs if risk aversion decreases.)

C. The beta of a stock reflects the firm's industry characteristics and its own management policies.

1. A firm can affect its beta risk through changes in the composition of its assets as well as through its use of debt financing.
2. A company's beta can also change as a result of external factors such as increased competition in its industry, the expiration of basic patents, major changes in technology, and the like.

D. Although logical in its development, the CAPM is not without deficiencies.

1. Betas are generally calculated for some past period, and the assumption is made that the relative volatility of a stock will remain constant in the future. However, conditions may change and alter a stock's future volatility, which is the item of real concern to investors.
2. The CAPM should use only expected data, yet only historic data are generally available.
3. Problems may arise when one attempts to forecast future events on the basis of past data.

VI. **With management's goal as stock price maximization, the overriding consideration is the riskiness of the firm's stock, and the relevant risk of any physical asset must be measured in terms of its effect on the stock's risk.**

DEFINITIONAL QUESTIONS

1. Investment risk is associated with the ________________ of low or negative returns; the greater the chance of loss, the ________ the investment.

2. A listing of all possible __________, with a probability assigned to each, is known as a(n) ________________ ________________.

3. Weighting each possible outcome of a distribution by its ________________ of occurrence and summing the results give the ____________ _________ of the distribution.

4. One measure of the tightness of a probability distribution is the ____________ ____________.

5. Investors who prefer outcomes with a high degree of certainty to those that are less certain are described as being ______ _________.

6. Owning a(n) ____________ of securities enables investors to benefit from ________________.

7. Diversification of a portfolio can result in lower ______ for the same level of _________.

8. Diversification of a portfolio is achieved by selecting securities that are not perfectly ____________ correlated with each other.

9. That part of a stock's risk that can be reduced by _________ _______ is known as _________-_________ risk, while the portion that cannot be eliminated is called _________ risk.

10. The ______ ______________ measures a stock's relative volatility as compared with a stock market index.

11. A stock that is twice as volatile as the market in general would have a beta coefficient of ______, while a stock with a beta of 0.5 would be only ______ as volatile as the market.

12. Another useful measure of risk is the _____________ ____ ____________, which is the standard deviation divided by the expected return.

13. An event's _____________ is defined as the chance that the event will occur.

14. The difference between the required rate of return on a risky asset and the _______ - ________ rate is referred to as a(n) ______ ___________.

15. The risk premium for a stock may be calculated by multiplying the stock's ______ ________________ times the __________ risk premium.

16. A stock's required rate of return is equal to the ______ - _______ rate plus the stock's ______ ___________.

17. The risk-free rate is made up of two parts: An inflation-free or ______ rate of return plus a(n) _____________ premium.

18. Changes in investors' ______ ______________ alter the _______ of the Security Market Line.

19. One drawback of the CAPM is that it uses only __________ data when expected data would be more accurate.

20. _____________ ______________ ________________ are used in determining the expected rate of return of the event when the number of possible outcomes is virtually unlimited.

21. The tendency of two variables to move together is called ______________, and the ______________ ______________ measures this tendency.

22. The ___________ _______ of an individual stock is its contribution to the riskiness of a well-diversified portfolio.

23. The ___________ _________ _______ quantifies the relationship between risk and rates of return within the CAPM framework.

24. The slope of the SML reflects the degree of risk aversion in the economy; the greater the average investors' aversion to risk, the __________ the slope of the line, the __________ the risk premium for any stock, and the higher the required rate of return on stocks.

25. An increase in the risk-free rate will cause an __________ ___________ shift in the SML.

CONCEPTUAL QUESTIONS

26. The Y-axis intercept of the Security Market Line (SML) indicates the required rate of return on an individual stock with a beta of 1.0.

a. True b. False

27. If a stock has a beta of zero, it will be riskless when held in isolation.

a. True b. False

28. A group of 200 stocks each has a beta of 1.0. We can be certain that each of the stocks was positively correlated with the market.

a. True b. False

29. Refer to Question 28. If we combined these same 200 stocks into a portfolio, market risk would be reduced below the average market risk of the stocks in the portfolio.

a. True b. False

30. Refer to Question 29. The standard deviation of the portfolio of these 200 stocks would be lower than the standard deviations of the individual stocks.

a. True b. False

31. Suppose k_{RF} = 7% and k_M = 12%. If investors became more risk averse, k_M would be likely to decrease.

a. True b. False

32. Refer to Question 31. The required rate of return for a stock with b = 0.5 would increase more than for a stock with b = 2.0.

a. True b. False

33. Refer to Questions 31 and 32. If the expected rate of inflation increased, the required rate of return on a b = 2.0 stock would rise by more than that of a b = 0.5 stock.

a. True b. False

34. Which is the best measure of risk for an asset held in a well-diversified portfolio?

a. Variance
b. Standard deviation
c. Beta
d. Semi-variance
e. Expected value

35. In a portfolio of three different stocks, which of the following could *not* be true?

a. The riskiness of the portfolio is less than the riskiness of each stock held in isolation.
b. The riskiness of the portfolio is greater than the riskiness of one or two of the stocks.
c. The beta of the portfolio is less than the beta of each of the individual stocks.
d. The beta of the portfolio is greater than the beta of one or two of the individual stocks.
e. The beta of the portfolio is equal to the beta of one of the individual stocks.

36. If investors expected inflation to increase in the future, and they also became more risk averse, what could be said about the change in the Security Market Line (SML)?

a. The SML would shift up and the slope would increase.
b. The SML would shift up and the slope would decrease.
c. The SML would shift down and the slope would increase.
d. The SML would shift down and the slope would decrease.
e. The SML would remain unchanged.

PROBLEMS

37. Stock A has the following probability distribution of expected returns:

Probability	Rate of Return
0.1	-15%
0.2	0
0.4	5
0.2	10
0.1	25

What is Stock A's expected rate of return, the standard deviation, and the coefficient of variation?

a. 8.0%; 9.5%; 1.1875
b. 8.0%; 6.5%; 0.8125
c. 5.0%; 3.5%; 0.7000
d. 5.0%; 6.5%; 1.3000
e. 5.0%; 9.5%; 1.9000

38. If k_{RF} = 5%, k_M = 11% and b = 1.3 for Stock X, what is k_X, the required rate of return for Stock X?

a. 18.7%
b. 16.7%
c. 14.8%
d. 12.8%
e. 11.9%

39. Refer to Problem 38. What would k_X be if investors expected the inflation rate to increase by 2 percentage points?

a. 18.7%
b. 16.7%
c. 14.8%
d. 12.8%
e. 11.9%

40. Refer to Problem 38. What would k_X be if an increase in investors' risk aversion caused the market risk premium to increase by 3 percentage points? k_{RF} remains at 5 percent.

a. 18.7%
b. 16.7%
c. 14.8%
d. 12.8%
e. 11.9%

41. Refer to Problem 38. What would k_x be if investors expected the inflation rate to increase by 2 percentage points *and* their risk aversion increased by 3 percentage points?

a. 18.7%
b. 16.7%
c. 14.8%
d. 12.8%
e. 11.9%

42. The Sure Thing Investment Fund has a total investment of $450 million in five stocks.

Stock	Investment (Millions)	Beta
1	$130	0.4
2	110	1.5
3	70	3.0
4	90	2.0
5	50	1.0
Total	$450	

What is the fund's overall, or weighted average, beta?

a. 1.14
b. 1.22
c. 1.35
d. 1.46
e. 1.53

43. Refer to Problem 42. If the risk-free rate is 7 percent and the market risk premium is 5 percent, what is the required rate of return on the Sure Thing Fund?

a. 12.5%
b. 13.6%
c. 14.3%
d. 15.4%
e. 16.1%

44. You are managing a portfolio of 10 stocks which are held in equal dollar amounts. The current beta of the portfolio is 1.8, and the beta of Stock A is 2.0. If Stock A is sold and the proceeds are used to purchase a replacement stock, what does the beta of the replacement stock have to be to lower the portfolio beta to 1.7?

a. 1.4
b. 1.3
c. 1.2
d. 1.1
e. 1.0

ANSWERS AND SOLUTIONS

1. probability; riskier
2. outcomes; probability distribution
3. probability; expected return
4. standard deviation
5. risk averse
6. portfolio; diversification
7. risk; return
8. positively
9. diversification; company-specific; market
10. beta coefficient
11. 2.0; half
12. coefficient of variation
13. probability
14. risk-free; risk premium
15. beta coefficient; market
16. risk-free; risk premium
17. real; inflation
18. risk aversion; slope
19. historical
20. Continuous probability distributions
21. correlation; correlation coefficient
22. relevant risk
23. Security Market Line
24. steeper; greater
25. upward parallel

26. b. The Y-axis intercept of the SML is k_{RF}, which is the required rate of return of an individual stock with a beta of zero.

27. b. A zero beta stock is riskless from a market risk viewpoint but still has company-specific risk and will be risky when held in isolation.

28. a. By definition, if a stock has a beta of 1.0 it moves exactly with the market. In other words, if the market moves up by 7 percent, the stock will also move up by 7 percent, while if the market falls by 7 percent the stock will fall by 7 percent.

29. b. Market risk is measured by the beta coefficient. The beta for the portfolio would be a weighted average of the betas of the stocks, so b_p would also be 1.0. Thus, the market risk for the portfolio would be the same as the market risk of the stocks in the portfolio.

30. a. Note that with a 200-stock portfolio, the actual returns would all be on or close to the regression line. However, when the portfolio (and the market) returns are quite high, some individual stocks wold have higher returns than the portfolio, and some would have much lower returns. Thus, the range of returns, and the standard deviation, would be higher for the individual stocks than for the portfolio.

31. b. RP_M, which is equal to $k_M - k_{RF}$, would rise, leading to an increase in k_M.

32. b. The required rate of return for a stock with b = 0.5 would increase less than for a stock with b = 2.0.

33. b. If the expected rate of inflation increased, the new SML would shift up parallel to the old SML due to an increase in k_{RF}. Thus, the effect on

the required rates of return for both the b = 0.5 and b = 2.0 stocks would be the same.

34. c. The beta coefficient is a measure of the extent to which the returns on a given stock move with the stock market.

35. c. The beta of the portfolio is a weighted average of the individual securities' betas, so it could not be less than the betas of all of the stocks.

36. a. The increase in inflation would cause the SML to shift up, and investors becoming more risk averse would cause the slope to increase.

37. e. $k_A = 0.1(-15\%) + 0.2(0\%) + 0.4(5\%) + 0.2(10\%) + 0.1(25\%) = 5.0\%.$

$$\text{Variance} = 0.1(-0.15 - 0.05)^2 + 0.2(0.0 - 0.05)^2 + 0.4(0.05 - 0.05)^2 + 0.2(0.10 - 0.05)^2 + 0.1(0.25 - 0.05)^2$$

$$\sigma^2 = 0.009.$$

$$\text{Standard deviation} = \sqrt{0.009} = 0.0949 = 9.5\%.$$

$$\text{Coefficient of variation} = 9.5\%/5.0\% = 1.90.$$

38. d. $k_X = k_{RF} + (k_M - k_{RF})b_X = 5\% + (11\% - 5\%)1.3 = 12.8\%.$

39. c. $k_X = k_{RF} + (k_M - k_{RF})b_X = 7\% + (13\% - 7\%)1.3 = 14.8\%.$

A change in the inflation premium does not change the market risk premium $(k_M - k_{RF})$ since both k_M and k_{RF} are affected.

40. b. $k_X = k_{RF} + (k_M - k_{RF})b_X = 5\% + (14\% - 5\%)1.3 = 16.7\%.$

41. a. $k_X = k_{RF} + (k_M - k_{RF})b_X = 7\% + (16\% - 7\%)1.3 = 18.7\%.$

42. d.

$$b_p = \sum_{i=1}^{5} w_i b_i$$
$$= \frac{\$130}{450}(0.4) + \frac{\$110}{\$450}(1.5) + \frac{\$70}{\$450}(3.0) + \frac{\$90}{\$450}(2.0) + \frac{\$50}{\$450}(1.0) = 1.46.$$

43. c. $k_p = k_{RF} + (k_M - k_{RF})b_p = 7\% + (5\%)1.46 = 14.3\%.$

44. e. First find the beta of the remaining 9 stocks:

$$1.8 = 0.9(b_R) + 0.1(b_A)$$
$$1.8 = 0.9(b_R) + 0.1(2.0)$$
$$1.8 = 0.9(b_R) + 0.2$$

$1.6 = 0.9(b_R)$
$b_R = 1.78.$

Now find the beta of the new stock that produces $b_p = 1.7$.

$1.7 = 0.9(1.78) + 0.1(b_N)$
$1.7 = 1.6 + 0.1(b_N)$
$0.1 = 0.1(b_N)$
$b_N = 1.0.$

CHAPTER 13
TIME VALUE OF MONEY

OVERVIEW

Of all the techniques used in finance, none is more important than the time value of money, or discounted cash flow (DCF) analysis. A dollar in the hand today is worth more than a dollar to be received in the future because, if you had it now, you could invest that dollar and earn interest. A knowledge of compound value, or future value, and present value techniques is essential to an understanding of many aspects of finance, such as security valuation and capital budgeting. Future value and present value techniques can be applied to lump sums, ordinary (deferred) annuities, annuities due, and uneven cash flow streams.

OUTLINE

I. **Future value (FV) is defined as the value to which a beginning lump sum or present value (PV) will grow in a certain number of periods, n, at a specified rate of interest, k. The amount of interest earned in each period is designated as I. The process of going from present values to future values is known as compounding.**

A. The formula for the future value after one period is found by

$$FV_1 = PV + I = PV + PV(k) = PV(1 + k).$$

B. However, for more than one period the formula is

$$FV_n = PV(1 + k)^n.$$

C. In the above equation, $(1 + k)^n$ is known as the *future value interest factor*, $FVIF_{k,n}$, which is the future value of one dollar left in an account for n periods paying k percent per period. Therefore,

$$FV_n = PV(FVIF_{k,n}).$$

D. These factors have been calculated for various interest rates and time periods and organized into tables to simplify future value calculations. FVIFs may be found in Table A-3 in the back of the text.

1. Select the appropriate $FVIF_{k,n}$ for the specified interest rate and the given number of periods.
2. Multiply the initial amount, PV, by the interest factor to determine the future value, or ending amount.
3. For example, the future value of \$100 at 8 percent for 5 years is $FV_5 = \$100(1.4693) = \$146.93$.

E. The same calculation can be made using a calculator. Using the exponential function, simply raise 1.08 to the 5th power, $1.08^5 = 1.4693$, then multiply by $100.

1. Using a financial calculator, simply enter PV = 100, k = i = 8, and n = 5, then press the FV key. Calculator results may differ from those using the interest factor tables due to rounding errors.

F. Another way to view this problem is through a *time line*. Time lines help to visualize what is happening.

Time:	**0**	**8%** **1**	**2**	**3**	**4**	**5**
Cash flows:	**100**					**FV_5=?**

G. The compounding process can be applied to anything that is growing--sales, population, earnings per share, and inflation.

II. **The concept of present value is the reverse of compounding and is often referred to as discounting.**

A. The *present value* is the value today of a future payment or series of payments discounted at the appropriate discount rate.

B. The formula for present value is

$$PV = \frac{FV_n}{(1 + k)^n} = FV_n\left(\frac{1}{(1 + k)^n}\right).$$

C. The term $[1/(1 + k)]^n$ is known as the *present value interest factor*, $PVIF_{k,n}$, and also has been determined for a wide range of interest rates and time periods, which may be found in Table A-1 in the back of the text. Therefore,

$$PV = FV_n(PVIF_{k,n}).$$

D. The present value of $146.93 to be received in 5 years discounted at an interest rate of 8 percent is $146.93(0.6806) = $100. This result can be compared with the future value calculation to confirm that these are *reciprocal processes*.

E. Using a financial calculator, you would input n = 5, k = i = 8, FV = 146.93, and then press the PV button to obtain $100.00.

F. The time line looks like this:

Time:	**0**	**8%** **1**	**2**	**3**	**4**	**5**
Cash flows:	**PV=?**					**FV_5=146.93**

G. Present and future values cannot be directly compared. Thus, one must either *compound* present amounts into the future or *discount* future dollars back to the present by using the appropriate formulas.

H. Present values are dependent on two factors, the discount rate and the number of periods until the payment will be received.
  1. If relatively *high* discount rates apply, funds due in the future are worth comparatively *little* today.
  2. Even at relatively low discount rates, the present values of funds due in the *distant future* are *quite small*.

III. **The interest rate (k) or time (n) can be found if three of the four variables (PV, FV, k, or n) are known, utilizing the above FV_n or PV equations.**

IV. **An annuity is defined as a series of payments of an equal, or constant, amount of money at fixed intervals for a specified number of periods. If the payments occur at the end of each period, as they typically do, the annuity is an ordinary (deferred) annuity. If the payments occur at the beginning of each period, the annuity is an annuity due.**

A. The *future value of an annuity* is the total amount one would have at the end of the annuity period if each payment were invested at a given periodic interest rate and held to the end of the annuity period.
  1. Defining FVA_n as the compound sum of an ordinary annuity of n years and PMT as the periodic payment, we can write

$$FVA_n = PMT(FVIFA_{k,n}).$$

  2. $FVIFA_{k,n}$ is the *future value interest factor for an annuity* at k percent for n periods. These factors may be found in Table A-4 in the back of the text.
  3. For example, the future value of a 3-year, 7 percent *ordinary annuity* of $1,000 per year would be $1,000(3.2149) = $3,214.90.
     a. Using a financial calculator, you would input n = 3, k = i = 7, PMT = 1,000, and then press the FV button to obtain $3,214.90.
  4. For an *annuity due*, each of the payments would have occurred at the *beginning* rather than the end of the period, thus each payment would be compounded for one more period. The equation is modified as

$$FVA_n(\text{Annuity due}) = PMT(FVIFA_{k,n})(1 + k).$$

  5. The future value of a 3-year, 7 percent annuity due of $1,000 per year is $1,000(3.2149)(1.07) = $3,439.94.
     a. Using a financial calculator, you would input n = 3, k = i= 7, PMT = 1,000, press BEG mode, and then press the FV button to obtain $3,439.94. (Remember to switch calculator back to END mode when finished.)

B. The *present value of an annuity* is the lump-sum payment required today that would be equivalent to the annuity payments spread over the annuity period. It is the amount today that would permit withdrawals of equal amounts (PMT) at the end (or beginning for an annuity due) of each period for n periods.

1. Defining PVA_n as the *present value of an ordinary annuity* of n years and PMT as the periodic payment, we can write

$$PVA_n = PMT(PVIFA_{k,n}).$$

2. $PVIFA_{k,n}$ is the *present value interest factor for an annuity* of n periodic payments discounted at k percent. These factors may be found in Table A-2 in the back of the text.
3. For example, an *annuity* of $1,000 per year for 4 years at 9 percent would have a present value of $1,000(3.2397) = $3,239.70.
   a. Using a financial calculator, you would input n = 4, k = i = 9, PMT = 1,000, and press the PV button to obtain $3,239.72.
4. The present value for an *annuity due* is

$$PVA_n(\text{Annuity due}) = PMT(PVIFA_{k,n})(1 + k).$$

5. The present value of a 4-year, 9 percent annuity due of $1,000 is $1,000(3.2397)(1.09) = $3,531.27.
   a. Using a financial calculator, you would input n = 4, k = i = 9, PMT = 1,000, press BEG mode, and then press the PV button to obtain $3,531.29. (Remember to switch calculator back to END mode when finished.)

V. **An annuity that calls for payments to go on indefinitely is called a perpetuity. These payments constitute an infinite series.**

A. The present value of a perpetuity is

$$PV(\text{perpetuity}) = \text{Payment/Interest rate} = PMT/k.$$

B. For example, if the discount rate were 8 percent, a perpetuity of $90 per year would have a present value of $90/0.08 = $1,125.

VI. **Many financial decisions require the analysis of uneven cash flow streams rather than a stream of constant payments such as an annuity. The present value of an uneven stream of future cash flows is equal to the sum of the PVs of the individual cash flow components. Similarly, the future value of an uneven stream of cash flows is the sum of the FVs of the individual cash flow components.**

A. To solve these types of problems with a financial calculator, you enter the individual cash flows, in chronological order, into the cash flow register, enter the interest rate, k = i, and then press the NPV key to find the present value of the cash flow stream.

VII. If one knows the relevant payment, the PVA_n or the FVA_n, then the number of periods of an annuity or the effective interest rate can be calculated.

A. For example, if one borrows $75,000 today, agrees to repay $7,635.48 each year at an interest rate of 9 percent, how many years does it take to pay off the loan?

$$PVA_n = PMT(PVIFA_{9\%,n})$$

$$PVIFA_{9\%,n} = \$75,000/\$7,635.48 = 9.8226.$$

Looking at the 9% column of Table A-2, we see that 9.8226 is the $PVIFA_{k,n}$ for 25 years.

B. For example, if one borrows $75,000 today, agrees to repay $7,635.48 each year for 25 years, what is the interest rate?

$$PVA_n = PMT(PVIFA_{k,25})$$

$$PVIFA_{k,25} = \$75,000/\$7,635.48 = 9.8226.$$

Looking at the Period 25 Row of Table A-2, we see that 9.8226 is the $PVIFA_{k,n}$ for 9 percent.

VIII. An amortized loan is one that is paid off in equal, periodic installments over time.

A. The amount of each payment, PMT, is found as follows:

$$\text{PV of annuity} = PMT(PVIFA_{k,n}).$$

$$PMT = \text{PV of annuity}/PVIFA_{k,n}.$$

B. Each payment consists partly of *interest* and partly of a repayment of *principal*. This breakdown is often depicted in the *amortization schedule*.

1. The interest component is largest in the first period and declines subsequently.
2. The repayment of principal is smallest in the first period and increases thereafter.

IX. Appendix 13A discusses semiannual, quarterly, and other compounding periods which are often used in financial transactions. Compounding on a non-annual basis requires an adjustment in the way in which the interest factors are determined.

A. The *effective annual rate* is the rate that would have produced the final compound value under annual compounding. The effective annual rate is given by the following formula:

$$\text{Effective annual rate} = \left(1 + \frac{k_{Nom}}{m}\right)^m - 1.0.$$

where k_{Nom} is the stated annual rate and m is the number of compounding periods per year.

B. Divide the *nominal, or stated, interest rate* by the number of times compounding occurs each year.

C. Use these adjusted values for k and n in the computations and when looking up interest factors in the tables.

D. For example, the effective annual rate for 12 percent, compounded quarterly, is as follows:

$$\text{Effective annual rate} = (1 + 0.12/4)^4 - 1.0 = 12.55\%.$$

E. For annual compounding use the formula:

$$FV_n = PV(1 + k)^n$$

to find the future value of a lump sum. But when compounding occurs more frequently than once a year, use the formula:

$$FV_n = PV\left(1 + \frac{k_{Nom}}{m}\right)^{mn}.$$

where m is the number of times per year compounding occurs and n is the number of years.

F. For example, the amount to which $1,000 will grow after 5 years if quarterly compounding is applied at a stated 8 percent interest rate is as follows:

$$FV = \$1,000(1 + 0.08/4)^{(4)(5)} = \$1,000(1.02)^{20} = \$1,485.95.$$

DEFINITIONAL QUESTIONS

1. The beginning value of an account or investment in a project is known as its __________ __________.

2. Using a savings account as an example, the difference between the account's __________ value and its __________ value at the end of a period is due to __________ earned during the period.

3. The equation $FV_n = PV(1 + k)^n$ determines the future value of a sum at the end of n periods. The factor $(1 + k)^n$ is known as the __________ __________ __________ __________.

4. The process of finding present values is often referred to as __________ and is the reverse of the __________ process.

5. The PVIF for a 5-year, 5 percent investment is 0.7835. This value is the __________ of the FVIF for 5 years at 5 percent.

6. For a given number of time periods, the PVIF will decline as the __________ __________ increases.

7. A series of payments of a constant amount for a specified number of periods is a(n) __________. If the payments occur at the end of each period it is a(n) __________ annuity, while if the payments occur at the beginning of each period it is an annuity ______.

8. The present value of an uneven stream of future payments is the ______ of the PVs of the individual payments.

9. Since different types of investments use different compounding periods, it is important to distinguish between the stated, or __________, rate and the __________ annual rate.

10. To use the interest factor tables when compounding occurs more than once a year, divide the __________ __________ by the number of times compounding occurs and multiply the years by the number of __________ __________ per year.

11. An annuity that calls for payments to go on indefinitely is called a(n) __________.

12. A(n) __________ __________ is one that is paid off in equal, periodic installments over time.

13. Each payment of an amortized loan consists partly of __________ and partly of a repayment of __________.

14. The breakdown of interest and principal on a loan is often depicted in the __________ __________.

15. The __________ __________ __________ is the rate that would have produced the final compound value under annual compounding.

CONCEPTUAL QUESTIONS

16. If a bank uses semiannual compounding for savings accounts, the nominal rate will be greater than the effective annual rate.

a. True b. False

17. If money has time value (that is, i > 0), the future value of some amount of money will always be more than the amount invested. The present value of some amount to be received in the future is always less than the amount to be received.

a. True b. False

18. You have determined the profitability of a planned project by finding the present value of all the cash flows from that project. Which of the following would cause the project to look less appealing, that is, to have a lower present value?

a. The interest rate decreases.
b. The cash flows are extended over a longer period of time.
c. The interest rate increases.
d. b and c are both correct.
e. a and b are both correct.

19. As the discount rate increases without limit, the present value of a future cash inflow

a. Gets larger without limit.
b. Stays unchanged.
c. Approaches zero.
d. Gets smaller without limit; that is, approaches minus infinity.
e. Goes to e^{in}.

PROBLEMS

(Note: In working these problems, you may get an answer which differs from ours by a few cents due to differences in rounding. This should not concern you; just pick the closest answer.)

20. Assume that you purchase a 6 year, 8 percent savings certificate for $1,000. If interest is compounded annually, what will be the value of the certificate when it matures?

a. $630.17
b. $1,469.33
c. $1,677.10
d. $1,586.90
e. $1,766.33

21. A savings certificate similar to the one in Problem 20 is available with the exception that interest is compounded semiannually. What is the difference between the ending value of the savings certificate compounded semiannually and the one compounded annually?

a. The semiannual is worth $14.10 more than the annual.
b. The semiannual is worth $14.10 less than the annual.
c. The semiannual is worth $21.54 more than the annual.
d. The semiannual is worth $21.54 less than the annual.
e. The semiannual is worth the same as the annual.

22. A friend promises to pay you $600 two years from now if you loan him $500 today. What annual interest rate is your friend offering?

a. 7.5%
b. 8.5%
c. 9.5%
d. 10.5%
e. 11.5%

23. You are offered an investment opportunity with the "guarantee" that your investment will double in 5 years. Assuming annual compounding, what annual rate of return would this investment provide?

a. 40.00%
b. 100.00%
c. 14.87%
d. 20.00%
e. 18.74%

24. You decide to begin saving toward the purchase of a new car in 5 years. If you put $1,000 in a savings account paying 6 percent compounded annually at the end of each of the next 5 years, how much will you accumulate after 5 years?

a. $6,691.13
b. $5,637.10
c. $1,338.23
d. $5,975.33
e. $5,731.95

25. Refer to Problem 24. What would be the ending amount if the payments were made at the beginning of each year?

a. $6.691.13
b. $5,637.10
c. $1,338.23
d. $5,975.33
e. $5,731.95

26. Refer to Problem 24. What would be the ending amount if $500 payments were made at the end of each 6-month period for 5 years and the account paid 6 percent compounded semiannually?

a. $6.691.13
b. $5,637.10
c. $1,338.23
d. $5,975.33
e. $5,732.00

27. Calculate the present value of $1,000 to be received at the end of 8 years. Assume an interest rate of 7 percent.

a. $582.00
b. $1,718.19
c. $531.82
d. $5,971.30
e. $649.37

28. How much would you be willing to pay today for an investment that would return $800 each year at the end of each of the next 6 years? Assume an interest rate of 5 percent.

a. $5,441.53
b. $4,800.00
c. $3,369.89
d. $4,060.56
e. $4,632.37

29. You have applied for a mortgage of $60,000 to finance the purchase of a new home. The bank will require you to make annual payments of $7,047.55 at the end of each of the next 20 years. Determine the interest rate in effect on this mortgage.

a. 8.0%
b. 9.8%
c. 10.0%
d. 51.0%
e. 11.2%

30. If you would like to accumulate $7,500 over the next 5 years, how much must you deposit each six months, starting six months from now, given a 6 percent interest rate and semiannual compounding?

a. $1,330.47
b. $879.23
c. $654.22
d. $569.00
e. $732.67

31. A company is offering bonds which pay $100 per year indefinitely. If you require a 12 percent return on these bonds--that is, the interest rate is 12 percent--what is the value of each bond?

a. $1,000.00
b. $962.00
c. $904.67
d. $866.67
e. $833.33

32. What is the present value (t = 0) of the following cash flows if the interest rate is 12 percent?

0	1	2	3	4	5
$0	$2,000	$2,000	$2,000	$3,000	-$4,000

a. $4,782.43
b. $4,440.50
c. $4,221.79
d. $4,041.23
e. $3,997.98

33. What is the effective annual rate of 12 percent compounded monthly?

a. 12.00%
b. 12.55%
c. 12.68%
d. 12.75%
e. 13.00%

34. Problem 29 refers to a 20-year mortgage of $60,000. This is an amortized loan. How much principal will be repaid in the second year?

a. $1,152.30
b. $1,725.70
c. $5,895.25
d. $7,047.55
e. $1,047.55

35. You have $1,000 invested in an account which pays 16 percent compounded annually. A commission agent (called a "finder") can locate for you an equally safe deposit which will pay 16 percent, compounded quarterly, for 2 years. What is the maximum amount you should be willing to pay him now as a fee for locating the new account?

a. $10.92
b. $13.78
c. $16.14
d. $16.80
e. $21.13

36. The present value (t = 0) of the following cash flow stream is $11,958.20 when discounted at 12 percent annually. What is the value of the missing t = 2 cash flow?

0	1	2	3	4
$0	$2,000	?	$4,000	$4,000

a. $4,000.00
b. $4,500.00
c. $5,000.00
d. $5,500.00
e. $6,000.00

37. A rare baseball card that you do not currently have in your collection is available, and you are seriously considering buying it. The dealer wants $50 for it and tells you that she bought it for $4.36 when she was just 12 years old. She also claims that the asking price would only yield her a 5 percent annual return on her original investment. If that is true, how old is the dealer now?

a. 44
b. 50
c. 56
d. 62
e. 70

38. Suppose that you have just graduated from college and have found a good job. You have decided to start saving up for the down payment on an expensive sports car that you have always wanted by setting aside $2,861.43 at the end of each year. You calculate that you need $15,000 for the down payment, so you will be able to afford the monthly car payments. You have found an investment where your savings should earn 4 percent annually. How many years must you save to have $15,000?

a. 3
b. 6
c. 8
d. 10
e. 11

ANSWERS AND SOLUTIONS

1. present value
2. present; future; interest (I)
3. future value interest factor
4. discounting; compounding
5. reciprocal
6. discount rate
7. annuity; ordinary; due
8. sum
9. nominal; effective
10. nominal rate; compounding periods
11. perpetuity
12. amortized loan
13. interest; principal
14. amortization schedule
15. effective annual rate

16. b. The effective annual rate is always greater than or equal to the nominal rate.

17. a. Both these statements are correct.

18. d. The slower the cash flows come in and the higher the interest rate, the lower the present value.

19. c. As the discount rate increases, the present value of a future sum decreases and eventually approaches zero.

20. d. $FV_n = PV(FVIF_{k,n}) = \$1,000(FVIF_{8\%,6}) = \$1,000(1.5869) = \$1,586.90$. (Calculator solution = $1,586.87.)

21. a. $FVIF_{4\%,12} = 1.6010$. Thus $FV_{12} = \$1,000(1.6010) = \$1.601.00$. The difference, $1,601.00 - $1,586.90 = $14.10, is the additional interest. (Calculator solution = $14.16.)

22. c.

$$FV_n = PV(FVIF_{k,n})$$
$$\$600 = \$500(FVIF_{k,2})$$
$$FVIF_{k,2} = 1.2000.$$

Looking across the Period 2 row in Table A-3 we see the FVIF for 2 years at 9% = 1.1881 and the FVIF for 2 years at 10% = 1.2100. Therefore, the annual interest rate is between 9% and 10%. (Calculator solution = 9.54%.)

23. c. Assume any value for the present value and double it:

$$FV_n = PV(FVIF_{k,n})$$
$$\$2 = \$1(FVIF_{k,5})$$
$$FVIF_{k,5} = 2.0000.$$

Looking across the Period 5 row in Table A-3 we see that 2.0000 occurs between 14% and 15%. (Calculator solution = 14.87%.)

24. b. $FVA_n = PMT(FVIFA_{6\%,5}) = \$1,000(5.6371) = \$5,637.10.$ (Calculator solution = $5,637.09.)

25. d. $FVA_n(\text{Annuity due}) = PMT(FVIFA_{6\%,5})(1 + k)$ $= \$1,000(5.6371)(1.06) = \$5,975.33.$ (Calculator solution = $5,975.32.)

26. e. $FVA_n = PMT(FVIFA_{3\%,10}) = \$500(11.464) = \$5,732.00.$ (Calculator solution = $5,731.94.)

(Note that to use the annuity tables the compounding period and payment period must be the same, in this case both are semiannual. If this is not the case, each cash flow must be treated individually.)

27. a. $PV = FV_n(PVIF_{7\%,8}) = \$1,000(0.5820) = \$582.00.$ (Calculator solution = $582.01.)

(Note that annual compounding is assumed if not otherwise specified.)

28. d. $PVA_6 = PMT(PVIFA_{5\%,6}) = \$800(5.0757) = \$4,060.56.$ (Calculator solution = $4,060.55.)

29. c. The amount of the mortgage ($60,000) is the present value of a 20-year ordinary annuity with payments of $7,047.55. Therefore,

$$PVA_{20} = PMT(PVIFA_{k,20})$$
$$\$60,000 = \$7,047.55(PVIFA_{k,20})$$
$$PVIFA_{k,20} = 8.5136$$
$$k = 10.00\%, \text{ exactly.}$$

(Calculator solution = 10.00%.)

30. c.

$$FVA_n = PMT(FVIFA_{k,n})$$
$$\$7,500 = PMT(11.464)$$
$$PMT = \$654.22.$$

(Calculator solution = $654.23.)

31. e. $PV(\text{perpetuity}) = PMT/k = \$100/0.12 = \$833.33.$

32. b. $PV = \$2,000(PVIFA_{12\%,3}) + \$3,000(PVIF_{12\%,4}) + (-\$4,000)(PVIF_{12\%,5})$
$= \$2,000(2.4018) + \$3,000(0.6355) - \$4,000(0.5674) = \$4,440.50.$
(Calculator solution = $4,440.51.)

33. c. Effective annual rate $= (1 + k_{Nom}/m)^{mn} - 1.0 = (1 + 0.12/12)^{12} - 1.0$
$= (1.01)^{12} - 1.0 = 1.1268 - 1.0 = 0.1268 = 12.68\%.$

34. a.

Year	Payment	Interest	Repayment on Principal	Remaining Principal Balance
1	$7,047.55	$6,000.00	$1,047.55	$58,952.45
2	7,047.55	5,895.25	1,152.30	57,800.15

35. d. Currently: $FV_n = \$1,000(FVIF_{16\%,2}) = \$1,000(1.3456) = \$1,345.60.$
New account: $FV_n = \$1,000(1 + k_{Nom}/m)^{mn} = \$1,000(1.3686) = \$1,368.60.$

Thus, the new account will be worth $23.00 more after 2 years.

PV of difference $= \$23(PVIF_{4\%,8}) = \$23(0.7307) = \$16.80.$
(Calculator solution = $16.78.)

Therefore, the most you should be willing to pay the finder for locating the new account is $16.80.

36. e. $\$11,958.20 = \$2,000(PVIF_{12\%,1}) + X(PVIF_{12\%,2}) + \$4,000(PVIF_{12\%,3}) + \$4,000(PVIF_{12\%,4})$
$\$11,958.20 = \$2,000(0.8929) + X(0.7972) + \$4,000(0.7118) + \$4,000(0.6355)$
$\$11,958.20 = \$7,175.00 + 0.7972(X)$
$0.7972(X) = \$4,783.20$
$X = \$6,000.00.$
(Calculator solution = $6,000.16.)

37. d. $FV_n = PV(FVIF_{k,n})$
$\$50 = \$4.36(FVIF_{5\%,n})$
$FVIF_{5\%,n} = 11.468.$

If you look under the 5% column in Table A-3 in the text, you will find that in the Period 50 row the FVIF is 11.467. Thus, the dealer bought the baseball card 50 years ago when she was 62 years old (12 years + 50 years). (Calculator solution = 50 years; thus the dealer is 62 years old.)

38. b. $PVA_n = PMT(PVIFA_{k,n})$
$\$15,000 = \$2,861.43(PVIFA_{4\%,n})$
$PVIFA_{4\%,n} = 5.2421.$

If you look under the 4% column in Table A-2 in the text, you will find that in the Period 6 row the PVIFA is 5.2421. Thus, it will take 6 years to save for the down payment for the sports car. (Calculator solution = 6 years.)

CHAPTER 14
THE PROCESS OF CAPITAL BUDGETING

OVERVIEW

The process of capital budgeting involves decisions concerning long-term investments. The term capital refers to fixed assets used in production, and a budget is a plan detailing projected inflows and outflows during some future period. Thus, the capital budget sets forth planned expenditures on fixed assets and other long-term projects, and capital budgeting is the entire process of analyzing projects, and deciding whether they should be included in the capital budget.

One of the most critical steps in capital budgeting analysis is cash flow estimation. The key to correct cash flow estimation is to consider only relevant incremental cash flows. However, the process is complicated by such factors as accurate sales forecasts, proper planning, and net working capital changes.

In capital budgeting future cash flows are estimated, risks are appraised and reflected in a cost of capital discount rate, and all cash flows are evaluated on a present value basis. Three methods are frequently used to determine which projects should be included in a firm's capital budget: (1) payback period, (2) net present value (NPV), and (3) internal rate of return (IRR). The payback period has deficiencies, and thus should not be used as the sole criterion for making capital budgeting decisions. The NPV and IRR methods both lead to the same accept/reject decisions on independent projects. However, these methods may conflict when ranking mutually exclusive projects which differ in scale or timing. When conflicts occur, the NPV method should be used to make the final decision.

OUTLINE

I. **Various factors combine to make capital budgeting decisions among the most important ones financial managers must make. A good decision can boost earnings sharply and increase the firm's stock price, but a bad decision can lead to bankruptcy.**

A. Capital expenditures limit the firm's future flexibility.

1. Behind every capital budget is an implicit sales forecast, and if projected cash flows fall far short of estimates, a firm is often in a situation where it can cancel a project only at a great loss.

B. Capital expenditures frequently require large sums of money.

1. Before a firm can spend a substantial sum, it must raise the funds; large amounts of money are not available automatically.
2. A firm contemplating a major capital expenditure program may need to arrange its financing several years in advance to be sure the needed funds can be obtained.

C. The impact of capital expenditures on the firm is significant.
   1. Not only is the firm's future flexibility influenced by the projects and assets in which it decides to invest, but the results of these decisions can also be seen directly in sales and in the standard ratios.

D. Timing is an important consideration in capital budgeting.
   1. Effective capital budgeting can improve not only the timing of asset acquisitions but also the quality of assets purchased.

II. **Capital budgeting is the process of identifying and then analyzing fixed asset investment proposals.**

A. Analyzing capital expenditure proposals has a cost, so firms classify projects into different categories to help differentiate the level of analysis required.
   1. Replacement: maintenance of business.
   2. Replacement: cost reduction.
   3. Expansion of existing products or markets.
   4. Expansion into new products or markets.
   5. Safety and environmental projects.
   6. Other miscellaneous projects.

B. Normally, a more detailed analysis is required for expansion and new product decisions than for simple replacement and maintenance decisions. Also, projects requiring larger investments will be analyzed more carefully than smaller projects.

III. **The financial manager does not usually initiate capital budgeting proposals; however, he or she evaluates and coordinates these requests.**

A. The capital budgeting process should follow these steps:
   1. Review of goals and objectives.
   2. Search for capital budgeting proposals.
   3. Estimation of project cash flows.
   4. Ranking of proposals.
   5. Selection of projects.
   6. Implementation.
   7. Post-audit.

B. The *post-audit* is the last, but by no means least important, step in the capital budgeting process. It involves a comparison of actual results with those predicted, and it explains any observed differences. We regard the post-audit as being one of the most important elements in a good capital budgeting system. It has two main purposes:
   1. Improve forecasts.
   2. Improve operations.

C. The post-audit is not a simple process--a number of factors can cause complications.

1. Recognize that each element of the cash flow forecast is subject to uncertainty, so a percentage of all projects undertaken by any reasonable venturesome firm will necessarily go awry.
2. Projects sometimes fail to meet expectations for reasons beyond the control of the operating executives and for reasons that no one could realistically be expected to anticipate.
3. It is often difficult to separate the operating results of one investment from those of a larger system.
4. It is often hard to hand out blame or praise because the executives who were actually responsible for a given decision may have moved on by the time the results of a long-term investment are known.

IV. **Estimating a project's relevant cash flows is the most important, as well as the most difficult, step in capital budgeting analysis.**

A. *Cash flow* is defined as the actual net cash that flows into, or out of, the firm during a specified period.

B. The better the firm's cash flow forecast, the more likely it is that poor projects will be rejected and good ones accepted.

C. The financial staff's role in the forecasting process includes:
1. Coordinating the efforts of the other departments.
2. Ensuring that everyone involved with the forecast uses a consistent set of economic assumptions.
3. Making sure that no biases are inherent in the forecasts.

D. An important element in cash flow estimation is the identification of *relevant cash flows*, defined as that set of cash flows which should be considered for the decision at hand.

E. Capital budgeting decisions must be based on cash flows. Cash flow must be distinguished from accounting income. A project's net cash flow in any year can be calculated as

$$\text{Net cash flow} = (\$REV - \$EXP)(1 - T) + DEP(T),$$

where \$REV = cash revenues, \$EXP = cash expenses, T = marginal tax rate, and DEP = depreciation expense.
1. Note that *interest expense* is not deducted in calculating cash flow. If interest charges were also deducted when determining the project's cash flow and the net cash flows later were discounted by the cost of capital, then double counting of this financing cost would occur.

F. In evaluating a capital project, we are concerned only with *incremental cash flows*, or those cash flows that result directly from the project. Incremental cash flows represent the change in the firm's total cash flows that occurs as a direct result of acquiring or not acquiring the asset. Several problems need to be considered in determining incremental cash flows.

1. *Sunk costs* are not incremental costs and should not be included in the analysis. These costs are outlays that have already been committed or have already occurred and thus are not affected by the accept/reject decision.
2. *Opportunity costs* are the dollar cash flows that can be generated from assets the firm already owns provided they are not used for the project in question. These costs need to be considered in evaluating capital projects even though no additional cash outlay is required.
3. *Externalities*, or the effects of a project on other parts of the firm, must be considered in the capital project evaluation. If the introduction of a new liquid detergent would reduce sales of a firm's existing line, then the reduction must be included in the analysis.
4. *Shipping and installation costs* need to be added to the cost of fixed assets and the combined total is used as the *depreciable basis* when depreciation charges are calculated.

G. Any *changes in net working capital* associated with the project must be added to the project's cost and will require additional financing. This additional financing is necessary and must be considered part of the required initial cost of the project. These net working capital dollars are recovered at the end of the project's life.

V. **A number of different methods can be used to rank projects and to decide whether or not they should be accepted for inclusion in the capital budget. The three ranking methods that are used by firms today are payback period, net present value (NPV), and internal rate of return (IRR).**

A. The *payback period* is defined as the expected number of years it takes a firm to recover its original investment in a project. It provides a measure of *project liquidity* or the speed with which cash invested in the project will be returned. While the payback period is easy and inexpensive to apply, it has two major weaknesses:

1. It ignores cash flows beyond the payback period, and therefore is biased against long-term projects.
2. It ignores the time value of money, because it assigns equal weight to cash flows received in each year during the payback period.

B. Methods that take into account the time value of money are called *discounted cash flow (DCF) techniques*. One such method is the *net present value (NPV) method*.

1. To calculate the NPV, find the present value of each cash flow, including the initial (negative) outflow, C, and sum these PVs to find the NPV. Thus, the NPV equation is as follows:

$$NPV = \sum_{t=1}^{n} \frac{CF_t}{(1+k)^t} - C.$$

Here CF_t is the expected net cash flow from the project at Period t, n is the project's expected life, and k is the appropriate discount rate, or the cost of capital.

2. If the NPV is positive, the project should be accepted; if negative, it should be rejected. By taking on a project with a positive NPV, the firm increases its value and improves the position of its stockholders.
3. If two projects are *mutually exclusive* (that is, if only one can be accepted), the one with the higher NPV should be chosen, assuming the NPV is positive. If both projects have negative NPVs, neither should be chosen.
4. *Independent* projects are those whose costs and revenues are independent of one another. When evaluating multiple independent projects with positive NPVs, all should be accepted.

C. The *internal rate of return (IRR)* is the discount rate which equates the present value of the expected future cash inflows to the investment's cost.
1. The equation for calculating the IRR is as follows, where CF_t is the cash flow for the year t:

$$\sum_{t=1}^{n} \frac{CF_t}{(1 + IRR)^t} - C = 0.$$

This is an equation with one unknown, IRR, and we can solve for the value of IRR that will make the equation equal to zero. This value will cause the sum of the discounted cash receipts to equal the initial cost of the project, making the equation equal to zero.
2. The IRR formula is simply the NPV formula solved for the particular discount rate that causes the NPV to equal zero.
3. The IRR can be found by trial and error, by using a graphical analysis of the net present value profile, or by using a financial calculator or computer.

D. A *net present value profile* is a plot of a project's net present value at various discount rates. It can be used to determine a single project's IRR, and also to choose between two mutually exclusive projects.
1. The point at which the NPV profile crosses the horizontal axis is the project's IRR.
2. The NPV and IRR criteria always lead to the same accept/reject decision for independent projects.
3. If two mutually exclusive projects have NPV profiles which intersect, there may be a conflict in project choice between the NPV and IRR methods. These conflicts are discussed in Appendix 14A.

VI. **The best method to use is the one that selects from all available projects that particular set of projects which maximizes the firm's value and hence shareholder wealth.**

A. There are three properties that must be exhibited by a capital budgeting method if it is to lead to consistently correct decisions:
1. Considers all cash flows throughout the life of the project.

2. Considers the time value of money.
3. Selects that project from a set of mutually exclusive projects which maximizes the firm's stock price.

B. Only the NPV method satisfies all three conditions.

VII. It is important not to lose sight of the long-range consequences of capital spending on a national level. Capital spending ebbs and flows with business cycles and interest rate levels, with utilization of existing capacity, with lenders' willingness to make funds available, and with tax incentives.

VIII. Appendix 14A discusses conflicts between NPV and IRR which arise in certain situations due to different underlying assumptions about the two methods.

A. Conflicts can occur under two circumstances.
1. The projects differ in scale; for example, one project costs $100,000 while the other project costs $1 million.
2. The projects differ in cash flow timing; that is, one project has larger cash flows in its early years, while the other has larger cash flows in its later years. Note that cash flow timing does not necessarily refer to project life, but rather to the relative sizes of the flows.

B. Whether due to timing or size differences, NPV and IRR conflicts should be resolved by using the NPV methodology. The NPV criteria avoids several problems.
1. NPV chooses the project with the highest true return in dollars, giving the highest absolute return versus the highest relative return.
2. A major underlying cause of conflicts in project rankings lies in differing *reinvestment rate assumptions*.
   a. The NPV method implicitly assumes that project cash flows are reinvested at the project's cost of capital.
   b. The IRR method implicitly assumes that project cash flows are reinvested at the project's IRR.
   c. The opportunity cost of project cash flows is the project's cost of capital. If these cash flows were not available to the firm, and if the firm needed capital to invest in new projects, then the funds would be obtained from the capital markets, and the cost would be the firm's overall cost of capital. Thus, the assumption of reinvestment at the cost of capital is the correct assumption, which makes the NPV decision rule superior to the IRR decision rule.
3. NPV avoids the problem of *multiple IRRs*, which occur in projects having *nonnormal cash flows*, where outflows are followed by inflows and then by more outflows.

DEFINITIONAL QUESTIONS

1. A firm's __________ __________ outlines its planned expenditures on fixed assets.

2. The most difficult step in the analysis of capital expenditure proposals involves estimating future __________ __________.

3. The number of years necessary to return the original investment in a project is known as the __________ __________.

4. One important weakness of payback analysis is the fact that ______ ______ beyond the payback period are __________.

5. The net present value (NPV) method of evaluating investment proposals takes into account the __________ value of __________.

6. A capital investment proposal should be accepted if its NPV is __________.

7. If two projects are __________ __________, the one with the __________ positive NPV should be selected.

8. In the IRR approach, a discount rate is sought which makes the value of the NPV equal to __________.

9. A net present value profile shows the relationship between a project's NPV and the __________ __________ used to calculate the NPV.

10. If an independent project's __________ is greater than the project's cost of capital, it should be accepted.

11. If two mutually exclusive projects are being evaluated, and one project has a higher NPV while the other project has a higher IRR, the project with the higher __________ should be preferred.

12. The NPV method implicitly assumes reinvestment at the project's ________ _____ __________, while the IRR method implicitly assumes reinvestment at the __________ ______ _____ ________.

13. The process of comparing a project's actual results with its projected results is known as a(n) _________-_________.

14. The primary objective of the post-audit is to improve __________ and __________.

15. The internal rate of return (IRR) is the __________ rate that equates the present value of the __________ __________ with the present value of the project's initial cost.

16. The term __________ refers to fixed assets used in production, while a(n) __________ is a plan detailing projected inflows and outflows during some future period.

17. Capital budgeting decisions must be based on _______ ________ as distinguished from accounting income.

18. ______________ _______ ________ are those cash flows that result directly from the project and represent the change in the firm's total cash flows that occurs as a direct result of acquiring or not acquiring the asset.

19. _______ ________ are outlays that have already been committed or have already occurred and thus are not affected by the accept/reject decision.

20. ________________, or the effects of a project on other parts of the firm, must be considered in the capital project evaluation.

CONCEPTUAL QUESTIONS

21. The NPV of a project with cash flows that come in relatively slowly is more sensitive to changes in the discount rate than is the NPV of a project with cash flows that come in more rapidly.

    a. True b. False

22. The NPV method is preferred over the IRR method because the NPV method's reinvestment rate assumption is better.

    a. True b. False

23. Other things held constant, a decrease in the cost of capital (discount rate) will cause an increase in a project's IRR.

    a. True b. False

24. The IRR method can be used in place of the NPV method for all independent projects, because the two methods then result in identical decisions.

    a. True b. False

25. Projects A and B each have an initial cost of $5,000, followed by a series of positive cash inflows. Project A has total undiscounted cash inflows of $12,000, while B has total undiscounted inflows of $10,000. Further, at a discount rate of 10 percent, the two projects have identical NPVs. Which project's NPV will be *more sensitive* to changes in the discount rate? (Hint: Projects with steeper NPV profiles are more sensitive to discount rate changes.)

a. Project A.
b. Project B.
c. Both projects are equally sensitive to changes in the discount rate since their NPVs are equal at all costs of capital.
d. Neither project is sensitive to changes in the discount rate, since both have NPV profiles which are horizontal.
e. The solution cannot be determined unless the timing of the cash flows is known.

PROBLEMS

26. Your firm is considering a fast-food concession at the 1994 World's Fair. The cash flow pattern is somewhat unusual since you must build the stands, operate them for 2 years, and then tear the stands down and restore the sites to their original condition. You estimate the net cash flows to be as follows:

Time	Expected Net Cash Flow
0	($800,000)
1	700,000
2	700,000
3	(400,000)

What is the approximate IRR of this venture?

a. 5%
b. 15%
c. 25%
d. 35%
e. 45%

(The following data apply to the next three problems.)

Toya Motors needs a new machine for production of its 1994-1995 models. The financial vice president has appointed you to do the capital budgeting analysis. You have identified two different machines that are capable of performing the job. You have completed the cash flow analysis, and the expected net cash flows are as follows:

Year	Expected Net Cash Flow Machine B	 Machine O
0	($5,000)	($5,000)
1	2,085	0
2	2,085	0
3	2,085	0
4	2,085	9,677

27. What is the payback period for Machine B?

a. 1.0 years
b. 2.0 years
c. 2.4 years
d. 2.6 years
e. 3.0 years

28. The cost of capital is uncertain at this time, so you construct NPV profiles to assist in the final decision. The profiles for Machines B and O cross at what cost of capital?

a. 6%
b. 10%
c. 18%
d. 24%
e. They do not cross.

29. If the cost of capital for the project is 14 percent at the time the decision is made, which machine would you choose?

a. Machine B; it has the higher positive NPV.
b. Machine O; it has the higher positive NPV.
c. Neither; both have negative NPVs.
d. Either; both have the same NPV.
e. Machine B; it has the higher IRR.

(The following data apply to the next four problems.)

The director of capital budgeting for Giant Inc. has identified two mutually exclusive projects, L and S, with the following expected net cash flows:

Year	Expected Net Cash Flow Project L	 Project S
0	($100)	($100)
1	10	70
2	60	50
3	80	20

Both projects have a cost of capital of 10 percent.

30. What is the payback period for Project S?

a. 1.6 years
b. 1.8 years
c. 2.1 years
d. 2.5 years
e. 2.8 years

31. What is Project L's NPV?

a. $50.00
b. $34.25
c. $22.64
d. $18.79
e. $10.06

32. What is Project L's IRR?

a. 18.1%
b. 19.7%
c. 21.4%
d. 23.6%
e. 24.2%

33. Plot the NPV profiles for the two projects. Where is the crossover point?

a. 6.9%
b. 7.8%
c. 8.7%
d. 9.6%
e. 9.9%

(The following data apply to the next two problems.)

Seven Sisters Cookies Inc. has the opportunity to invest in a new type of oven which cooks the cookie dough more evenly resulting in a tastier cookie. The company expects this to result in higher sales. The initial outlay is $100,000, and the before-tax cash revenues generated by the investment in the oven are expected to be $25,000 per year for the next 10 years, after which it will be scrapped as potentially unreliable. There will be no additional annual cash expenses associated with the oven. Seven Sisters uses straight line depreciation (no salvage), the firm's tax rate is 40 percent, and the required rate of return on this asset is 12 percent.

34. What are the estimated annual net cash flows?

a. $10,000
b. $12,500
c. $15,000
d. $17,000
e. $19,000

35. What is the NPV of the oven?

a. $7,353.80
b. $7,736.96
c. $8,214.33
d. $8,897.25
e. $9,375.00

ANSWERS AND SOLUTIONS

1. capital budget
2. cash flows
3. payback period
4. cash flows; ignored
5. time; money
6. positive
7. mutually exclusive; higher
8. zero
9. discount rate
10. IRR
11. NPV
12. cost of capital; internal rate of return
13. post-audit
14. forecasts; operations
15. discount; cash inflows
16. capital; budget
17. cash flows
18. Incremental cash flows
19. Sunk costs
20. Externalities

21. a. The more the cash flows are spread over time, the greater is the effect of a change in discount rate. This is because the compounding process has a greater effect on distant cash flows than on cash flows that come in earlier.

22. a. Project cash flows are substitutes for outside capital. Thus, the opportunity cost of cash flows is the firm's cost of capital, adjusted for risk. The NPV method uses this cost as the reinvestment rate, while the IRR method assumes reinvestment at the IRR.

23. b. The computation of IRR is independent of the project's cost of capital.

24. a. Both the NPV and IRR methods lead to the same accept/reject decisions for independent projects. Thus, the IRR method can be used as a proxy for the NPV method when choosing independent projects.

25. a. If we were to begin graphing the NPV profiles for each of these projects, we would know two of the points for each project. The Y-intercepts for Projects A and B would be $7,000 and $5,000, respectively, and the

crossover rate would be 10 percent. Thus, from this information we can conclude that Project A's NPV profile would have the steeper slope and would be more sensitive to changes in the discount rate.

26. c. Unless you have a calculator that performs IRR calculations, the IRR must be obtained by trial and error or graphically. (The calculator solution is 25.48 percent.)

27. c. After Year 1, there is \$5,000 - \$2,085 = \$2,915 remaining to pay back. After Year 2, only \$2,915 - \$2,085 = \$830 is remaining. In Year 3, another \$2,085 is collected. Assuming that the Year 3 cash flow occurs evenly over time, then payback occurs \$830/\$2,085 = 0.4 of the way through Year 3. Thus, the payback period is 2.4 years.

28. b. To solve graphically, construct the NPV profiles:

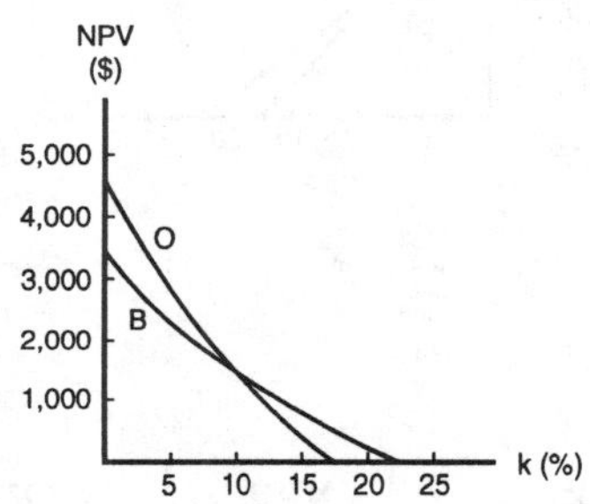

The Y intercept is the NPV when k = 0%. For B, 4(\$2,085) - \$5,000 = \$3,340. For O, \$9,677 - \$5,000 = \$4,677. The X intercept is the discount rate when NPV = \$0, or the IRR. For B, \$5,000 = \$2,085($PVIFA_{IRR,4}$); IRR = 24%. For O, \$5,000 = \$9,677($PVIF_{IRR,4}$); IRR = 18%. The graph is an approximation since we are only using two points to plot lines that are curvilinear. However, it shows that there is a crossover point, and that it occurs somewhere in the vicinity of k = 10%.

29. a. Refer to the NPV profiles. When k = 14%, we are to the right of the crossover point and Machine B has the higher NPV. You can verify this fact by calculating the NPVs. NPV_B = \$1,075 and NPV_O = \$730. Note that Machine B also has the higher IRR. However, the NPV method should be used when evaluating mutually exclusive projects. Note that had the project cost of capital been 8 percent, then Machine O would be chosen on the basis of the higher NPV.

30. a. After the first year, there is only \$30 remaining to be repaid, and \$50 is received in Year 2. Assuming an even cash flow throughout the year, the payback period is 1 + \$30/\$50 = 1.6 years.

31. d. $NPV_L = -\$100 + \$10/1.10 + \$60/(1.10)^2 + \$80/(1.10)^3$
$= -\$100 + \$9.09 + \$49.59 + \$60.11 = \$18.79.$
(Calculator solution is \$18.78.)

32. a. We used a calculator to find IRR_L = 18.1%.

33. c. The NPV profiles plot as follows:

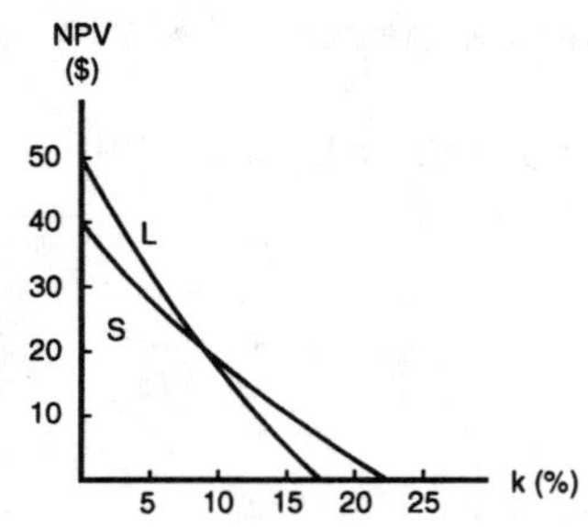

k	NPV_L	NPV_S
0%	\$50	\$40
5	33	29
10	19	20
15	7	12
20	(4)	5
25	(13)	(2)

By looking at the graph, we see that the approximate crossover rate is 8.7 percent.

34. e. Net cash flow = \$25,000(1 - 0.40) + (\$100,000/10)(0.40)
= \$15,000 + \$4,000 = \$19,000.

35. a. NPV = CF($PVIFA_{12\%,10}$) - Initial Outlay
= \$19,000(5.6502) - \$100,000
= \$107,353.80 - \$100,000 = \$7,353.80.

CHAPTER 15
DECISIONS IN CAPITAL BUDGETING

OVERVIEW

The analysis of project risk focuses on three types of risk: (1) stand-alone risk, (2) corporate, or within-firm, risk, and (3) beta, or market, risk. While some are more difficult to measure than others, each is important to estimate for proper capital budgeting analysis. In practice, both measuring risk and incorporating risk into capital budgeting decisions involves judgment.

In this chapter, we combine the topics of risk and capital budgeting to explain how managers incorporate risk measures into capital budgeting decisions. In addition, we cover several special topics in capital budgeting, including replacement analysis, evaluation of projects with unequal lives, and effects of inflation on capital budgeting decisions.

OUTLINE

I. **Risk analysis is important in all financial decisions, especially those relating to capital budgeting. There are three separate and distinct types of project risk: stand-alone risk, corporate (or within-firm risk), and beta (or market) risk.**

A. *Stand-alone risk* is that project's risk disregarding the facts that it is but one asset within the firm's portfolio of assets and that the firm in question is but one stock in most investors' stock portfolios. It is measured by the variability of the project's expected returns. Stand-alone risk is important for several reasons:

1. It is much easier to estimate a project's stand-alone risk than its corporate risk and beta risk.
2. In the majority of cases, all three types of risk are highly correlated; thus, stand-alone risk is generally a good proxy for hard-to-measure beta risk.
3. Management should spend considerable effort on ascertaining the riskiness of the project's own cash flows -- its stand-alone risk -- in order to obtain a reasonably accurate assessment of a project's riskiness.

B. *Corporate, or within-firm, risk* is the effect a project has on the company's risk without consideration for the effects of the stockholders' own personal diversification. It is measured by the project's impact on the firm's earnings variability. Corporate risk is important for three primary reasons:

1. Undiversified stockholders, including owners of small businesses, are more concerned about corporate risk than beta risk.

2. Empirical studies show that even well-diversified investors consider both beta and corporate risk to be important when setting required returns.
3. A firm that is relatively unstable will find it difficult to attract and retain good employees, and both customers and suppliers will be reluctant to depend on the firm. These facts lower the sales and profits of a firm with excessive corporate risk.

C. *Beta, or market, risk* is project risk assessed from the standpoint of an equity investor who holds a highly diversified portfolio. It is measured by the project's effect on the firm's beta coefficient.

1. The *Capital Asset Pricing Model (CAPM)* provides a framework for analyzing the relationship between risk and return, and can be used to evaluate projects as portfolios and thus determine the required rate of return.
2. The required rate of return is equal to the risk-free rate of return, k_{RF}, plus the market risk premium, $k_M - k_{RF}$, times the stock's beta coefficient, b:

$$k = k_{RF} + (k_M - k_{RF})b.$$

3. For example, if a firm has a beta of 1.1, $k_M = 12\%$, and $k_{RF} = 8\%$, then its required rate of return will be $k = 8\% + (12\% - 8\%)1.1 = 12.4\%$. Stockholders should be willing to let the firm invest in average-risk projects if the firm can earn 12.4 percent or more on this money.
4. The acceptance of a particular capital budgeting project may cause a firm's overall beta to rise or fall, causing a change in the required rate of return.
   a. The impact of any one project on a firm's beta will depend upon the size of the project relative to the existing "portfolio" of projects.
   b. An increase in the firm's beta coefficient will cause the stock price to decline unless the increased beta is offset by a higher expected rate of return.
   c. Given the proportions of the new investment and the existing projects, it is possible to calculate the required return on a new investment needed to offset the project's effect on the firm's beta.
5. If the beta coefficient for each project can be determined, then an individual project's cost of capital can be found as follows:

$$k_{Project} = k_{RF} + (k_M - k_{RF})b_{Project}.$$

   High beta (or high-risk) projects will have a relatively high cost of equity capital, while low beta (or low-risk) projects will have a correspondingly low cost of capital.
6. The *Security Market Line* can be used to illustrate this concept graphically. It shows how investors are willing to make tradeoffs between risk, as measured by beta, and expected returns. If the expected rate of return on a given capital project lies above the SML,

the expected rate of return on the project is more than enough to compensate for its risk, so it should be accepted. Conversely, if the project's rate of return lies below the SML, it should be rejected. Projects that lie on the SML should be accepted, as their returns exactly compensate for their risk.

II. Portfolio considerations play an important role in the overall capital budgeting process.

A. The returns on an individual project may be very uncertain, but if the project is small in relation to the total firm, and if its returns are not highly correlated with the firm's other assets, then the project may not be very risky in either the corporate or beta sense.

B. Through planned diversification, corporations can stabilize earnings and reduce corporate risk. However, investors can diversify their stock portfolios more easily than firms can diversify their assets, so corporate diversification just to reduce risk is not likely to raise stock prices.

1. Corporations have experienced some complications from their rush to diversify.
   a. A corporate culture clash which hurts both firms.
   b. A management which is spread "too thin."
   c. A situation in which top management of the acquiring firm has insufficient expertise in the business of the acquired firm to direct its operations.

III. Financial managers must assess the relative stand-alone, corporate, and beta risk for each proposed project. Although it is difficult to assign weights to the importance of each, they should be included.

IV. Financial managers must also consider several other important topics in analyzing capital budgeting projects. Among these are replacement decisions and the comparison of projects with unequal lives.

A. *Replacement decision analysis* is somewhat different from that for expansion projects. The replacement decision involves whether or not to replace an existing asset that is still productive with a new one. (Note that it involves comparing two *mutually exclusive* projects.) A replacement decision worksheet is used which shows net cash flows made at the time the investment is made (t = 0), incremental cash flows over the life of the project, and the net present value (NPV) of all these cash flows. A positive NPV would indicate that the replacement should be made.

1. Additional cash flows must be considered at time = 0.
   a. The cash received from the sale of the old equipment is an inflow.
   b. However, the sale of the old machine will usually have tax effects. If the old equipment is sold below book value, there will be a *tax savings;* if the equipment is sold at a profit, taxes

must be paid. The tax effect is equal to the loss or gain times the firm's marginal tax rate.

2. Additional considerations must be made in arriving at the cash flow from operations.
   a. The effects of the new equipment on revenues and costs must be looked at. An incremental increase in revenues would produce a cash inflow, while an incremental increase in costs would produce a cash outflow. The incremental flows must be based on the flows generated by the old asset. The revenue and cost effects are combined into a single incremental cash inflow and multiplied by (1 - T) to obtain the after-tax cash inflow.
   b. The depreciation expense on the old equipment must be subtracted from the depreciation expense on the new equipment to get the *net change in depreciation*. This amount is then multiplied by the tax rate to find the tax savings or loss from the change in depreciation.
   c. Any *salvage value* on the old machine, including tax effects, must be included as a cash outflow at the end of the project's life. Accepting the new project causes the firm to forgo the old machine's salvage value. Thus, it must be included as an *opportunity cost*. Of course, any salvage value on the new machine must also be included in the analysis.

B. Special consideration must be given to replacement decisions that involve two alternatives with different lives. To adjust for *unequal lives*, a series of *replacement chains* extending out to the "common denominator" year may be set up. Thus, a 6-year machine would have a 2-chain cycle if compared to a 4-year machine with a 3-chain cycle, the common denominator year being 12. The proper comparison for the *replacement chain (common life) method* can be made as follows:
1. Find the NPV for each machine.
2. Determine the NPV for each chain out to its common denominator year. If the NPV of the 6-year machine = $250, and the NPV of the 4-year machine = $150, then the 6-year machine will have an NPV of $250 in Years 0 and 6, while the 4-year machine will have an NPV of $150 in Years 0, 4, and 8.
3. Discount these NPVs back to the present.
4. Sum the component NPVs for each machine to find the "true" NPV.

C. As a general rule, the unequal life issue does not arise for *independent projects* but can arise if mutually exclusive projects with significantly different lives are being evaluated. However, even for mutually exclusive projects, it is not always appropriate to extend the analysis to a common life. This should only be done if there is a high probability that the projects will actually be replicated beyond their initial lives.

D. There are several potentially serious weaknesses inherent in this type of unequal life analysis:

1. If inflation is expected, then replacement equipment will have a higher price, and both sales prices and operating costs will probably change. Thus, the static conditions built into the analysis would be invalid.
2. Replacements that occur down the road would probably employ new technology, which in turn might change the cash flows. This factor is not built into the replacement chain analysis.
3. It is difficult enough to estimate the lives of most projects, so estimating the lives of a series of projects is often just speculation.
4. If reasonably strong competition is present, the profitability of projects will be eroded over time and that would reduce the need to extend the analysis beyond the projects' initial lives.

E. When the problems above occur, expected inflation and/or possible efficiency gains are built directly into the cash flow estimates, and then the replacement chain approach is used.

V. **The effects of inflation on capital budgeting may be handled in two ways: (1) explicitly adjust the discount rate and (2) make no explicit adjustment in the discount rate but adjust the expected cash flows to reflect expected inflation.**

A. As long as sales prices and costs are expected to rise at the same rate of inflation that investors have built into the cost of capital, then the inflation-adjusted NPV will be equal to the NPV calculated in real terms.

B. If only the cost of capital is adjusted for inflation and the expected cash flows are not, the NPV will be downward biased.
1. If sales prices and all costs are expected to rise at approximately the same rate, the bias can be corrected by having current cash flows increase at the inflation rate, or by using the real rate as the cost of capital.
2. In any situation where both revenues and all costs are not expected to rise at exactly the same inflation rate as is built into the cost of capital, the best procedure is to build inflation into the basic cash flow component projections for each year.

DEFINITIONAL QUESTIONS

1. Three types of risk have been identified in capital budgeting decisions: ________ - ________ risk, ____________ risk, and ________ risk.

2. The required rate of return on a company's stock is equal to the _______ - _______ rate plus a(n) __________ for risk.

3. The risk premium on a stock is equal to the market risk premium times the stock's _______ ______________.

4. An increase in the overall beta coefficient will cause the firm's stock price to _______ unless this increase is offset by a(n) _________ expected rate of return.

5. Measuring corporate risk involves determining the uncertainty of a project's ________ ______.

6. The __________ the risk associated with an investment, the greater the _______ _____ _________ needed to compensate investors.

7. A project with a high degree of corporate risk will not necessarily affect the firm's _______ to any great extent.

8. ________-________ _______ is that project's risk disregarding the facts that it is but one asset within the firm's portfolio of assets and that the firm in question is but one stock in most investors' stock portfolios.

9. ____________ _______ is the effect a project has on the company's risk without consideration for the effects of the stockholders' own personal diversification.

10. Riskier projects should be evaluated with a higher _______ ____ __________ than average-risk projects.

11. _______ _______ is project risk assessed from the standpoint of an equity investor who holds a highly diversified portfolio.

12. In replacement analysis, two cash flows that occur at t = 0 that are not present in expansion projects are the price received from the sale of the ______ equipment and the ______ effects of the sale.

13. In replacement analysis, the depreciation tax savings or loss is based on the _____________ in depreciation expense between the old and new asset.

14. The __________ ________ __________ ________ provides a framework for analyzing the relationship between risk and return, and can be used to evaluate projects as portfolios and thus determine the required rate of return.

15. The ___________ _________ _______ shows how investors are willing to make tradeoffs between risk, as measured by beta, and expected returns.

16. Through planned __________________, corporations can stabilize earnings and reduce corporate risk.

17. ______________ ___________ ___________ involves whether or not to replace an existing asset that is still productive with a new one.

18. In a replacement decision, any salvage value on the old machine, including tax effects, must be included as a cash outflow at the end of the project's

life. Accepting the project causes the firm to forgo the old machine's salvage value; thus, it must be included as a(n) ____________ ______.

19. To adjust for unequal lives, a series of ____________ __________ extending out to the common denominator year may be set up. As a general rule, the unequal life issue can arise if __________ ___________ projects with significantly different lives are being evaluated.

20. The effects of inflation on capital budgeting may be handled in two ways: (1) explicitly adjust the __________ _______ and (2) make no explicit adjustment in the discount rate but adjust the __________ _______ _______ to reflect expected inflation.

CONCEPTUAL QUESTIONS

21. McDonald's is planning to open a new store across from the student union. Annual revenues are expected to be $5 million. However, opening the new location will cause annual revenues to drop by $3 million at McDonald's existing stadium location. The relevant sales revenues for the capital budgeting analysis are $2 million per year.

    a. True b. False

22. In a replacement decision, the salvage value of the old asset need not be considered since the current market value of the asset is included in the analysis.

    a. True b. False

23. Even if the beta of a project being considered has a value of zero, acceptance of the project will affect the market risk of the firm.

    a. True b. False

24. In capital budgeting decisions, corporate risk will be of least interest to

    a. Employees.
    b. Stockholders with few shares.
    c. Institutional investors.
    d. Creditors.
    e. The local community.

PROBLEMS

(The following data apply to the next three problems.)

As the capital budgeting director of Union Mills Inc. you are analyzing the replacement of an automated loom system. The old system was purchased 5 years ago for $200,000; it falls into the MACRS 5-year class; and it has 5 years of remaining life and a $50,000 salvage value five years from now. The current market value of the old system is $100,000. The new system has a price of $300,000, plus an additional $50,000 in installation costs. The new system falls into the MACRS 5-year class, has a 5-year economic life, and a $100,000 salvage value. The new system will require a $40,000 increase in the spare parts inventory. The primary advantage of the new system is that it will decrease operating costs by $40,000 per year. Union Mills has a 12 percent cost of capital and a marginal tax rate of 40 percent.

25. What is the net cash investment at Year 0?

a. $350,000
b. $325,200
c. $295,000
d. $40,000
e. $23,200

26. What is the annual net operating cash inflow in Year 1?

a. $47,200
b. $43,950
c. $39,825
d. $33,350
e. $50,200

27. What is the net cash flow in the final year (Year 5)?

a. $31,360
b. $43,060
c. $117,800
d. $121,930
e. $117,200

28. Initially, United Products has a beta of 1.30. The risk-free rate is 7 percent, and the required rate of return on the market is 13 percent. The firm now sells 10 percent of its assets, having a beta of 1.30, and uses the proceeds to purchase a new product line with a beta of 1.00. What is the new overall required rate of return for United Products?

a. 15.11%
b. 16.24%
c. 17.48%
d. 18.00%
e. 14.62%

29. Consolidated Inc. uses a weighted average cost of capital of 12 percent to evaluate average-risk projects and adds/subtracts two percentage points to evaluate projects of greater/lesser risk. Currently, two mutually exclusive projects are under consideration. Both have a net cost of $200,000 and last 4 years. Project A, which is riskier than average, will produce yearly after-tax net cash flows of $71,000. Project B, which has less-than-average risk, will produce an after-tax net cash flow of $146,000 in Years 3 and 4 only. What should Consolidated do?

a. Accept Project B with an NPV of $9,412.
b. Accept both projects since both NPVs are greater than zero.
c. Accept Project A with an NPV of $6,874.
d. Accept neither project since both NPVs are less than zero.
e. Accept Project A with an NPV of $15,652.

30. Union Industries, an all-equity financed firm, is considering the purchase of a plant that produces plastic products. The plant is expected to generate a rate of return of 17 percent, and the plant's estimated beta is 2.00. The risk-free rate is 8 percent, and the market risk premium is 6 percent. Union should make the investment.

a. True b. False

31. Diversified Products (DP) is considering the formation of a new division which will double the assets of the firm. DP is an all-equity firm which has a current required rate of return of 16 percent. The risk-free rate is 8 percent, and the market risk premium is 5 percent. If DP wants to reduce its required rate of return to 14 percent, what is the maximum beta the new division could have?

a. 0.80
b. 0.90
c. 1.00
d. 1.15
e. 1.25

32. Midwest Motors is choosing between two automobile washing/waxing machines on the basis of cost. The expected net costs of the two machines are as follows:

Year	Machine A	Machine B
0	($20,000)	($10,000)
1	(5,000)	(8,000)
2	(5,000)	(8,000)
3	(5,000)	(8,000)
4	(5,000)	(8,000)

The firm's cost of capital is 10 percent. Machine B is judged to be a riskier-than-average project, while Machine A is considered less risky than average. The firm's policy is to add or subtract 2 percentage points to adjust for risk. The firm should choose Machine B.

a. True b. False

33. The Evans-Smythe Company is evaluating an average-risk capital project that has a 4-year economic life and falls into the 3-year MACRS class life. The initial net investment outlay (in Time 0) is $56,400. The expected end-of-year cash flows, expressed in Time 0 dollars, are listed below:

	Year 1	Year 2	Year 3	Year 4
Revenues	$84,000	$84,000	$84,000	$84,000
Operating costs (excl. depr.)	64,500	64,500	64,500	64,500
Depreciation	18,612	25,380	8,460	3,948

The firm has a marginal tax rate of 40 percent. Evans-Smythe's current cost of capital is 13 percent, which includes an inflation premium of 5 percent. For simplicity, assume that the firm's cost of capital is calculated as a real rate of return plus an inflation premium. What is the NPV of this project calculated in Time 0 dollars?

a. -$3,745.97
b. -$1,822.43
c. $519.78
d. $1,089.65
e. $1,796.05

ANSWERS AND SOLUTIONS

1. stand-alone; corporate (or within-firm); beta (or market)
2. risk-free; premium
3. beta coefficient
4. fall; higher
5. cash flows
6. greater; rate of return
7. beta
8. Stand-alone risk
9. Corporate risk
10. cost of capital (or discount rate)
11. Beta risk
12. old; tax
13. difference
14. Capital Asset Pricing Model
15. Security Market Line
16. diversification
17. Replacement decision analysis
18. opportunity cost
19. replacement chains; mutually exclusive
20. discount rate; expected cash flows

21. a. Incremental revenues, which are relevant in a capital budgeting decision, must be considered if they affect other parts of the firm.

22. b. In an incremental analysis, the cash flows assuming replacement are compared with the cash flows assuming the old asset is retained. If the old asset is retained, it will produce a salvage value cash flow which must be included, with tax effects, in the replacement analysis.

23. a. The addition of an asset with a beta of zero would normally lower the beta of the firm, thus lowering the firm's market risk. (The beginning beta of most firms is greater than zero.)

24. c. Institutional investors are well diversified and, therefore, more concerned with beta risk.

25. b.

Price of new machine	($300,000)
Installation	(50,000)
Sale of old machine	100,000
Tax on sale*	(35,200)
Increase in net working capital	(40,000)
	($325,200)

*The old machine has been depreciated down to $12,000, since it falls into the MACRS 5-year class and it has been in operation for 5 years. Now, the old machine has a market value of $100,000. The $88,000 (purchase price minus book value) is treated as ordinary income and is taxed at 40 percent. Thus, Union Mills must pay a tax of 0.40($88,000) = $35,200 on the sale of the old asset.

26. a. The after-tax revenue/cost component is 0.60($40,000) = $24,000. As for the tax savings due to depreciation, the depreciable basis for the new machine is $350,000. Further, the MACRS depreciation allowance for Year 1 of a 5-year class asset is 20 percent. Thus, the depreciation expense on the new machine is 0.20($350,000) = $70,000. The old machine still has 1 year of depreciation left equal to 0.06 x $200,000 = $12,000, so the change in depreciation due to the replacement decision is an increase of $70,000 - $12,000 = $58,000. The tax savings is 0.40($58,000) = $23,200. Therefore, the Year 1 net cash flow from operations is $24,000 + $23,200 = $47,200.

27. c. In the final year, Year 5, the net cash flow is composed of 0.60($40,000) = $24,000 in after-tax cost decrease and 0.40(0.11)($350,000) = $15,400 in depreciation tax savings, for a total of $39,400, plus the applicable nonoperating cash flows. Thus, we have the following:

From operations	$ 39,400
Salvage value of new machine	100,000
Tax on new machine salvage value	(31,600)
Salvage value of old machine	(50,000)
Tax on old machine salvage value	20,000
Change in working capital	40,000
Net cash flow	$117,800

Note that the salvage value of the old machine is a cash outflow. This is an opportunity cost, since buying the new machine deprives Union Mills of the salvage value of the old machine. Additionally, salvage tax effects must be considered. Also note that the change in working capital considered at t = 0, an outflow, is exactly offset by an inflow at the end of the project. This is because it is assumed that the project will terminate and the increase in working capital is no longer required.

28. e. New b = 0.9(1.30) + 0.1(1.00) = 1.27.
New k = 7% + (13% - 7%)1.27 = 14.62%.

29. a. Look at the time lines:

A:	0	1	2	3	4
	($200,000)	$71,000	$71,000	$71,000	$71,000

206,874 ← @ 14% (years 1–4)
$ 6,874 = NPV

B:	0	1	2	3	4
	($200,000)	0	0	$146,000	$146,000

109,692 ← @ 10% (year 3)
99,720 ← @ 10% (year 4)
$ 9,412 = NPV

Note that both discount rates are adjusted for risk. Since the projects are mutually exclusive, the project with the higher NPV is chosen.

30. b. The project's required rate of return on equity and overall cost of capital is 20 percent:

$$k_{Project} = 8\% + (6\%)2 = 20\%.$$

Since the expected return is only 17 percent, the plant should not be purchased.

31. a. First, find the current beta of the firm:

$$k = 8\% + (5\%)b = 16\%$$
$$b = 1.60.$$

Now find the beta required to lower the required rate of return to 14 percent:

$k = 8\% + (5\%)b = 14\%$
$b = 1.20.$

Finally, if the firm doubles with the formation of the new division, 50 percent of the expanded firm's assets will be old assets, while 50 percent will be assets from the new division. Thus, $0.5(1.60) + 0.5(b_{Div.}) = 1.20$; $b_{Div.} = 0.80$.

32. b. These are cash outflows, so the risk adjustment process is reversed. Thus, the project cost of capital for Machine A is 12 percent, while the project cost of capital for B is 8 percent.

$$PV_{Project\ A} = (\$35{,}187).$$

$$PV_{Project\ B} = (\$36{,}497).$$

We see that with the correct risk adjustment, the PV of costs for Machine A is less than the PV of costs for Machine B, and hence Machine A should be selected.

33. e. $k_n = k_r + i$
$13\% = k_r + 5\%$
$k_r = 8\%.$

The relevant real cash flows are calculated as follows:

	1	2	3	4
Revenues	$84,000	$84,000	$84,000	$84,000
Op. costs	64,500	64,500	64,500	64,500
	$19,500	$19,500	$19,500	$19,500
Taxes	7,800	7,800	7,800	7,800
	$11,700	$11,700	$11,700	$11,700
Dep. tax sav.[a]	7,445	10,152	3,384	1,579
NCF	$19,145	$21,852	$15,084	$13,279

[a] Depreciation tax savings = (DEP)T.

The NPV is calculated as:

$$\begin{aligned} NPV &= \$19{,}145(PVIF_{8\%,1}) + \$21{,}852(PVIF_{8\%,2}) + \$15{,}084(PVIF_{8\%,3}) \\ &\quad + \$13{,}279(PVIF_{8\%,4}) - \$56{,}400 \\ &= \$17{,}726.85 + \$18{,}734.57 + \$11{,}974.17 + \$9{,}760.46 - \$56{,}400 \\ &= \$1{,}796.05. \end{aligned}$$

Because the NPV is positive, the project should be accepted. (Note that if the nominal cost of capital had been used, the NPV would have been biased downward resulting in a negative NPV and a rejection of the project. This would have been an incorrect decision.)

CHAPTER 16
BONDS AND PREFERRED STOCK

OVERVIEW

Most firms find it desirable to use long-term debt financing. The two most important classes of fixed-income securities are term loans and bonds. These securities come in many types: secured and unsecured, zero-coupon and normal coupon, floating rate and fixed rate, and so on. Firms can also use preferred stock, which is a hybrid security that represents a cross between debt and equity. The variety stems from the fact that different groups of investors favor different types of securities, and their tastes change over time. The astute financial manager knows how to "package" securities at a given point in time to attract the greatest number of potential investors, thereby keeping the firm's cost of capital to a minimum.

OUTLINE

I. **A bond is a long-term promissory note issued by a business or governmental unit; it is a contract under which a borrower agrees to make payments of interest and principal, on specific dates, to the holder of the bond.**

A. Bonds differ from term loans in that they are generally offered to the public rather than to a single lender or a small group of lenders.

B. The *par value* is the stated face (nominal) value of a bond. The par value generally represents the amount of money the firm borrows and promises to repay at some future date.

C. The specified number of dollars of interest that the issuer of the bond is required to pay each period is the *coupon payment*. The stated annual rate of interest on a bond is the *coupon interest rate*.

D. A bond's *maturity date* is the specified date on which the par value of the bond must be repaid. Most bonds have original maturities (the number of years to maturity at the time the bond is issued) of from 10 to 40 years.

E. A *call provision* gives the issuing corporation the right to call the entire bond issue for redemption before its regular maturity.

F. A bond that has just been issued is known as a *new issue*. Once a bond has been on the market for a while, it is classified as an *outstanding bond* or *seasoned issue.* Although newly issued bonds generally sell very close to par, the prices for outstanding bonds may vary widely from par.

II. **A bond is a contractual debt instrument, calling for the payment of a specified amount of interest for a stated number of years, and for the repayment of the par value on the bond's maturity date.**

A. Bonds with annual coupon payments represent an *annuity* of I dollars per year for n years, plus a final payment of M dollars at the end of n years.

B. The present value of this payment stream determines the value of the bond.

C. As an example, consider a 3 year, $1,000 bond paying $50 annually, when the appropriate interest rate, k_d, is 8 percent:

$$V = I(PVIFA_{k_d,n}) + M(PVIF_{k_d,n}) = \$50(2.5771) + \$1,000(0.7938) = \$922.66.$$

1. Suppose that this bond paid $25 semiannually, the value of the bond would be

$$V = I/2(PVIFA_{k_d/2,2n}) + M(PVIF_{k_d/2,2n})$$

$$= \$25(5.2421) + \$1,000(0.7903)$$

$$= \$921.35.$$

D. The percentage rate of return on the bonds consists of an *interest,* or *current, yield* and a *capital gains yield.*
1. The current yield is calculated as the annual interest payment on the bond divided by the bond's current market price.
2. The capital gains yield is calculated as the capital gain during any one year (the difference between the ending and beginning price) divided by the beginning price.

E. Bond prices and interest rates are *inversely related;* that is, they tend to move in the opposite direction from one another.
1. A bond will sell *at par* when its coupon rate is equal to the going rate of interest, k_d.
2. When the going rate of interest is above the coupon rate, the bond will sell at a *"discount"* from its par value, as in the example above.
3. If current interest rates are below the coupon rate, the bond will sell at a *"premium"* above its par value.
4. An increase in interest rates causes the prices of outstanding bonds to fall, while a decrease in interest rates causes bond prices to rise.
5. The market value of a bond will approach its par value as its maturity date approaches.

F. The longer a bond's maturity, the larger the price change in response to a given movement in market interest rates. This means that the prices of long-term bonds are more sensitive to interest rate changes than are short-term bond prices.

G. Interest rates fluctuate over time, and people or firms who invest in bonds are exposed to risk from changing interest rates, or *interest rate risk*.

H. The rate of interest earned on a bond if it is held until redeemed by the issuer is known as the *yield to maturity (YTM)*.

I. If current interest rates are well below an outstanding bond's coupon rate, then a callable bond is likely to be called, and investors should estimate the expected rate of return on the bond as the *yield to call (YTC)* rather than the yield to maturity.

1. The YTC is calculated for an annual coupon bond as follows:

$$V_B = \sum_{t=1}^{n} I \frac{1}{(1 + k_d)^t} + \text{Call price} \frac{1}{(1 + k_d)^n}.$$

The value for k_d that solves this equation is the YTC.

III. **Funded debt is simply another name for long-term debt. When a firm "funds" its floating debt, it replaces short-term debt with securities of longer maturities.**

IV. **Bond holders attempt to reduce agency problems by use of legal restrictions designed to ensure, insofar as possible, that the company does nothing to cause the quality of its bonds to deteriorate after they have been issued. These legal restrictions are listed in the bond indenture.**

A. A bond's *indenture* is a legal document that spells out the rights of both the bondholders and the issuing corporation. A *trustee* is an official, usually of a bank, who represents the bondholders and makes sure the terms of the indenture are carried out.

B. The Securities and Exchange Commission approves indentures and makes sure that all indenture provisions are met before allowing a company to sell new securities to the public.

C. A *restrictive covenant* is a provision in a bond issue that requires the issuer to meet certain stated conditions.

1. Standard provisions typically include minimum levels for the current ratio and the debt-to-assets ratio.
2. These requirements are designed to help insure that the credit standing of the firm and the bond issue remains high.

D. A *sinking fund provision* requires that a firm retire a portion of a bond issue each year.

1. Failure to make a sinking fund payment constitutes *technical default,* so lenders can require immediate payment on the entire issue and possibly force the firm into bankruptcy.
2. Generally, sinking funds permit the firm to call a specific number of bonds for redemption or to buy the required number of bonds in the open market. The firm will select whichever method is the least expensive.

E. A *call provision* gives the issuing corporation the right to call the entire bond issue for redemption before its regular maturity.
1. When a bond is called, the company must normally pay an amount greater than the par value. This extra payment is referred to as a *call premium.*
2. Bonds are frequently called when the issuing firm can refund the issue at a lower interest rate. The call premium is thus a penalty for depriving investors of the higher rate of interest.
3. A call for refunding purposes is quite different from a call for sinking fund purposes. A sinking fund call generally has no call premium and only involves a small percentage of the issue, while a regular call involves the entire issue.

V. **There are various types of bonds. Some of the more important ones are discussed below.**

A. When real estate or other property is pledged as collateral for a bond issue, the bond is referred to as a mortgage bond. In case of bankruptcy, the mortgage bondholders have first claim on the proceeds from the sale of the pledged assets.
1. Holders of *second mortgage bonds* have a claim against the property only after the first mortgage bondholders have been paid off in full. Second mortgages are sometimes called *junior mortgages* because they are junior in priority to the claims of *senior mortgages,* or first mortgage bonds.

B. A *debenture* is an unsecured bond, and holders are general creditors of the corporation. The use of debentures depends on the firm's general credit strength and the nature of its assets.

C. Subordinated debentures have claims on assets, in the event of bankruptcy, only after senior debt as named in the subordinate debenture's indenture has been paid off.

D. There are several other important types of bonds.
1. *Convertible bonds* are securities that are convertible into shares of common stock, at a fixed price, at the option of the bondholder.
2. *Warrants* are options that permit the holder to buy stock for a stated price, thereby providing a capital gain if the price of the stock increases.
3. *Income bonds* pay interest only when covered by the earnings of the firm.

4. *Indexed,* or *purchasing power, bonds* have interest payments based on an inflation index so as to protect the holder from inflation. It is used most commonly in countries with high rates of inflation.

VI. **There have been several innovations in long-term financing.**

A. *Zero coupon bonds* pay no interest but are offered at substantial discounts below their par values and hence provide capital appreciation rather than interest income.

1. The advantages to the issuer are as follows:
   a. No cash outlays are required until maturity.
   b. These bonds often have a relatively lower yield to maturity than regular coupon bonds.
   c. The issuer receives an annual tax deduction equal to the yearly amortization of the discount, which means that the bonds have a positive cash flow in the form of tax savings over their life.
2. The major disadvantage to the issuer is that the firm will have a very large nondeductible cash outlay coming up in the year the bonds mature.
3. The main advantage to investors is that zero coupon bonds guarantee a "true" yield to maturity since there is no *reinvestment rate risk*.

B. When interest rates are volatile, lenders are reluctant to lend long term at fixed interest rates. Thus, they charge very high maturity risk premiums. On the other hand, borrowers, in general, would rather borrow long term so that they do not have to worry about having to continually refund their debt.

1. The answer to the dilemma is long-term, *floating rate debt.*
2. The debt may have a 5- or 10-year maturity, but the interest rate changes periodically to reflect current market conditions.
3. Floating rate debt is advantageous to lenders because it causes the market value of the debt to be stabilized, and it provides lenders with more income to meet their own obligations.
4. Floating rate debt is also advantageous to corporations because they can obtain debt with a long maturity without committing themselves to paying a historically high rate of interest for the entire term of the loan. However, if interest rates rise, borrowers will face increasing interest expense.

C. A *junk bond* is a high risk, high yield bond used to finance mergers, leveraged buyouts, and troubled companies.

VII. **Bond issues are normally assigned quality ratings by both Moody's Investors Service and Standard & Poor's Corporation. These ratings reflect the probability that a bond will go into default. Aaa (Moody's) and AAA (S&P) are the highest ratings.**

A. *Bond ratings* influence investors' perceptions of default risk and therefore have an impact on the interest rate paid, and hence on the firm's cost of capital.

B. Institutions are often limited to investing in *investment grade securities,* that is, those rated BBB or Baa, or higher. It is important, therefore, that a firm maintain a good quality rating on its bond issues.

C. Rating agencies review outstanding bonds on a periodic basis, occasionally *upgrading* or *downgrading* a bond as the issuer's circumstances change. Also, as a company issues more bonds, this will trigger a review by the rating agencies.

D. A change in a firm's bond rating will have a significant effect on its ability to borrow long-term capital and on the cost of that capital.

VIII. A term loan is long-term debt where the borrower negotiates directly with a financial institution. This type of financing is, therefore, called direct financing.

A. The financial institution which lends the funds is usually a bank, an insurance company, or a pension fund.

B. The maturity of a term loan is generally from 3 to 15 years, but it may be as short as 2 or as long as 30 years.

C. *Term loans* have several advantages over publicly issued securities.
   1. Loan provisions can be worked out more quickly between the lender and the borrower.
   2. Loan provisions can also be more flexible.
   3. It is not necessary for a term loan to go through the SEC registration process.
   4. If necessary or desirable, changes in the contract can be negotiated with the lender.
   5. Issuance costs are generally lower for term loans.

D. Most term loans are *amortized,* or paid off, in equal installments over the life of the loan.

E. The interest rate on a term loan can either be fixed for the life of the loan or be variable.

F. Among the recent developments is the trend toward firms selling junk bonds instead of taking out bank term loans, thus causing banks to lose a large slice of their traditional business.

IX. Long-term debt instruments have both advantages and disadvantages from both the issuer's and investor's viewpoints.

A. There are several advantages to the corporation from the use of long-term debt, as opposed to equity financing.
   1. The cost of debt is limited.
   2. Because creditors, including bondholders, have prior claims on the firm's earnings and assets, this lowers the risk to these lenders.

Therefore, the cost to the firm is lower on debt than on preferred and common stock.

3. Owners of the firm do not have to give up any of their control of the firm since bondholders typically do not vote.
4. It is possible for the firm to build some flexibility into the bond indenture by including a call provision.

B. The disadvantages associated with the use of long-term debt include:

1. Debt must be serviced. The fixed interest charge must be paid, whether the firm is having a good or a bad year.
2. Most debt has a fixed maturity date so that the firm must have a plan to repay lenders or refinance the debt.
3. The indenture provisions are likely to be much more severe than any restrictions that apply to short-term loans.
4. There are limits to the amount of funds that can be raised through debt.

C. Bondholders and other long-term lenders are likely to focus on three aspects of debt: risk, return, and control.

1. Compared with the preferred and common stockholders of a given firm, investors holding the firm's debt have less risk due to prior claims on earnings and assets and protective covenants of indenture.
2. With lower risk, the expected return to lenders should also be lower than what common stockholders hope to realize.
3. Bondholders and other creditors do not have the right to vote. However, if the bonds go into default, the bondholders in effect take control of the firm.

X. **Preferred stock is a hybrid type of long-term financing. It is called a hybrid because it represents an equity investment in a business, yet it has many of the characteristics associated with debt.**

A. If an analysis is being made by a common stockholder, preferred is treated like debt, because it entails fixed charges which must be paid ahead of common stock dividends.

B. However, if the analysis is being made by a creditor studying a firm's vulnerability to failure, preferred stock is viewed as part of the equity base.

C. From management's perspective, preferred stock lies between debt and common equity. Since failure to pay dividends on preferred stock will not force the firm into bankruptcy, preferred stock is safer to use than debt. At the same time, if the firm is highly successful, the common stockholders will not have to share that success with the preferred stockholders because preferred dividends are fixed.

D. Preferred stock has the following characteristics:

1. Preferred stock has a par value.

2. The preferred dividend can be stated as a percentage of the par value or in dollars.
3. Dividends on preferred stock must be paid before dividends can be paid on common stock. For protection, dividends on most preferred stock are *cumulative* from year to year; thus, unpaid preferred dividends (arrearages) accumulate and must be paid before common stockholders can receive dividends.
4. Nonpayment of preferred stock dividends, however, does not force a company into bankruptcy.
5. In the event of bankruptcy, preferred stockholders have priority over common stockholders but below creditors.
6. Some preferred stock is convertible into common stock.

E. Some other provisions one occasionally encounters in preferred stock include:
1. Voting rights
2. Participating with common stock in sharing the firm's earnings
3. Sinking funds
4. Call provisions
5. Effective maturity dates

F. The current market price for preferred stock, V_{ps}, is determined by discounting future dividend payments, D_t, at the required rate of return, k_d. This gives us

$$V_p = \frac{D}{k_p}.$$

G. There are advantages and disadvantages associated with preferred stock financing for both issuers and investors.
1. Preferred stock is a fixed cost form of financing, yet the firm avoids the danger of bankruptcy if earnings are too low to pay the preferred dividend. Preferred also allows a firm to avoid sharing control, as it must do when selling common stock.
2. Although advantageous to a firm, preferred stock does have a higher after-tax cost of capital than debt, mainly because preferred dividends are not tax deductible.
3. For the investor, preferred stock provides reasonably assured income. Also, for corporate investors, 70 percent of preferred dividends received are not taxable.
4. The disadvantages to the investors are: (1) returns are limited on preferred stock even though a substantial portion of ownership risk is borne by the preferred stockholders, (2) preferred stockholders have legally enforceable rights to dividends, even if a company earns a profit, and (3) companies often manage to avoid paying off all accumulated dividends when they emerge from a troubled, low-income period.

H. Because preferred dividends are not tax deductible, many companies have retired their preferred stock and replaced them with debentures or subordinated debentures. However, some firms still find it advantageous to use preferred to raise long-term capital when conditions are such that neither common stock nor long-term debt can be issued on reasonable terms.

DEFINITIONAL QUESTIONS

1. A(n) ______ loan is long-term debt where the borrower negotiates directly with a financial institution. This type of financing is, therefore, called _________ _________.

2. The process of paying off a term loan in equal _________ over the life of the loan is called __________.

3. A(n) ______ is a long-term contract under which the __________ agrees to make payments of interest and principal, on specific dates, to the holder of the bond.

4. A bond with annual coupon payments represents an annuity of I dollars per year for n years, plus a lump sum of M dollars at the end of n years, and its value, V, is the ____________ ______________ of this payment stream.

5. At the time a bond is issued, the coupon interest rate is generally set at a level that will cause the __________ __________ and the __________ __________ of the bond to be approximately equal.

6. Market interest rates and bond prices move in _____________ directions from one another.

7. The total return, or yield, on a bond is calculated as the sum of the _________ yield plus the __________ _________ yield.

8. The interest rate earned by purchasing a bond and holding it until maturity is known as the bond's _____________ _______ _____________.

9. If current interest rates are well below an outstanding bond's coupon rate, then a callable bond is likely to be called, and investors should estimate the expected rate of return on the bond as the _________ _____ _________ rather than the yield to maturity.

10. Long-term debt is sometimes referred to as _____________ debt.

11. The legal document setting forth the terms and conditions of a bond issue is known as the _______________.

12. The ______ represents the bondholders and sees that the terms of the indenture are carried out.

13. Failure to make a sinking fund payment places the company in _________ _________, and could ultimately lead to _________.

14. In meeting its sinking fund requirements, a firm may ______ the bonds or purchase them on the ______ ______.

15. Except when the call is for sinking fund purposes, when a bond issue is called, the firm must pay a ______ __________, or an amount in excess of the ______ value of the bond.

16. A bond issue is most likely to be called if interest rates have ______ substantially since the time of issue.

17. A restrictive __________ is a provision in the bond's ___________ which requires the issuer to meet certain stated conditions.

18. A bond secured by real estate is known as a(n) __________ bond.

19. A(n) __________ __________ bond is a bond that pays no interest but is offered at a substantial discount below their par values and hence provides capital appreciation rather than interest income.

20. Preferred stock is referred to as a hybrid because it is similar to ______ in some respects and to __________ __________ in others.

21. The dividend on a share of _____________ stock may be indicated as a ______________ of par or in dollars.

22. Most preferred stock dividends are __________, and thus must be paid before dividends can be paid to common stockholders.

23. Preferred stocks are attractive to __________ investors because of the 70 percent dividend exclusion.

24. Issuing preferred stock decreases the danger of __________ if operating income is low.

CONCEPTUAL QUESTIONS

25. There is a direct relationship between bond ratings and the required rate of return of bonds; that is, the higher the rating, the higher is the required rate of return.

    a. True   b. False

26. Which of the following would tend to increase the coupon interest rate on a bond that is to be issued?

a. Adding a sinking fund.
b. Adding a restrictive covenant.
c. Adding a call provision.
d. A change in the bond's rating from Aa to Aaa.
e. Both a and c above.

27. Zero coupon bonds have become quite popular over the last several years. These bonds are advantageous to the issuer because

a. The bond is, in effect, not callable.
b. These bonds generally have a higher yield to maturity than normal coupon bonds.
c. The bond's cash outflows are spread over the life of the bond.
d. The bonds are initially sold above par value.
e. None of the above statements is the correct answer.

28. Whenever the going rate of interest is less than the coupon rate, a bond's price will rise above its par value. Such a bond is called

a. A junk bond.
b. A convertible bond.
c. A discount bond.
d. A premium bond.
e. None of the above.

PROBLEMS

29. John Williams has just inherited 100 bonds (maturity value per bond = $1,000). For the past three years, he has been writing a book in his spare time. Now that he has received these bonds, he is considering cashing them in, quitting his job, and continuing to work on his book with the goal of completing it over a two-year period. The 8 percent bonds mature on January 1, 2014, and it is now January 1, 1984. Interest on these bonds is paid annually on December 31, and new bonds issued by the same company with the same maturity have a 12 percent coupon rate. If John sells his bonds now and puts the proceeds in an account paying 10 percent compounded annually, what would be the largest equal annual amounts he could withdraw for two years beginning next year, January 1, 1995?

a. $40,406
b. $50,616
c. $25,308
d. $34,570
e. $41,950

30. A major auto manufacturer has experienced a market re-evaluation lately due to a number of lawsuits. The firm has a bond issue outstanding with 15 years to maturity, a maturity value of $1,000, and a coupon rate of 4 percent. The required rate has now risen to 8 percent. At what price can these individual securities be purchased on the market?

a. $1,273.26
b. $1,000.02
c. $549.71
d. $657.58
e. $340.31

31. Nedermeyer Inc. has 100 bonds outstanding (maturity value per bond = $1,000). The required rate of return on these bonds is currently 10 percent, and interest is paid annually. The bonds mature in 5 years, and their current market value is $772.55 per bond. What is the annual coupon interest rate?

a. 9%
b. 6%
c. 4%
d. 2%
e. None of the above

32. Interest rates have fallen since ACC Industries sold an issue of $1,000 par value bonds with a coupon rate of 18 percent. With 20 years left to maturity, investors are willing to purchase these bonds for a 14 percent yield to maturity. What is the current market price of these bonds?

a. $1,585
b. $1,265
c. $1,000
d. $965
e. $785

33. You are considering the purchase of a zero coupon bond which matures in 10 years at a maturity value of $1,000. If you can buy the bond today for $247.20, what pre-tax rate of return would you receive?

a. 12%
b. 14%
c. 15%
d. 16%
e. 18%

34. Acme Products has a bond outstanding with 8 years remaining to maturity, a 10 percent coupon, and a par value of $1,000. If the current market price is $811.07 and interest is paid semiannually, what is the bond's yield to maturity?

a. 12%
b. 13%
c. 14%
d. 15%
e. 16%

35. Given your answer to the previous question, what are the current yield and the capital gains yield of the bond?

a. 14% ; 0%
b. 12.3% ; 1.7%
c. 10% ; 4%
d. 15.8% ; -1.8%
e. The answer cannot be determined from the information provided.

36. Ten years ago, TNT Company sold a 30 year bond issue. The bonds were sold at their par value of $1,000 and carry an 8 percent coupon rate payable annually. However, since the bonds were issued, interest rates have increased to 10 percent. A very good friend of yours bought some these bonds when they were originally issued and has offered to sell you one of the bonds for $850. Should you accept your friend's offer?

a. Accept the offer. The bond originally sold for $1,000, thus, for $850 you are getting a bargain.
b. Reject the offer. Since the current interest rate is 2% higher than the coupon rate on the bond, you should get a 2 percent discount on the purchase. Therefore, you should pay no more than $800 for the bond.
c. Accept the offer. You expect interest rates to go back down some time within the remaining life of the bond. Even if the bond is currently over priced, if interest rates go down and hold that level for a long period of time you will easily recoup any present losses.
d. Reject the offer. Your "friend" is trying to pull a fast one on you. The bond has a current market value of $830. If you buy the bond from your friend you will lose about $20.
e. Of course you should accept the offer. Your good friend would never try to cheat you out of money.

37. Suppose the bond in the previous problem had a market value of $1,229.40. What is the current market rate required by investors?

a. 6%
b. 7%
c. 8%
d. 9%
e. 10%

38. The Privy Company has just issued a 10-year bond with a 10 percent annual coupon. The $100,000 issue sold at its par value of $1,000 per bond. The indenture has a sinking fund provision which stipulates that one-tenth of the issue will be redeemed at the end of each year. Assume that interest rates fall after the issue date, causing the market value of the bonds to rise, and that Privy exercises the sinking fund provision by calling one-tenth of the issue (10 bonds) each year. What is the effective before-tax cost of the issue?

a. 8.0%
b. 9.2%
c. 10.0%
d. 11.2%
e. 12.0%

ANSWERS AND SOLUTIONS

1. term; direct financing
2. installments; amortization
3. bond; borrower
4. present value
5. market price; par value
6. opposite
7. current; capital gains
8. yield to maturity
9. yield to call
10. funded
11. indenture
12. trustee
13. technical default; bankruptcy
14. call; open market
15. call premium; par
16. fallen
17. covenant; indenture
18. mortgage
19. zero coupon
20. bonds; common stock
21. preferred; percentage
22. cumulative
23. corporate
24. bankruptcy

25. b. The relationship is an inverse one. The higher the rating, the lower is the default risk, and hence the lower is the required rate of return. Aaa/AAA is the highest rating, and as we go down the alphabet, the ratings are lower.

26. c. Sinking funds, restrictive covenants, and an improvement in the bond rating all indicate lower risk for the bond, and hence would lower the coupon rate.

27. e. The primary advantages to the issuer are (1) that zero coupons have a lower required rate of return, and (2) that annual interest payments are avoided.

28. d. This is the definition of a premium bond.

29. a. $V = \$8,000(PVIFA_{k_d,n}) + \$100,000(PVIF_{k_d,n})$

$= \$8,000(7.4694) + \$100,000(0.1037)$

$= \$59,755.20 + \$10,370.00 = \$70,125.20.$

1/1/94	10%	1/1/95	1/1/96
$70,125.20		PMT	PMT

$PMT = \$70,125.20/PVIFA_{k_d,n} = \$70,125.20/1.7355 = \$40,406.34 \approx \$40,406.$

30. d. $V = \$40(PVIFA_{k_d,n}) + \$1,000(PVIF_{k_d,n})$

$= \$40(8.5595) + \$1,000(0.3152) = \$657.58.$

31. c. $V = I(PVIFA_{k_d,n}) + M(PVIF_{k_d,n})$

$\$772.55 = I(3.7908) + \$1,000(0.6209)$
$3.7908I = \$151.65$
$I = \$40$; therefore, the annual coupon interest rate = 4%.

32. b. $V = I(PVIFA_{k_d,n}) + M(PVIF_{k_d,n})$

$= \$180(6.6231) + \$1,000(0.0728)$

$= \$1,192.16 + \$72.80 = \$1,264.96 \approx \$1,265.$

33. c. $PV = FV_{10}(PVIF_{k,10})$

$\$247.20 = \$1,000(PVIF_{k,10})$

$PVIF_{k,10} = \$247.20/\$1,000 = 0.2472.$

In Table A-1 the present value interest factor, 0.2472, occurs in the 10 period row, 15 percent column. Therefore, the bond's rate of return is 15 percent.

34. c. This question may be answered by the trial-and-error method exclusively. However, the YTM approximation formula may be used to determine a beginning value for the required return:

$$k_d = \frac{\$100 + \dfrac{\$1,000 - \$811.07}{8}}{\dfrac{\$1,000 + \$1,622.14}{3}} = \frac{\$123.62}{\$874.05} = 14.14\%.$$

Since this is a semiannual coupon bond, k_d must be divided by 2. So, try the 7 percent interest factors:

$V = I/2(PVIFA_{k_d/2,2n}) + M(PVIF_{k_d/2,2n})$
$= \$50(9.4466) + \$1,000(0.3387)$
$= \$472.33 + \$338.70 = \$811.03.$

This is close enough to conclude that k_d = Yield to maturity = $k_d/2 \times 2$ = 14%.

35. b. The current yield is simply the annual interest payment on the bond divided by its current market price. At this point you can calculate the capital gains yield by subtracting the current yield from the total yield.

Current Yield = \$100/\$811.07 = 12.33%.

Capital Gains Yield = 14% - 12.33% = 1.67%.

36. d. $V = I(PVIFA_{kd,n}) + M(PVIF_{kd,n})$

$= \$80(8.5136) + \$1,000(0.1486)$

$= \$681.09 + \$148.60 = \$829.69 \approx \$830.$

37. a. This problem must be solved by using the trial-and-error method. Since the market value of the bond is greater than its par value, the current market rate must be lower than the coupon rate. This automatically eliminates answers c, d, and e.

$V = I(PVIFA_{kd,n}) + M(PVIF_{kd,n})$

Using the factors for 7%:

$V = \$80(10.5940) + \$1,000(0.2584) = \$1,105.92.$

Using the factors for 6%:

$V = \$80(11.4699) + \$1,000(0.3118) = \$1,229.40.$

38. c. Each year, Privy will retire \$10,000 face value in bonds. Thus, its interest expense would also decrease by one-tenth each year:

Year	Debt Outstanding at Beginning of Year	Interest Expense
1	\$100,000	\$10,000
2	90,000	9,000
-	------	-----
9	20,000	2,000
10	10,000	1,000

Thus, Privy pays 10 percent on the outstanding balance throughout the life of the issue and it is being retired at par value. Its effective before-tax cost is also 10 percent.

CHAPTER 17
COMMON STOCK

OVERVIEW

Common stock represents the ownership position in a firm. As owners, the common stockholders have certain rights and privileges, including (1) the right to control the firm through election of directors and (2) the right to the residual earnings of the firm. The value of a share of common stock is the present value of the expected future dividend stream. The total rate of return on a stock is comprised of a dividend yield plus a capital gains yield.

Firms generally begin their corporate life as closely held companies, with all the common stock held by the founding managers. Then, as the company grows, it is often necessary to sell stock to the general public (that is, go public) to raise more funds. There are several advantages and disadvantages to stock financing and to going public from management's viewpoint, as well as from the investor's perspective. To go public, the firm's managers must be familiar with the investment banking process by which the new securities are offered.

OUTLINE

I. **Common stock represents the ownership of an incorporated business. It corresponds to the proprietor's capital or to the partners' capital for an unincorporated business.**

A. The common stockholders are the owners of the corporation, and they have certain rights and privileges.

1. Common stockholders have control of the firm through their election of the firm's directors, who in turn select officers to manage the business.

a. In a large, publicly owned firm, neither the managers nor any individual shareholders normally have the 51 percent necessary for absolute control of the company.

b. Thus, stockholders must vote for directors, and the voting process is regulated by both state and federal laws.

c. Stockholders who are unable to attend annual meetings may still vote by means of a *proxy*. Proxies can be solicited by any party seeking to control the firm.

d. If earnings are poor and stockholders are dissatisfied, an outside, or inside, group may solicit the proxies in an effort to overthrow management and take control of the business. This is known as a *proxy fight*.

2. The *preemptive right* gives the current shareholders the right to purchase any new shares issued, in proportion to their current holdings.

a. The preemptive right may or may not be required by state law.
b. When granted, the preemptive right enables current owners to maintain their proportionate share of ownership and control of the business.
c. It also prevents the sale of shares at low prices to new stockholders, which would dilute the value of the previously issued shares.

B. Although most firms have only one type of common stock, in some instances *classified stock* is sometimes created by a firm to meet its special needs and circumstances. If two classes of stock were desired, one would normally be called "Class A" and the other "Class B."
1. Class A might be non-voting stock but holders would be entitled to receive dividends before dividends would be paid on Class B stock.
2. Class B could be called *founders' shares* and given sole voting rights in the firm's formative years.
3. Note that Class A and Class B have no standard meanings.

II. **Common stock represents participation in the ownership of a firm. However, to a vast majority of shareholders, it is more valued for the returns that can be gained from its purchase.**

A. People typically buy common stock expecting to receive dividends plus a capital gain when they sell their shares at the end of some holding period. The capital gain may or may not be realized, but most people expect a gain or else they would not buy stocks.

B. The *expected dividend yield* on a stock during the coming year is equal to the expected dividend, D_1, divided by the current stock price, P_0. The term $(\hat{P}_1 - P_0)/P_0$ is the *expected capital gains yield.* The expected dividend yield plus the expected capital gains yield equals the *expected total return,* $\hat{k}_s$.

C. The value of the stock today is calculated as the present value of an infinite stream of dividends. For any investor, cash flows consist of dividends plus the expected future sales price of the stock. This sales price, however, is dependent upon dividends expected by future investors:

$$\hat{P}_0 = \frac{D_1}{(1 + k_s)^1} + \frac{D_2}{(1 + k_s)^2} + \dots + \frac{D_\infty}{(1 + k_s)^\infty} = \sum_{t=1}^{\infty} \frac{D_t}{(1 + k_s)^t}.$$

Here k_s is the discount rate used to find the present value of the dividends.
1. This equation makes two simplifying assumptions:
a. The growth in the firm's earnings and dividends will progress at a constant rate into the future.
b. k_s is greater than g.

D. For many companies, earnings and dividends are expected to grow at some *normal (constant) rate.* Dividends in any future Year t may be forecast as $D_t = D_0(1 + g)^t$, where D_0 is the last dividend paid and g is the expected rate of growth. For a company which last paid a $2.00 dividend and which has an expected 6 percent growth rate, the estimated dividend 1 year from now would be $D_1 = \$2.00(1.06) = \$2.12$; D_2 would be $\$2.00(1.06)^2 = \$2.25$, and the estimated dividend 4 years hence would be $D_t = D_0(1 + g)^t = \$2.00(1.06)^4 = \$2.525$. Using this method of estimating future dividends, and assuming a constant growth rate, the value of the firm's common stock is as follows:

$$\hat{P}_0 = \frac{D_1}{k_s - g}.$$

This *constant growth model* is often called the *Gordon Model*, after Myron J. Gordon, who developed it.

1. Note that this equation is sufficiently general to encompass cases where growth is zero or even negative.

E. When investors purchase stock that they expect to sell in the future, their expected rate of return is determined by the stock's expected dividend yield and the expected capital gains yield. Thus, $\hat{k}_s$ = Dividend yield + Capital gains yield = $D_1/P_0 + g$. For a constant growth stock, both the dividend yield and the capital gains yield remain a constant percentage over time.

F. Firms typically go through periods of *supernormal, or nonconstant, growth*, after which time their growth rate settles to a rate close to that of the economy as a whole. The value of such a firm is equal to the present value of its expected future dividends. To find the value of such a stock, we proceed in three steps:

1. Find the dividends expected at the end of each year during the period of nonconstant growth.

2. Find the expected price of the stock at the end of the nonconstant growth period, at which point it has become a normal, constant growth stock.

3. Discount all the expected cash flows through the end of the supernormal growth period and sum to find the intrinsic value of the stock, $\hat{P}_0$.

III. Thus far the main characteristics and the valuation model for common stock have been presented. There are advantages and disadvantages of stock financing from the point of view of the issuing corporation, investors, and society in general.

A. Advantages of common stock financing from the issuer's viewpoint include:

1. Common stock does not carry a fixed obligation to pay periodic dividends to stockholders.

2. Common stock never matures; hence it never has to be repaid. And yet, the issuer always has the option of buying back some portion of its common stock in the open market.

3. Common stock increases the proportion of equity financing and thus the firm's creditworthiness. This increases its future ability to use debt.

4. Common stock can often be sold on better terms than debt when a company's prospects look bright.
5. Financing with common stock serves as a way to maintain a *reserve borrowing capacity,* which is unused debt capacity that permits borrowing if a firm needs capital in troubled times.

B. Disadvantages of common stock financing from the issuer's viewpoint include:
1. Issuing common stock extends voting rights, and perhaps even control, to new stockholders.
2. Common stock gives new stockholders the right to a percentage of profits rather than to a fixed payment as in the case of creditors.
3. The costs of underwriting and distributing common stock are usually higher than those for preferred stock or debt.
4. If common stock is sold to the point where the equity ratio exceeds that in the optimal capital structure, a firm's average cost of capital will increase, and its stock price will not be maximized.
5. Common stock dividends are not tax deductible as an expense for calculating the corporation's taxable income, but bond interest is deductible.

C. Advantages of common stock ownership include:
1. Higher expected total return than bonds or preferred stock.
2. Unlimited ownership rights to remaining profits after payment of contractual obligations.
3. Provides a relatively good hedge against inflation.
4. No danger of a call.
5. Right to vote.

D. Disadvantages of common stock ownership include:
1. Common stock is riskier than bonds or preferred stock.
2. Common stockholders have no legal rights to dividends.
3. In the event of bankruptcy, common stockholders' claims on assets come last.
4. The issuing corporation has made no promise to buy back the stock.
5. Common stock prices are quite volatile.

E. From a social viewpoint, common stock is a desirable form of financing because it makes business firms less vulnerable to the consequences of declines in sales and earnings.

IV. **Most businesses begin life as proprietorships, partnerships, or closely held corporations. However, if the business prospers and grows, at some point the decision must be made as to whether to go public. The market for stock that has recently gone public is called the initial public offering (IPO) market. There are advantages and disadvantages to public ownership.**

A. Going public has the following advantages:
1. The original owners are able to diversify their holdings by selling some of their stock in a public offering.

2. Public ownership increases the liquidity of the stock.
3. New corporate cash is more easily raised by a publicly owned company.
4. Going public establishes the firm's value in the marketplace.

B. Going public has the following disadvantages:
1. A publicly owned company must file quarterly and annual reports, which can be costly, especially for small firms.
2. Publicly owned firms must disclose operating and ownership data.
3. The opportunities for owners/managers to engage in questionable, but legal, self-dealings are reduced.
4. If a publicly held firm is very small, its shares will be traded very infrequently, and a liquid market will not really exist.
5. Managers of publicly owned firms with less than 50 percent control must be concerned about tender offers and proxy fights. This sometimes leads to operating decisions that are not in the best long-run interests of the shareholders.

C. The decision to go public should be made on the basis of the company's and its stockholders' unique circumstances.

V. **The financial manager must have a knowledge of the investment banking process, the process by which new securities are issued. The firm must make its decisions about raising capital in two stages.**

A. The firm makes some initial, preliminary decisions on its own: Stage I Decisions.
1. The dollar amount of new capital to be raised.
2. The type of securities to be offered.
3. The actual procedure to follow must be decided, that is, whether the securities should be offered as a *competitive bid* or a *negotiated deal*.
4. Finally, the investment banking firm must be selected.

B. The firm then makes decisions jointly with its selected investment banker: Stage II Decisions.
1. First, the two parties will reevaluate the firm's initial decisions about the size of the issue and the type of securities to use.
2. The firm and its investment banker must decide whether the banker will work on a *best efforts arrangement* or on an *underwritten arrangement*.
   a. On a best efforts sale, the banker does not guarantee that the securities will be sold or that the company will get the cash it needs.
   b. On an underwritten issue, the company does get a guarantee. Essentially, the banker purchases the issue, then resells the securities at a higher price. The banker bears significant risks in underwritten offerings.
3. *Flotation costs*, those costs associated with issuing new securities, must be negotiated. These costs include compensation to the investment banker plus legal, accounting, printing, and other costs

borne by the issuer. Flotation costs depend on the type of security issued and the size of the issue.

4. The offering price needs to be set.
   a. If the firm is already publicly owned, the offering price will be based upon the existing market price.
   b. If the firm is going public for the first time, there will be no established price, so the investment bankers will have to estimate the *equilibrium price*, the price that will be low enough to induce investors to buy the stock, but not so low that it will rise sharply immediately after it is issued.

C. Because they are exposed to potentially large losses, investment bankers typically do not handle the purchase and distribution of an issue singlehandedly unless it is a very small one. Groups of investment bankers form an *underwriting syndicate* to spread the risk and minimize individual losses.
   1. The investment banking house that sets up the deal is called the *lead, or managing, underwriter.*
   2. In addition to the underwriting syndicate, on larger offerings still more investment bankers are included in a *selling group*, which handles the distribution of securities to individual investors.

D. *Shelf registrations* are used by large, well-known companies to facilitate selling securities to investors by putting them "on the shelf" and then selling them to investors when the company determines the market is right. A *master registration statement* is filed with the SEC and then updated by a *short-form statement* just prior to each individual offering.

E. For new issues, the investment banker will normally *maintain the secondary market* in the shares after the public offering. This is done in order to provide liquidity for the shares and to maintain a good relationship with both the issuer and the investors who purchased the shares.

DEFINITIONAL QUESTIONS

1. One of the fundamental rights of common stockholders is to elect a firm's __________, who in turn select officers to manage the business.

2. If a stockholder cannot vote in person, participation in the annual meeting is still possible through a(n) ______.

3. The preemptive right protects stockholders against loss of __________ of the corporation as well as __________ of market value from the sale of new shares below market value.

4. Firms may find it desirable to separate the common stock into different ______. Generally, this classification is designed to differentiate stock in terms of the right to receive __________ and the right to ______.

5. Like other financial assets, the value of common stock is the __________ value of a future stream of income.

6. The income stream expected from a common stock consists of a(n) __________ yield and a(n) __________ __________ yield.

7. The market for stock that has recently gone public is called the __________ __________ __________ market.

8. ______ __________ refers to the sale of shares of a closely held business to the general public.

9. Setting the __________ price for an issue of stock may present a conflict of interest between the issuer and the __________ __________.

10. In order to spread the risk of underwriting a sizable common stock issue, investment bankers will form a(n) __________ __________.

11. If earnings are poor and stockholders are dissatisfied, an outside, or inside, group may solicit the proxies in an effort to overthrow management and take control of the business; this is known as a(n) __________ __________.

12. The __________ __________ model is often called the Gordon Model, after Myron J. Gordon, who developed it. It is sufficiently general to encompass cases where growth is ______ or even __________.

13. One of the advantages of common stock financing from the issuer's viewpoint is that it serves as a way to maintain a(n) __________ __________ __________, which is unused debt capacity that permits borrowing if a firm needs capital in troubled times.

14. With a(n) ________ __________ __________, the investment banker does not guarantee that the securities will be sold or that the company will get the cash it needs.

15. With a(n) __________ __________, the investment banker gives a guarantee that the securities will be sold and that the company will get the cash it needs.

CONCEPTUAL QUESTIONS

16. A firm may go public, yet the firm itself may not receive any additional funds in the process.

    a. True b. False

17. According to the valuation model developed in this chapter, the value that an investor assigns to a share of stock is independent of the length of time the investor plans to hold the stock.

a. True b. False

18. When new shares are being sold, if it appears that the investment bankers will be unable to sell the entire issue at the initial offering price, the only way the entire issue can be sold is to lower the price.

a. True b. False

19. Flotation costs are generally higher for bond issues than for stock issues.

a. True b. False

20. When stockholders assign their right to vote to another party, this is called

a. A privilege.
b. A preemptive right.
c. An ex right.
d. A proxy.
e. A prospectus.

21. Which of the following assumptions would cause the constant growth stock valuation model to be invalid?

$$\hat{P}_0 = \frac{D_1}{k_s - g}$$

a. The growth rate is negative.
b. The growth rate is zero.
c. The growth rate is less than the required rate of return.
d. The required rate of return is above 30 percent.
e. None of the above assumptions would invalidate the model.

PROBLEMS

22. Your sister-in-law, a stockbroker at Invest Inc., is trying to sell you a stock with a current market price of $25. The stock's last dividend (D_0) was $2.00, and earnings and dividends are expected to increase at a constant growth rate of 10 percent. Your required return on this stock is 20 percent. From a strict valuation standpoint, you should:

a. Buy the stock; it is fairly valued.
b. Buy the stock; it is undervalued by $3.00.
c. Buy the stock; it is undervalued by $2.00.
d. Not buy the stock; it is overvalued by $2.00.
e. Not buy the stock; it is overvalued by $3.00.

23. Lucas Labs' last dividend was $1.50. Its current equilibrium stock price is $15.75, and its expected growth rate is a constant 5 percent. If the stockholders' required rate of return is 15 percent, what is the expected dividend yield and expected capital gains yield for the coming year?

a. 0%; 15%
b. 5%; 10%
c. 10%; 5%
d. 15%; 0%
e. 15%; 15%

24. The Canning Company has been hard hit by increased competition. Analysts predict that earnings (and dividends) will decline at a rate of 5 percent annually into the foreseeable future. If Canning's last dividend (D_0) was $2.00, and investors' required rate of return is 15 percent, what will be Canning's stock price in 3 years?

a. $8.15
b. $9.50
c. $10.00
d. $10.42
e. $10.96

(The following data are used in the next three problems.)

The Club Auto Parts Company has just recently been organized. It is expected to experience no growth for the next 2 years as it identifies its market and acquires its inventory. However, Club will grow at an annual rate of 5 percent in the third year, and, beginning with the fourth year, should attain a 10 percent growth rate which it will sustain thereafter. The first dividend (D_1) to be paid at the end of the first year is expected to be $0.50 per share. Investors require a 15 percent rate of return on Club's stock.

25. What is the current equilibrium stock price?

a. $5.00
b. $8.75
c. $9.57
d. $12.43
e. $15.00

26. What will Club's stock price be at the end of the first year (P_1)?

a. $5.00
b. $8.76
c. $9.56
d. $12.43
e. $15.00

27. What dividend yield and capital gains yield should an investor in Club expect for the first year?

a. 0%; 15%
b. 3%; 12%
c. 6%; 9%
d. 10%; 5%
e. 12%; 3%

28. Johnson Corporation's stock is currently selling at $45.83 per share. The last dividend paid (D_0) was $2.50. Johnson is a constant growth firm. If investors require a return of 16 percent on Johnson's stock, what do they think Johnson's growth rate will be?

a. 6%
b. 7%
c. 8%
d. 9%
e. 10%

29. Susie Goldsmith is an analyst with Trulock Investments and is currently evaluating the common stock of Fantastic Software Company. Fantastic's earnings and dividends have been growing at an annual rate of 9 percent in the past and this rate of growth is expected to continue. Fantastic's earnings per share were $5.00 last year and the company follows a policy of paying out 45 percent in dividends. If the required rate of return on Fantastic is 15 percent, what is the stock worth today?

a. $36.925
b. $40.875
c. $45.000
d. $48.750
e. $52.000

30. Barak-Gapenski Inc. paid dividends of $3.00 recently. The risk-free rate of return is 7 percent and the required rate of return on the market is 13 percent. Barak-Gapenski has a beta of 0.90 and is expected to have constant annual growth of 6 percent. What is a fair price for the company's common stock?

a. $32.6000
b. $38.9275
c. $44.0000
d. $49.6875
e. $56.9500

ANSWERS AND SOLUTIONS

1. directors
2. proxy
3. control; dilution
4. classes; dividends; vote
5. present
6. dividend; capital gains
7. initial public offering
8. Going public
9. offering; investment banker
10. underwriting syndicate
11. proxy fight
12. constant growth; zero; negative
13. reserve borrowing capacity
14. best efforts arrangement
15. underwritten arrangement

16\. a. A firm may go public if its managers sell off a portion of their stock holdings. Then, the funds obtained go to the managers rather than the firm.

17\. a. The model considers all future dividends. This produces a current value which is appropriate for all investors independent of their expected holding period.

18\. b. The investment bankers may be able to increase the demand for the stock by "promoting" the issue. If not, then a price reduction may be required.

19\. b. The investment banker normally must expend greater effort in selling stocks, thus must charge a higher fee.

20\. d. Recently, there has been a spate of proxy fights, whereby a dissident group of stockholders solicits proxies in competition with the firm's management. If the dissident group gets a majority of the proxies, then it can gain control of the board of directors and oust existing management.

21\. e. The model would be invalid, however, if the growth rate exceeded the required rate of return.

22\. e.

$$\hat{P}_0 = \frac{D_0(1 + g)}{k_s - g} = \frac{\$2.00(1.10)}{0.20 - 0.10} = \$22.00.$$

Since the stock is currently selling for \$25.00, the stock is not in equilibrium and is overvalued by \$3.00.

23\. c.

$$\text{Dividend yield} = \frac{D_1}{P_0} = \frac{D_0(1 + g)}{P_0}$$

$$= \frac{\$1.50(1.05)}{\$15.75} = 0.10 = 10\%.$$

For a constant growth stock the capital gains yield is equal to g.

$$\text{Capital gains yield} = \frac{P_1 - P_0}{P_0} = \frac{P_0(1 + g) - P_0}{P_0}$$

$$= \frac{\$16.54 - \$15.75}{\$15.75} = g = 5\%.$$

24. a.

$$P_0 = \frac{D_0(1 + g)}{k_s - g} = \frac{\$2.00(0.95)}{0.15 - (-0.05)} = \frac{\$1.90}{0.20} = \$9.50.$$

$$\hat{P}_3 = P_0(1 + g)^3 = \$9.50(0.95)^3 = \$9.50(0.8574) = \$8.15.$$

The Gordon model also can be used:

$$P_3 = \frac{D_4}{k_s - g} = \frac{D_0(1 + g)^4}{0.15 - (-0.05)} = \frac{\$2.00(0.95)^4}{0.20} = \$8.15.$$

25. b. To calculate the current value of a nonconstant growth stock, follow these steps:

(1) Determine the expected stream of dividends during the nonconstant growth period. Also calculate the expected dividend at the end of the first year of constant growth that will be used later to calculate stock price.

$$D_1 = \$0.50.$$
$$D_2 = D_1(1 + g) = \$0.50(1 + 0.0) = \$0.50.$$
$$D_3 = D_2(1 + g) = \$0.50(1.05) = \$0.525.$$
$$D_4 = D_3(1 + g) = \$0.525(1.10) = \$0.5775.$$

(2) Discount the expected dividends during the nonconstant growth period at the investor's required rate of return to find their present value.

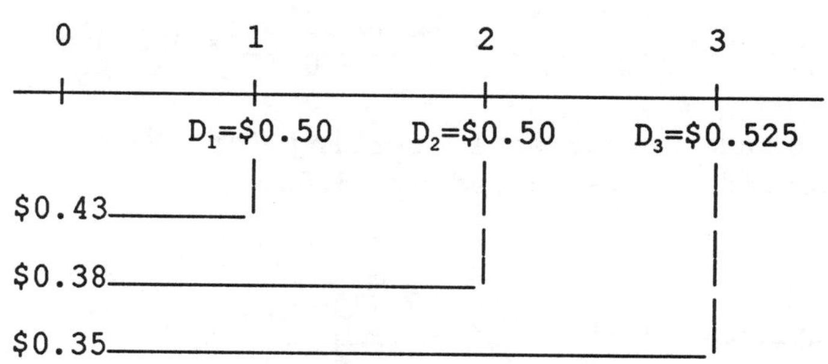

(3) Calculate the expected stock price at the end of the final year of nonconstant growth. This occurs at the end of Year 3. Use the Gordon model for this calculation.

$$\hat{P}_3 = \frac{D_4}{k_s - g} = \frac{\$0.5775}{0.15 - 0.10} = \$11.55.$$

Then discount this stock price 3 periods at the investor's required rate of return to find its present value.

$$PV = \$11.55(PVIF_{15\%,3}) = \$11.55(0.6575) = \$7.59.$$

(4) Add the present value of the stock price expected at the end of Year 3 plus the dividends expected in Years 1, 2 and 3 to find the present value of the stock, P_0.

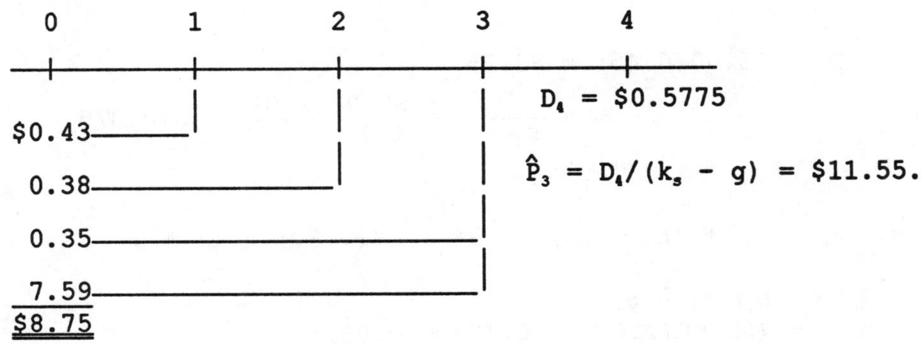

26. c. To calculate the expected stock price at the end of Year 1, P_1, follow the same procedure you would to find the value of a nonconstant growth stock. However, discount values to Year 1 instead of Year 0. Also, remember that the dividend in Year 1, D_1, is not included in the valuation because it has already been paid and therefore adds nothing to the wealth of the investor buying the stock at the end of Year 1.

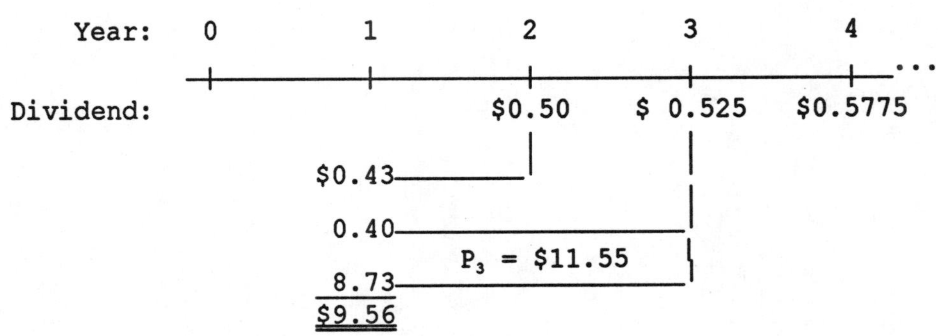

27. c. Dividend yield = D_1/P_0 = \$0.50/\$8.75 = 0.057 ≈ 6%.

Capital gains yield = $(\hat{P}_1 - P_0)/P_0$ = (\$9.56 - \$8.75)/\$8.75 = 0.093 ≈ 9%.

Total yield = Dividend yield + Capital gains yield = 6% + 9% = 15%. The total yield must equal the required rate of return. Also, the capital gains yield is not equal to the growth rate during the nonconstant growth

phase of a nonconstant growth stock. Finally, the dividend and capital gains yields are not constant until the constant growth phase is reached.

28. e.

$$\hat{P}_0 = \frac{D_0(1 + g)}{k_s - g}$$

$$\$45.83 = \frac{\$2.50(1 + g)}{0.16 - g}$$

$$\$7.33 - \$45.83g = \$2.50 + \$2.50g$$

$$\$48.33g = \$4.83$$

$$g = 0.0999 = 10\%.$$

29. b. $D_0 = \$5.00(0.45) = \$2.25.$

$$P_0 = \frac{D_1}{k_s - g} = \frac{\$2.25(1.09)}{0.15 - 0.09} = \$40.875.$$

30. d. $k_s = k_{RF} + (k_M - k_{RF})b = 7\% + 6\%(0.90) = 12.4\%.$

$$\begin{aligned} P_0 &= D_1/(k_s - g) \\ &= (\$3.00(1.06))/(0.124 - 0.06) \\ &= \$3.18/0.064 = \$49.6875. \end{aligned}$$

CHAPTER 18
HYBRID FINANCING:
LEASING, OPTIONS, AND CONVERTIBLE SECURITIES

OVERVIEW

Firms can use different types of long-term financing other than common stock, preferred stock, and debt. Other types of long-term capital include: (1) leasing, which is an alternative to borrowing, and (2) options, especially warrants and convertibles, which are attractive to investors because they allow debtholders to acquire common stock at bargain prices and thus to share in the capital gains if a company is especially successful. All of these methods are widely used today, and an understanding of them is essential for the financial manager.

OUTLINE

I. **The ownership of assets is not as important as the ability to use them in a profitable manner. Leasing provides the same ability to use capital assets as outright ownership. Leasing is similar to borrowing, and it provides the same type of financial leverage.**

A. Historically, land and buildings were the types of assets most often leased, but today it is possible to lease almost any kind of fixed asset.

1. The *lessor* is the owner of the leased property and receives such tax benefits of ownership as the depreciation write-offs and, when they apply, investment tax credits.
2. The *lessee* buys the right to use the property by making lease payments to the lessor.

B. There are three common types of leasing arrangements.

1. Under a *sale and leaseback*, a firm owning an asset sells the property and simultaneously leases it back for a specified period at specific terms.
   a. This arrangement provides an alternative to simply borrowing against the property on a mortgage loan basis.

2. *Operating, or service, leases* provide for both financing and maintenance. Ordinarily, these leases call for the lessor to maintain and service the leased equipment, and the cost of maintenance is built into the lease payments.
   a. These leases are frequently *not fully amortized*; that is, the payments required under the lease contract are not sufficient to recover the full cost of the equipment.

b. They frequently contain a *cancellation clause,* which gives the lessee the right to cancel the lease before the expiration of the basic agreement.

3. *Financial, or capital, leases* are fully amortized; however, they do not provide for maintenance and are not cancelable.
   a. They differ from a sale and leaseback only in that new equipment is purchased by the lessor from a manufacturer rather than from the user-lessee.

C. Leasing is often referred to as *off balance sheet financing* because often neither the leased assets nor the lease liabilities appear on the firm's balance sheet.
   1. A firm with extensive lease arrangements would have both its assets and its liabilities understated in comparison with a firm which borrowed to purchase the assets. The firm that leases would show a lower debt ratio.
   2. *FASB #13* requires firms to *capitalize* certain financial leases and thus to restate their balance sheets to report leased assets as fixed assets and the present value of future lease payments as debt.

D. A lease will be classified as a capital lease and shown directly on the balance sheet if any one of the following conditions exists:
   1. Ownership of the property is effectively transferred from the lessor to the lessee.
   2. The lessee can purchase the property or renew the lease at less than a fair market price when the lease expires.
   3. The lease runs for a period equal to or greater than 75 percent of the asset's life.
   4. The present value of the lease payments is equal to or greater than 90 percent of the initial value of the asset.

E. Any prospective lease must be evaluated by both the lessee and the lessor. The lessee must determine whether leasing an asset is less costly than buying it, and the lessor must decide whether or not the lease will provide a reasonable rate of return.

F. For the lessee, leasing is a substitute for debt financing. In an NPV-type analysis, the lessee estimates the cost of leasing and the cost of owning. If the PV cost of leasing is less than the PV cost of owning, the asset should be leased.
   1. All cash flows must reflect tax effects.
   2. Since leasing is a substitute for debt financing and since lease cash flows have approximately the same risk as debt cash flows, the *appropriate discount rate is the after-tax cost of debt.*

G. Other factors often arise in leasing decisions.
   1. The value of the asset at lease termination is called its *residual value.*

a. It might first appear that assets with large residual values would most likely be owned since the owner gets the residual value.
b. However, competition among leasing companies forces lease contracts to reflect expected residual values. Thus, large residual value assets do not necessarily imply that firms should buy them rather than lease them.

2. Leasing is sometimes said to have an advantage for firms that are seeking the maximum degree of financial leverage.
a. It is sometimes argued that a firm can obtain more money, and for a longer period, under a lease arrangement than under a loan secured by the asset.
b. Because some leases do not appear on the balance sheet, lease financing has been said to give the firm a stronger appearance in a superficial credit analysis, thus permitting it to use more leverage than it could if it did not lease.
c. However, this contention is of questionable validity for firms with audited financial statements.

II. An option is a contract that gives its holder the right, but not the obligation, to buy (or sell) an asset at some predetermined price within a specified period of time.

A. There are many types of options and option markets.

1. *Call options* convey the right to buy a share of stock at a set price called the *exercise, or striking, price*.

2. *Put options* give the holder the right to sell the stock at the striking price.

3. An option, whether a call or a put, has both a buyer and a seller.
a. The buyer has the right to exercise the option.
b. The seller, who is called the *option writer,* must execute the transaction if the option is exercised.
c. A seller who writes call options on stock he or she holds is said to write *covered options*. A similar option written by someone who does not hold the stock is called a *naked option*.

4. Corporations on whose stock options are written have nothing to do with the options market--they do not raise money in this market nor have any direct transactions in it.

B. The *formula value* of an option is defined as follows: Formula value = Current (market) stock price - Striking price. The formula value can be thought of as the value of the option if it expired today.

1. For example, if a stock sells for \$25 and the option's exercise price is \$20, the option's formula value is \$25 - \$20 = \$5.

2. However, the actual price as set in the options market will be higher than the formula value.

3. An option's market price is higher than its formula value because options offer investors greater leverage and less loss potential than do the underlying stocks.

C. In addition to the stock price and the striking price, the value of an option also depends on the following:
   1. *Time to maturity.* The longer the option period, the greater its market value over its formula value (premium).
   2. *Stock price volatility.* The greater the volatility of the underlying stock's price, the greater the premium.

III. **A warrant is an option issued by a company which gives the holder the right to buy a stated number of shares of common stock at a specified price. Thus, warrants are essentially company-issued call options.**

A. Often warrants are attached to debt instruments as an incentive for investors to buy the combined issue at a lower interest rate than would otherwise be the case. Additionally, warrants may eliminate the need for extremely restrictive indenture provisions.

B. Warrants were originally used as "sweeteners" by small, risky firms to help sell either debt or preferred stocks. However, some strong firms have also used warrants.

C. The price paid for a bond with warrants is determined as follows: Price paid for bond with warrants = Straight-debt value of bond + Value of warrants.

D. Most warrants are *detachable* and can be traded separately from the bond or preferred stock with which they were issued.

E. The warrants' exercise price is generally set at from 10 to 30 percent above the market price of the stock on the date the bond is issued.

F. The issuing firm benefits from financing by issuing bonds with warrants in two ways:
   1. The before-tax cost of debt is reduced.
   2. The exercise of warrants results in the issuance of new common shares, representing new equity capital for the firm.

G. There are three conditions which encourage holders to exercise their warrants:
   1. Warrant holders will surely exercise warrants and buy stock if the warrants are about to expire with the market price of the stock above the exercise price.
   2. Warrant holders will tend to exercise voluntarily and buy stock if the company raises the dividend on the common stock by a sufficient amount.
   3. Warrants sometimes have *stepped-up exercise prices,* which prod owners into exercising them.

H. Warrants generally produce additional funds when needed for growth. This occurs because as a company becomes successful and grows, the stock price increases over the exercise price and the warrants are exercised providing an inflow of funds.

IV. **Convertible securities are bonds or preferred stocks that can be exchanged for common stock at the option of the holder.**

A. Conversion of a bond or preferred stock, unlike exercise of a warrant, does not produce additional funds for the firm. However, conversion does lower the debt ratio.

B. The *conversion ratio (CR)* specifies the number of common shares that will be received for each bond or share of preferred stock that is converted: CR = (Par value)/P_c.

C. The *conversion price*, P_c, is the effective price paid for the common stock when conversion occurs: Conversion Price = P_c = (Par value)/CR. For example, if a bond is issued at its par value of $1,000 and can be converted into 40 shares of common stock, the conversion price would be:

$$\text{Conversion price} = P_c = \$1{,}000/40 = \$25 \text{ per share.}$$

Someone buying the bond for $1,000 and then converting it would, in effect, be paying $25 per share for the stock.

D. The conversion price is typically set at about 10 to 30 percent above the market price of common stock when the bond is sold. Thus, if the common stock is selling for $20.83 at the time the convertible is issued, the conversion price might be set at 1.2($20.83) = $25. This would produce a *conversion ratio* of CR = 40:

$$CR = \$1{,}000/P_c = \$1{,}000/\$25 = 40.$$

E. A typical provision protecting the convertible against *dilution* from stock splits, stock dividends, and the sale of common stock at prices below the conversion price, states that if common stock is sold at a price below the conversion price, the conversion price must be lowered to the price at which the new stock was issued.

F. The bond's *conversion value*, C_t, is the value of common stock obtained by converting a convertible security: Conversion value = C_t = Initial stock price $(1 + g)^t$(CR).

G. The actual market price of a convertible bond will always be *equal to or greater than* the higher of its straight-debt value or its conversion value. The higher of these two values is called the *floor value*.

1. The market value of a convertible generally will exceed the floor price because investors are willing to pay a premium over the straight-debt value because of the possibility of earning large capital gains if the stock price increases.

H. Convertibles have certain advantages and disadvantages to the issuing corporation.

1. Advantages:
   a. Convertibles permit a company to sell debt with a lower interest rate and with less restrictive covenants than straight bonds.
   b. Convertibles are generally subordinated to mortgage bonds, bank loans, and other senior debt, so financing with convertibles leaves the company's access to regular debt unimpaired.
   c. Convertibles provide a way of selling common stock at prices higher than those currently prevailing.
2. Disadvantages:
   a. The use of a convertible security may give the issuer the opportunity to sell common stock at a price higher than it could sell stock otherwise. However, if the stock price increases greatly, the company would probably have been better off if it had used straight debt in spite of its higher interest rate and then later sold common stock to refund the debt.
   b. If the company truly wants to raise equity capital, and if the stock price does not rise sufficiently after the bond is issued, then the firm will be stuck with debt.
   c. The convertible issue's low coupon interest rate advantage will be lost when conversion occurs.

I. The expected rate of return on a company's convertible debt should lie between its cost of straight debt and its cost of common equity.

V. **Firms with warrants or convertible securities outstanding must reflect these securities when they calculate and report earnings per share (EPS) to stockholders. Firms can theoretically report EPS in one of three ways:**

A. *Simple EPS.* Earnings available to common stockholders are divided by the average number of shares actually outstanding during the period.

B. *Primary EPS.* The earnings available are divided by the average number of shares that would have been outstanding if warrants and convertibles likely to be converted in the near future had actually been exercised or converted.

C. *Fully diluted EPS.* This is similar to primary EPS except that *all* warrants and convertibles are assumed to be exercised or converted, regardless of the likelihood of either occurring.

D. Simple EPS is virtually never reported by firms which have warrants or convertibles likely to be exercised or converted; the SEC prohibits use of this figure, and it requires that primary and fully diluted earnings be shown on the income statement.

DEFINITIONAL QUESTIONS

1. Conceptually, leasing is similar to __________, and it provides the same type of financial __________.

2. Under a(n) _______ ______ __________ arrangement, the seller receives the purchase price of the asset but retains the ______ of the property.

3. __________ leases include both financing and maintenance arrangements.

4. A(n) __________, or __________, lease is similar to a sale and leaseback arrangement, except that they generally apply to the purchase of ______ equipment directly from a manufacturer.

5. Capitalizing a lease requires that the asset be listed under ________ ________, and that the __________ ________ of the future lease payments be shown as _______.

6. ____________ among leasing companies will tend to force leasing rates down to the point where expected __________ values are fully reflected in the lease rates.

7. Since some leases do not appear on the __________ ________, a firm may be able to use more __________ than if it did not lease.

8. A firm with low profits may be able to transfer the depreciation write-off to another firm and be compensated in the form of lower ________ __________.

9. The leasing decision is normally a(n) __________ decision rather than a(n) __________ __________ decision.

10. Warrants and convertible securities may make a company's securities more attractive to a broader range of __________ and lower the firm's _______ _____ __________.

11. A(n) __________ is an option sold with debt permitting the owner to buy a stated number of shares of _________ ________ at a specified ________.

12. The formula value of an option equals the _________ price minus the __________, or __________, price.

13. When they are exercised, warrants add additional _________ _________ to a firm's capital structure.

14. Warrants will certainly be exercised if the stock price is above the __________ price and the warrant is about to _________.

15. Holders of warrants will have an extra incentive to exercise the warrants if the company sharply increases the __________ on its common shares.

16. Almost all warrants are ____________ and can be traded separately from the debt with which they were issued.

17. Convertible bonds or preferred stocks may be exchanged for _________ _______ at the option of the _________.

18. The _____________ ________ specifies the number of shares of common stock that will be received for each bond that is converted.

19. Selling a convertible issue may be thought of as selling _________ ________ at a price higher than the market price prevailing at the time the convertible is issued.

20. In reporting its earnings, a firm with warrants and convertible securities must report both __________ EPS and ________ __________ EPS.

21. In a leasing arrangement, the _________ is the owner of the leased property and receives such tax benefits of ownership as the depreciation write-offs and, when they apply, investment tax credits.

22. In a leasing arrangement, the _________ buys the right to use the property by making lease payments.

23. Leasing is often referred to as ______ _________ _______ _________ because often neither the leased assets nor the lease liabilities appear on the firm's balance sheet.

24. Since leasing is a substitute for debt financing and since lease cash flows have approximately the same risk as debt cash flows, the appropriate discount rate is the ________-______ _______ _____ _______.

25. A(n) _________ is a contract that gives its holder the right, but not the obligation, to buy (or sell) an asset at some predetermined price within a specified period of time.

26. _______ _________ convey the right to buy a share of stock at a set price, while ______ _________ give the holder the right to sell the stock at a set price.

27. A seller who writes call options on stock he or she holds is said to write __________ __________; while similar options written by someone who does not hold the stock are called ________ _________.

28. Warrants sometimes have __________-_____ ___________ _________, which prod owners into exercising them.

29. _____________ _____________ are bonds or preferred stocks that can be exchanged for common stock at the option of the holder.

30. The actual market price of a convertible bond will always be ________ _____ or __________ _______ the higher of its straight-debt value or its conversion value.

CONCEPTUAL QUESTIONS

31. When one is evaluating a lease proposal, cash flows should be discounted at a relatively high rate because lease flows are fairly certain.

a. True b. False

32. Generally, operating leases are fully amortized, and the lease is written for the expected life of the asset.

a. True b. False

33. A firm which uses extensive lease financing and does not capitalize its leases will have a substantially lower debt ratio than an otherwise similar firm which borrows to finance its assets.

a. True b. False

34. Firms may or may not capitalize a financial lease, at their own option.

a. True b. False

35. The coupon interest rate on convertible bonds is generally higher than the rate on nonconvertible bonds of the same riskiness and rating.

a. True b. False

36. Primary EPS shows what EPS would have been if all warrants and convertibles outstanding had been converted, regardless of the likelihood of either occurring.

a. True b. False

37. Investors are willing to accept lower interest (or dividend) yields on convertible securities in the hopes of later realizing capital gains.

a. True b. False

38. The conversion of a convertible bond replaces debt with common equity on a firm's balance sheet, but it does not bring in any additional capital.

a. True b. False

PROBLEMS

(The following data apply to the next three problems.)

Treadmill Trucking Company is negotiating a lease for five new tractor/trailer rigs with International Leasing. Treadmill has received its best offer from Betterbilt Trucks for a total price of $900,000. The terms of the lease offered by International Leasing call for 4 payments of $260,000, with each payment occurring at the beginning of each year. As an alternative to leasing, the firm can borrow from a large insurance company and buy the trucks. The $900,000 would be borrowed on an amortized term loan at a 10 percent interest rate for 4 years. Assume the trucks fall into the MACRS 3-year class and have an expected residual value of $100,000. Maintenance costs would be included in the lease. If the trucks are owned, a maintenance contract would be purchased at the beginning of each year for $10,000 per year. Treadmill plans to buy a new fleet of trucks at the end of the fourth year. Treadmill Trucking has an effective tax rate of 40 percent.

39. What is Treadmill's present value of the cost of owning?

a. $453,225
b. $510,354
c. $552,957
d. $601,717
e. $694,676

40. What is Treadmill's present value of the cost of leasing?

a. $502,468
b. $523,265
c. $551,036
d. $572,990
e. $608,419

41. Treadmill should lease the trucks.

a. True b. False

42. The Clayton Corporation has warrants outstanding that permit the holder to purchase one share of common stock per warrant at $30. What is the formula value of Clayton's warrants if the common stock is currently selling at $20 per share?

a. -$20
b. -$10
c. $5
d. $10
e. $20

43. Refer to Problem 42. Calculate the formula value if the common stock is now selling at $40 per share.

a. -$20
b. -$10
c. $0
d. $10
e. $20

44. White Corporation has just sold a bond issue with 10 warrants attached to each bond. The bonds have a 20-year maturity, an annual coupon rate of 12 percent, and they sold at the $1,000 initial offering price. The current yield to maturity on bonds of equal risk, but without warrants, is 15 percent. What is the value of each warrant?

a. $22.56
b. $21.20
c. $20.21
d. $19.24
e. $18.78

(The following data apply to the next three problems.)

Central Food Brokers is considering issuing a 20-year convertible bond that will be priced at its par value of $1,000 per bond. The bonds have a 12 percent annual coupon interest rate, and each bond could be converted into 40 shares of common stock. The stock currently sells at $20 per share, has an expected annual dividend of $3.00, and is growing at a constant 5 percent rate per year. The bonds are callable after 10 years at a price of $1,050, with the price declining by $5 per year. If, after 10 years, the conversion exceeds the call price by at least 20 percent, management will probably call the bonds.

45. What is the conversion price?

a. $20
b. $25
c. $33
d. $40
e. $50

46. If the yield to maturity on nonconvertible bonds of similar risk is 16 percent, what is the straight-debt value?

a. $1,000.00
b. $907.83
c. $812.22
d. $762.85
e. $692.37

47. If an investor expects the bond issue to be called in Year 10, and he plans on converting it at that time, what is the investor's expected rate of return upon conversion?

a. 12.0%
b. 12.2%
c. 13.6%
d. 14.4%
e. 15.3%

ANSWERS AND SOLUTIONS

1. borrowing; leverage
2. sale and leaseback; use
3. Operating
4. financial; capital; new
5. fixed assets; present value; debt
6. Competition; residual
7. balance sheet; leverage
8. lease payments
9. financing; capital budgeting
10. investors; cost of capital
11. warrant; common stock; price
12. market; striking; exercise
13. common equity
14. exercise (striking); expire
15. dividend
16. detachable
17. common stock; holder
18. conversion ratio
19. common stock
20. primary; fully diluted
21. lessor
22. lessee
23. off balance sheet financing
24. after-tax cost of debt
25. option
26. Call options; put options
27. covered options; naked options
28. stepped-up exercise prices
29. Convertible securities
30. equal to; greater than

31. b. The cash flows are fairly certain, so they should be discounted at a relatively low rate, generally, the after-tax cost of debt.

32. b. Operating leases are frequently not fully amortized. The lessor expects to recover all costs either in subsequent leases or through the sale of the used equipment at its residual value.

33. a. However, analysts would recognize that leases are as risky as debt financing, and thus include the impact of lease financing on the firm's debt costs and capital structure. Also, if the company which leases capitalizes the leases, then the debt ratios will be similar.

34. b. FASB #13 spells out in detail the conditions under which leases must be capitalized for an unqualified audit opinion.

35. b. The coupon interest rate is lower because investors expect some capital gains return upon conversion. Note, however, that the overall required rate of return is probably higher for the convertible issue than the straight debt issue because the capital gains portions of the convertible's total return is more risky.

36. b. Primary EPS includes only those shares from warrants and convertibles likely to be converted in the near future. Fully diluted EPS includes all shares.

37. a. However, the investor is including the expected capital gain as part of his required return, so the total required return on convertibles is higher than on a straight-debt security.

38. a. The bond is turned into the company and replaced with common stock. No cash is exchanged. When a warrant is exercised, the firm gets additional capital.

39. c. Place the cash flows associated with ownership on a time line:

	0	1	2	3	4
Net purchase price	$900,000				
Dep tax savings[a]		118,800	162,000	54,000	25,200
Maintenance Pymt (AT)[b]	(6,000)	(6,000)	(6,000)	(6,000)	
Salvage value[c]					60,000
Net cash flow	($906,000)	$112,800	$156,000	$48,000	$85,200

PV cost of owning at 6 percent after-tax cost of debt is $552,957.

[a]Depreciable basis = $900,000.

Year	Factor	Depreciation Expense	Tax Savings
1	0.33	$297,000	$118,800
2	0.45	405,000	162,000
3	0.15	135,000	54,000
4	0.07	63,000	25,200
		$900,000	

[b]After-tax maintenance cash flow = $10,000(1 - T) = $10,000(0.6) = $6,000.

[c]After-tax residual value = $100,000(1 - T) = ($100,000)(0.6) = $60,000.

40. d. Place the cash flows associated with leasing on a time line:

0	1	2	3
($156,000)[a]	($156,000)[a]	($156,000)[a]	($156,000)[a]

[a]$260,000(1 - T) = ($260,000)(0.6) = $156,000.

PV cost of leasing at 6 percent after-tax cost of debt is \$572,990.

41. b. The PV cost of leasing is \$572,990 - \$552,957 = \$20,033 more than the cost of owning.

42. b. Formula value = Market price - Exercise price. When P_0 = \$20, Formula value = \$20 - \$30 = -\$10. Note that negative prices cannot actually exist, so the formula value would be considered to be zero.

43. d. When P_0 = \$40, Formula value = \$40 - \$30 = \$10.

44. e. First, find the straight-debt value:

$$V = I(PVIFA_{k,n}) + M(PVIF_{k,n})$$

$$= \$120(PVIFA_{15\%,20}) + \$1,000(PVIF_{15\%,20}) = \$812.22.$$

Thus the value of the attached warrants is \$1,000 - \$812.22 = \$187.78. Since each bond has 10 warrants, each warrant must have a value of \$18.78.

45. b. P_c = Par value/Shares received = \$1,000/40 = \$25.00.

46. d. $V = I(PVIFA_{k,n}) + M(PVIF_{k,n})$

$$= \$120(PVIFA_{16\%,20}) + \$1,000(PVIF_{16\%,20}) = \$762.85.$$

47. c. This is solved by finding the value of k_c in the equation:

Price paid = $I(PVIFA_{k_c,n}) + M(PVIF_{k_c,n})$.

$M = (1.05)^{10} \times \$20 \times 40$ shares = \$1,303.12.

Therefore, find the value of k_c for the following:

$$\$1,000 = \$120(PVIFA_{k_c,10}) + \$1,303.12(PVIF_{k_c,10})$$

$$k_c = 13.6\%.$$

CHAPTER 19
THE COST OF CAPITAL

OVERVIEW

The cost of capital is critically important in finance for several reasons. First, capital budgeting decisions have a major impact on a firm, and correct capital budgeting decisions require an estimate of the cost of capital. Second, many other types of decisions, including those related to leasing and to bond refunding, require estimates of the cost of capital. Finally, maximizing the value of a firm requires that the costs of all inputs, including capital, be minimized, and to minimize the cost of capital managers must be able to measure it.

The firm's marginal cost of capital (MCC) schedule is developed in the following manner. First, the cost of capital must be estimated for each component of the firm's capital structure. These components are normally debt, preferred equity, and common equity. The next task is to combine the component costs to form a weighted average cost of capital. The weights are based on the firm's target capital structure. Capital typically has an increasing cost if the firm expands beyond certain limits. The point at which the cost of capital increases is called a break point, and the MCC schedule is often drawn as a step-function which increases due to increases in one or more of the capital components.

The investment opportunity schedule (IOS) is a plot of the firm's potential projects arrayed in descending order of IRRs. The intersection of the MCC and the IOS schedules defines the firm's optimal capital budget as well as the relevant marginal cost of capital used to evaluate all new projects with the same risk as the firm's other assets.

OUTLINE

I. **Determination of an estimate of the cost of capital is an important tool in making correct capital budgeting decisions.**

   A. Because firms tend to utilize a mix of debt and equity to finance their new assets, the appropriate cost of capital must reflect the average costs of the various sources of long-term funds used, and not just the firm's cost of equity. Thus, the cost of capital should be calculated as a *weighted average*, or composite, of the various types of funds it generally uses, regardless of the specific financing used to fund a particular project.

   B. *Capital components* are the long-term items on the right-hand side of the balance sheet such as debt, preferred stock, common stock, and retained earnings.

1. Any increase in total assets must be financed by an increase in one or more of these capital components.

C. Each element of capital has a *component cost* which can be identified as follows:
1. k_d = interest rate on new debt, before tax.
2. $k_d(1 - T)$ = after-tax cost of debt, where T is the marginal tax rate.
3. k_p = component cost of preferred stock.
4. k_s = component cost of retained earnings.
5. k_e = component cost of external equity obtained by issuing new common stock as opposed to retained earnings. It is necessary to distinguish between equity raised by retained earnings and that raised by selling new stock.
6. k_a = the weighted average cost of capital (WACC).

II. **The cost of each capital component can be determined as follows:**

A. The *after-tax component cost of debt,* $k_d(1 - T)$, is defined as the interest rate to be paid on new debt capital, reduced by (1 - T) because interest payments are tax deductible.
1. For example, if Firm A has a tax rate of 40 percent and can borrow at a rate of 11 percent, then its after-tax cost of debt is $k_d = 11\%(1 - 0.4) = 11\%(0.6) = 6.6\%$.
2. In effect, the government pays part of the cost of debt because interest is *tax deductible.*
   a. Because of its tax deductibility, tax savings result which reduce the net cost of debt. The value of the firm's stock depends on *after-tax cash flows,* and because cash flows and rates of return should be on a comparable basis, the interest rate is adjusted downward to account for the preferential tax treatment of debt.
3. k_d is applicable to *new debt* only, not to any previously outstanding debt.
   a. We are interested in the cost of the next dollar borrowed, or the *marginal cost of debt.* The rate at which the firm has borrowed in the past is a *sunk cost,* and it is irrelevant for cost of capital purposes.

B. The component *cost of preferred stock,* k_p, is the preferred dividend, D_p, divided by the issuance price net of flotation costs, P_n; thus, $k_p = D_p/P_n$. Note that *no tax adjustment is made* since preferred stock dividends are paid from after-tax earnings.

C. The *cost of retaining earnings,* k_s, is the rate of return stockholders require on equity capital the firm obtains by retaining earnings. A cost of capital must be assigned to retained earnings because of the *opportunity cost principle.*
1. Opportunity cost is the rate of return available on the best alternative investment of equal risk.
2. The cost of equity is the most difficult of the cost of capital components to determine. Unlike debt and preferred stock, the cash

flows resulting from the purchase of common stock are difficult to forecast.

3. For stocks in *equilibrium*, the *required rate of return* is equal to the *expected rate of return*.

III. There are three approaches used to determine k_s.

A. One approach to calculating the cost of equity is to use the *Capital Asset Pricing Model (CAPM)* as follows:

1. Estimate the risk-free rate, k_{RF}, usually based on U.S. Treasury securities.
2. Estimate the stock's beta coefficient, b_i, as an index of the stock's market risk.
3. Estimate the required rate of return on the market, or on an "average" stock, designating this return as k_M.
4. Substitute these values into the CAPM equation to estimate the required rate of return on a firm's stock as follows:

$$k_s = k_{RF} + (k_M - k_{RF})b_i.$$

5. If k_{RF} = 8%, k_M = 13%, and the beta of Firm A is 1.3, then k_s = 8% + (5%)1.3 = 14.5%.
6. Although the CAPM appears to yield accurate, precise estimates of k_s, there are several problems with this approach:
   a. If a firm's stockholders are not well diversified, they may be concerned with *total risk* rather than beta, or market, risk. In this case the CAPM will understate the correct value of k_s.
   b. Even if the CAPM is valid, it is hard to obtain correct estimates of the inputs required to make it operational.

B. The required rate of return, k_s, may be estimated by the *discounted cash flow (DCF) approach*. This approach combines the expected dividend yield, D_1/P_0, with the expected future growth rate, g, of earnings and dividends, or

$$k_s = D_1/P_0 + g.$$

1. The DCF approach assumes that stocks are normally in equilibrium and that growth is expected to be at a constant rate. If growth is not constant, then a nonconstant growth model must be used.
2. The expected growth rate may be based on projections of past growth rates, if they have been relatively stable, or on expected future growth rates as estimated in some other manner.
3. If Firm A last paid $4.00 in annual dividends which are expected to grow at a constant 8 percent per year, and Firm A's stock is selling for $61.89 per share, then

$$k_s = \frac{\$4(1.08)}{\$61.89} + 8\% = 14.98\%.$$

C. A simple approach to determine k_s is the *bond-yield-plus-risk-premium approach* in which a judgmental estimate of a risk premium is added to the firm's own cost of long-term debt.

1. Using this approach, k_s is found as follows:

$$k_s = \text{Bond rate} + \text{Risk premium}.$$

2. If Firm A uses a risk premium of 4 percentage points, and its bond rate is 11 percent, then $k_s = 11\% + 4\% = 15\%$.

3. It is logical to think that firms with risky, low-rated, and consequently high-interest-rate debt will also have risky, high-cost equity, and the procedure of basing the cost of equity on a readily observable debt cost utilizes this precept.

4. Low risk premiums occur when interest rates are quite high and people are reluctant to invest in long-term bonds for fear of runaway inflation, further increases in interest rates, and losses on bond investments. High risk premiums occur when interest rates are relatively low.

D. It is recommended that all three approaches be used in estimating the required rate of return on common stock. When the methods produce differing results, judgment must be used in selecting the best estimate.

IV. **The cost of new common stock, or external equity capital, k_e, is higher than the cost of retained earnings, k_s, because of flotation costs involved in selling new common stock.**

A. To allow for *flotation costs, F,* we must adjust the DCF formula for the required rate of return as follows:

$$k_e = \frac{D_1}{P_0(1 - F)} + g.$$

1. If Firm A incurred flotation costs of 12 percent in issuing new common shares, the required rate of return would be as follows:

$$k_e = \frac{\$4.00(1.08)}{\$61.89(1 - 0.12)} + 8\% = 7.93\% + 8\% = 15.93\%.$$

2. If Firm A can earn 15.93 percent on investments financed by new common stock, then earnings, dividends, and the growth rate will be maintained, and the price per share will not fall. If it earns more than 15.93 percent, the price will rise; while if it earns less, the price will fall.

V. The target proportions of debt, preferred stock, and common equity, along with the component costs of capital, are used to calculate the firm's weighted average cost of capital (WACC), which is equal to k_a.

A. The calculation of the *weighted average cost of capital* is shown below for a firm which finances 30 percent with debt, 10 percent with preferred stock, and 60 percent with common equity and which has the following after-tax component costs:

Component	Weight	×	After-Tax Cost	Weighted Cost
Debt	0.3		6.6%	1.98%
Preferred	0.1		12.6	1.26
Common	0.6		15.0	9.00
			k_a =	12.24%

B. In more general terms, and in equation format,

$$WACC = k_a = w_d k_d(1 - T) + w_p k_p + w_s k_s.$$

Here w_d, w_p, and w_s are weights used for debt, preferred, and common equity, respectively.

C. The weights could be based either on the accounting values shown on the firm's balance sheet, book values, or on the market values of the different securities. *Theoretically, the weights should be based on market values,* but if a firm's book value weights are reasonably close to its market value weights, book value weights can be used as a proxy for market value weights.

D. The capital structure that minimizes a firm's weighted average cost of capital also maximizes its stock price.

VI. The marginal cost of capital (MCC) is defined as the cost of the last dollar of new capital that the firm raises, and the marginal cost increases as more and more capital is raised during a given period.

A. Firms raise capital in accordance with their *target capital structures.* The *optimal capital structure* is the one that produces the lowest WACC.

B. As companies raise larger and larger sums during a given time period, the component costs begin to rise. This causes an increase in the weighted average cost of obtaining new capital.

C. Suppose that a firm (different from the firm previously discussed) needs \$500,000 in new capital. Its capital structure is 60 percent common equity, 30 percent debt, and 10 percent preferred stock. Its marginal tax rate is 40 percent. The before-tax cost of debt is 14 percent, and the cost of preferred stock is 12.6 percent. The firm will need to raise 0.6(\$500,000) = \$300,000 in common equity. It expects retained earnings for the year to be \$100,000; therefore, it needs to sell \$300,000 -

$100,000 = $200,000 of new common stock. The cost of retained earnings is 16.0 percent, but the cost of new equity is 16.8 percent. The average cost of capital for this firm, using retained earnings, is

$$k_a = WACC = w_d k_d(1 - T) + w_p k_p + w_s k_s$$

$$= 0.3(14\%)(0.60) + 0.1(12.6\%) + 0.6(16.0\%) = 13.38\%.$$

The average cost of capital, using new equity, is

$$k_a = WACC = w_d k_d(1 - T) + w_p k_p + w_s k_e$$

$$= 0.3(14\%)(0.60) + 0.1(12.6\%) + 0.6(16.8\%) = 13.86\%.$$

D. Only *long-term debt* is included in the capital structure. The capital budgeting process involves long-term assets, and it finances those assets with long-term capital. Thus, current liabilities do not enter the calculation.

E. The point at which the marginal cost of capital increases is called a *break point*. The *retained earnings break point* is calculated as Retained earnings/Equity fraction. For the firm discussed above, this break point is $100,000/0.6 = $166,667. That is, when $166,667 of new capital is raised, the firm will have used 0.6($166,667) = $100,000 of retained earnings. After that, more costly new common equity must be used.

F. The *marginal cost of capital (MCC) schedule* shows the relationship between the cost of each dollar raised, k_a, and the total amount of capital raised during the year.

G. The *optimal capital structure* is the one that produces the lowest MCC schedule.

H. In general, a break will occur in the MCC schedule any time the cost of one of the components rises.

1. The break point is determined by the following equation:

$$\text{Break point} = \frac{\text{Total amount of lower-cost capital of a given type}}{\text{Fraction of this type of capital in the optimal structure}}.$$

2. If there are no break points, there will be one MCC. If there are n break points, there will be n + 1 different MCCs.

I. For ease in calculating the MCC schedule, first identify the points where breaks occur, then determine the cost of capital for each component in the intervals between breaks, and, finally, calculate the weighted averages of these costs for each interval.

VII. The optimal capital budget and a firm's marginal cost of capital are interrelated.

A. The *investment opportunity schedule (IOS)* is a plot of the firm's potential projects in descending order of IRRs.

B. The *marginal cost of capital (MCC) schedule* is a plot of the firm's weighted average cost of capital.

C. The *intersection* of the IOS and MCC schedules determines the cost of capital that is used in the capital budgeting process.

1. If the cost of capital at the intersection of the IOS and MCC schedules is used, then the firm will make correct accept/reject decisions, and its level of financing and investment will be optimal.

2. This discount rate is influenced both by the shape of the MCC curve and by the set of available projects.

D. The discount rate determined by the intersection of the MCC curve and IOS should be used to find the NPV of new projects that are as risky as the firm's existing assets, but it should be adjusted upward or downward to find NPVs for projects with higher or lower risk.

VIII. A number of issues relating to the cost of capital present some problems in this area.

A. The largest single source of capital for many firms is depreciation. The *cost of depreciation-generated funds* is approximately equal to the weighted average cost of capital in the interval in which capital comes from retained earnings and low-cost debt.

B. There is a serious question about how one should measure the cost of equity for a privately owned firm (whose stock is not traded).

C. One cannot overemphasize the practical difficulties encountered when one actually attempts to estimate the cost of equity.

D. It is difficult to assign proper risk-adjusted discount rates to capital budgeting projects of differing degrees of riskiness.

E. The target capital structure was given in this chapter; however, establishing the target capital structure is a major task in itself.

F. Capital budgeting and cost of capital estimates are *dynamic considerations*, as they are part of the planning process. They deal with ex ante, or estimated, data rather than ex post, or historical, data.

DEFINITIONAL QUESTIONS

1. The firm should calculate its cost of capital as a __________ __________ of the various types of funds it generally uses, regardless of the specific financing used to fund a particular project.

2. Capital components are items on the right-hand side the balance sheet such as (1) _______, (2) _________ ________, (3) _________ ________, and (4) __________ __________.

3. The cost of equity capital is defined as the _______ _____ _________ stockholders require on the firm's common stock.

4. There are ________ approaches that can be used to determine the cost of retained earnings.

5. Assigning a cost to retained earnings is based on the ______________ _______ principle.

6. The cost of external equity capital is higher than the cost of retained earnings due to ____________ ________.

7. Using the Capital Asset Pricing Model (CAPM), the required rate of return on common stock is found as a function of the _______-_______ _______, the firm's _______ ______________, and the required rate of return on an average ________.

8. The cost of common equity may also be found by adding a _______ __________ to the interest rate on the firm's own _______-________ _______.

9. The required rate of return may also be estimated as the expected __________ ________ on the common stock plus the expected _________ _______ in dividends.

10. The proportions of _______, ___________ ________, and _________ _________ in the target capital structure should be used to calculate the __________ __________ cost of capital.

11. The ___________ cost of capital is the cost of raising another dollar of capital.

12. The MCC schedule can be used to help determine the ___________ _______ to be used in the capital budgeting process.

13. The _____________ ______________ ___________ graphs a firm's capital projects in descending order of each project's ___________ _______ _____ _________.

14. The ________-______ _______ _____ _______ is defined as the interest rate to be paid on new debt capital, reduced by (1 - T) because interest payments are tax deductible.

15. For stocks in _____________, the required rate of return is equal to the expected rate of return.

16. Firms raise capital in accordance with their ________ _________ ___________.

17. The __________ capital structure is the one that produces the lowest WACC.

18. The point at which the marginal cost of capital increases is called a ________ ________.

19. The ___________ _______ _____ __________ ___________ shows the relationship between the cost of each dollar raised and the total amount of capital raised during the year.

20. The component _______ _____ ____________ ________ is the preferred dividend divided by the issuance price net of flotation costs. No ______ _____________ is made since preferred stock dividends are paid from after-tax earnings.

CONCEPTUAL QUESTIONS

21. If a firm obtained all of its common equity from retained earnings, its MCC schedule would always be flat; that is, there would be no break points.

a. True b. False

22. If there are n break points in the MCC schedule, there will be n + 1 different MCCs.

a. True b. False

23. Funds acquired by the firm through preferred stock have a cost to the firm equal to the preferred dividend divided by the price investors paid for one share.

a. True b. False

24. Which of the following statements could be true concerning the costs of debt and equity?

a. Firm A's cost of debt is greater than Firm A's cost of equity.
b. Firm A's cost of debt is greater than Firm B's cost of equity.
c. The cost of retained earnings for Firm A is less than the cost of external equity for Firm A.
d. The cost of retained earnings for Firm A is less than the cost of debt for Firm A.
e. Statements b and c could both be true.

25. The first break point in the WACC:

a. Always results from using up retained earnings.
b. Always results from using up cheap debt.
c. Depends jointly on the capital structure and the amount of each type of low-cost funds that are available.
d. Assuming net income is held constant, the first break point is directly affected by the tax rate because the cost of debt is reduced due to the deductibility of interest.
e. Statements c and d are both true.

26. Which of the following statements is most *correct*?

a. Dividends must be paid with after-tax dollars, but interest is paid with before-tax dollars. This situation encourages corporations to finance with stock rather than with debt.
b. If a company accepts a new project which is expected to earn exactly the cost of the capital used to finance it, then the investment decision should not affect the value of the firm's stock.
c. The cost of retained earnings is higher than the cost of newly issued common equity because of the taxes that must be paid on income before earnings are available for retention.
d. Since the CAPM cost of common equity is affected by the interest rate on Treasury securities, if interest rates in the economy rise sharply, then the CAPM estimate of the cost of equity should, in theory, rise to a level above the DCF cost estimate if equilibrium is to exist.
e. Statements a, b, c, and d are all true.

PROBLEMS

27. Roland Corporation's next expected dividend (D_1) is $2.50. The firm has maintained a constant payout ratio of 50 percent during the past 7 years. Seven years ago its EPS was $1.50. The firm's beta coefficient is 1.2. The required return on an average stock in the market is 13 percent, and the risk-free rate is 7 percent. Roland's A-rated bonds are yielding 10 percent, and its current stock price is $30. Which of the following values is the most reasonable estimate of Roland's cost of retained earnings, k_s?

a. 10%
b. 12%
c. 14%
d. 20%
e. 26%

28. The director of capital budgeting for See-Saw Inc., a manufacturer of playground equipment, is considering a plan to expand production facilities in order to meet an increase in demand. He estimates that this expansion will produce an IRR of 11 percent. The firm's target capital structure calls for a debt/equity ratio of 0.8. See-Saw currently has a bond issue outstanding which will mature in 25 years and has a 7 percent annual coupon rate. The bonds are currently selling for $804. The firm has maintained a constant 6% growth rate; its next expected dividend is $2; its current stock price is $40; and its tax rate is 40 percent. Should it undertake the expansion? (Assume that there is no preferred stock outstanding and that any new debt will have a 25-year maturity.)

a. No; the expected return is 2.5 percentage points lower than the cost of capital.
b. No; the expected return is 1.0 percentage points lower than the cost of capital.
c. Yes; the expected return is 0.5 percentage points higher than the cost of capital.
d. Yes; the expected return is 1.0 percentage points higher than the cost of capital.
e. Yes; the expected return is 2.5 percentage points higher than the cost of capital.

29. Midterm Corporation's present capital structure, which is also its target capital structure, calls for 50 percent debt and 50 percent common equity. The firm has only one potential project, an expansion program with a 10.2 percent IRR and a cost of $20 million but which is completely divisible; that is, Midterm can invest any amount up to $20 million. Midterm expects to retain $3 million of earnings next year. It can raise up to $5 million in new debt at a before-tax cost of 8 percent, and all debt after the first $5 million will have a cost of 10 percent. The cost of retained earnings is 12 percent; Midterm can sell any amount of new common stock desired at a constant cost of new equity of 15 percent. The firm's marginal tax rate is 40 percent. What is Midterm's optimal capital budget?

a. $0 million
b. $5 million
c. $6 million
d. $10 million
e. $20 million

30. The management of Florida Phosphate Industries is planning next year's capital budget. FPI projects net income of $10,500, and its payout ratio is 40 percent. The company's earnings and dividends are growing at a constant rate of 5 percent; the last dividend, D_0, was $0.90; and the current equilibrium stock price is $8.59. FPI can raise up to $10,000 of debt at a 12 percent before-tax cost, the next $10,000 will cost 14 percent, and all debt after $20,000 will cost 16 percent. If FPI issues new common stock, a 10 percent flotation cost will be incurred on the first $16,000 issued, while flotation costs will be 20 percent on all new stock issued after the first $16,000. FPI is at its optimal capital structure, which is 40 percent debt and 60 percent equity, and the firm's marginal tax rate is 40 percent. FPI has the following independent, indivisible, and equally risky investment opportunities:

Project	Cost	IRR
A	$15,000	17%
B	20,000	14
C	15,000	16
D	12,000	15

What is FPI's optimal capital budget?

a. $62,000
b. $42,000
c. $30,000
d. $15,000
e. $0

31. Refer to Problem 30. Management neglected to incorporate project risk differentials into the analysis. FPI's policy is to add 2 percentage points to the IRR of those projects significantly less risky than average and to subtract 2 percentage points from the IRR of those which are substantially more risky than average. Management judges Project A to be of high risk, Projects C and D to be of average risk, and Project B to be of low risk. No projects are divisible. What is the optimal capital budget after adjustment for project risk? Assume that if the Company has a choice between two projects of equal risk (after adjustment), and one project uses all the available funds at a certain cost whereas the other project does not, the Company will choose the project that uses all the available funds.

a. $62,000
b. $50,000
c. $42,000
d. $30,000
e. $15,000

32. Gator Products Company (GPC) is at its optimal capital structure of 70 percent common equity and 30 percent debt. GPC's MCC and IOS schedules for next year intersect at a 14 percent marginal cost of capital. At the intersection, the IOS schedule is vertical and the MCC schedule is horizontal. GPC has a marginal tax rate of 40 percent. Next year's dividend is expected to be $2.00 per share, and GPC has a constant growth in earnings and dividends of 6 percent. The after-tax cost of equity used in the MCC at the intersection is based on new equity with a flotation cost of 10 percent, while the before-tax cost of debt is 12 percent. What is GPC's current equilibrium stock price?

a. $12.73
b. $17.23
c. $20.37
d. $23.70
e. $37.20

33. Stacy Paints Corporation has a target capital structure of 50 percent debt and 50 percent common equity. The company expects to have $500 of after-tax income during the coming year, and it plans to retain 60 percent of its earnings. The current stock price is P_0 = $32; the last dividend was D_0 = $2.10; and the dividend is expected to grow at a constant rate of 8 percent. New stock can be sold at a flotation cost of F = 25%. What will Stacy Paints' marginal cost of *equity* capital (not the WACC) be if it raises a total of $700 of new capital?

a. 15.09%
b. 16.51%
c. 17.46%
d. 16.25%
e. 17.18%

ANSWERS AND SOLUTIONS

1. weighted average
2. debt; preferred stock; common stock; retained earnings
3. rate of return
4. three
5. opportunity cost
6. flotation costs
7. risk-free rate (k_{RF}); beta coefficient (b_i); stock (k_M)
8. risk premium; long-term debt
9. dividend yield; growth rate
10. debt; preferred stock; common equity; weighted average
11. marginal
12. discount rate
13. investment opportunity schedule (IOS); internal rate of return (IRR)
14. after-tax cost of debt
15. equilibrium
16. target capital structures
17. optimal
18. break point
19. marginal cost of capital schedule
20. cost of preferred stock; tax adjustment

21. b. The component cost of debt and/or preferred equity might increase, thus causing break points in the MCC schedule.

22. a. This statement is correct.

23. b. Flotation costs must be subtracted from the investor's cost to get the net issuance price, which is then used to calculate the cost of preferred stock.

24. e. If Firm A has more business risk than Firm B, Firm A's cost of debt could be greater than Firm B's cost of equity. Also, the cost of retained earnings is less than the cost of external equity because of flotation costs.

25. c. Look at the break point formula; it is obvious that the capital structure and the amount of low-cost funds of each type affect the break point. The tax rate affects the after-tax cost of debt, but it does not directly affect the break point, so statement d is incorrect. Therefore, statement c is the correct response.

26. b. Statement b is correct. If a project's return exceeds its cost of capital, the value of the firm, and the stock price, will rise, and vice versa if the project's return is less than the cost of capital. Therefore, if the project's return is just equal to the cost of capital used to finance it, accepting the project should have no effect on the value of the stock. The other statements are all false. Note that an increase in interest rates will cause the CAPM cost of equity to rise, but the interest rate increase will also cause the DCF cost to increase. The stock price would decline, causing the dividend yield to increase. Equilibrium requires the two cost of equity estimates to be equal.

27. c. Use all three methods to estimate k_s.

(1) CAPM: $k_s = k_{RF} + (k_M - k_{RF})b_i = 7\% + (13\% - 7\%)1.2 = 14.2\%$.

(2) Risk Premium: k_s = Bond yield + Risk premium = 10% + approximately 4% = 14%.

(3) DCF: $k_s = D_1/P_0 + g = \$2.50/\$30 + g$, where g can be estimated as follows:

$$\$0.75 = \$2.50(PVIF_{k,7})$$
$$PVIF_{k,7} = \$0.75/\$2.50 = 0.3000.$$

Thus k, which is the compound growth rate, g, is about 19%, or, using a calculator, 18.8%. Therefore, $k_s = 0.083 + 0.188 = 27.1\%$.

Roland Corporation has apparently been experiencing supernormal growth during the past 7 years, and it is not reasonable to assume that this growth will continue. The first two methods yield a k_s of about 14 percent, which appears reasonable.

28. e. Cost of equity = k_s = \$2/\$40 + 0.06 = 0.11 = 11%.

Cost of debt = k_d = Yield to maturity on outstanding bonds based on current market price.

$$V = I(PVIFA_{k,25}) + M(PVIF_{k,25})$$
$$\$804 = \$70(PVIFA_{k,25}) + \$1,000(PVIF_{k,25}).$$

Solving by trial and error gives k_d = 9%. In determining the capital structure weights, note that debt/equity = 0.8 or, for example, 4/5. Therefore, debt/assets is

$$\frac{D}{A} = \frac{\text{Debt}}{\text{Debt + Equity}} = \frac{4}{4 + 5} = \frac{4}{9}.$$

and equity/assets = 5/9. Hence, the weighted average cost of capital is

$$k_a = WACC = k_d(1 - T)(D/A) + k_s(1 - D/A)$$

$$= 0.09(1 - 0.4)(4/9) + 0.11(5/9)$$

$$= 0.024 + 0.061 = 0.085 = 8.5\%.$$

The cost of capital is 8.5 percent, while the expansion project's IRR is 11.0 percent. Since the expected return is 2.5 percentage points higher than the cost, the expansion should be undertaken.

29. d. First, look only at debt:

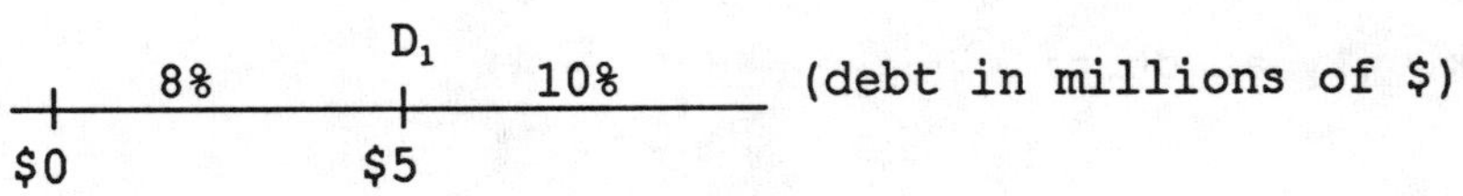

Now, look only at equity:

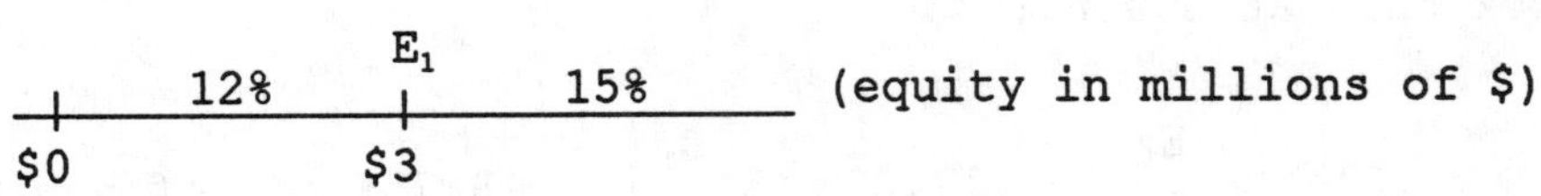

Now combine debt and equity and look at total capital:

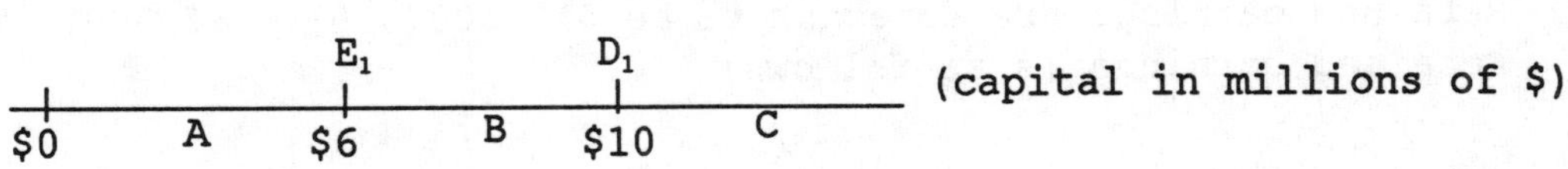

The break points are calculated as follows:

E_1 = \$3,000,000/0.5 = \$6,000,000.

D_1 = \$5,000,000/0.5 = \$10,000,000.

Now, determine the weighted average cost of capital for intervals A, B, and C:

$k_a = WACC = w_d(k_d)(1 - T) + w_s(k_s \text{ or } k_e)$.

A = 0.5(8%)(0.6) + 0.5(12%) = 8.4%.

B = 0.5(8%)(0.6) + 0.5(15%) = 9.9%.

C = 0.5(10%)(0.6) + 0.5(15%) = 10.5%.

Finally, graph the IOS and MCC schedules.

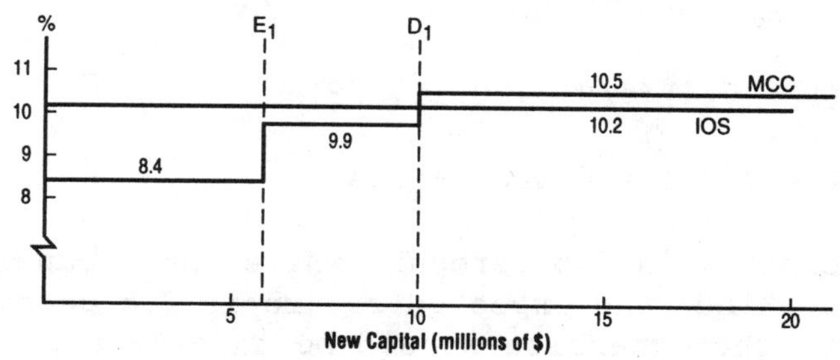

Thus, the optimal capital budget is \$10 million.

30. b. First look only at debt:

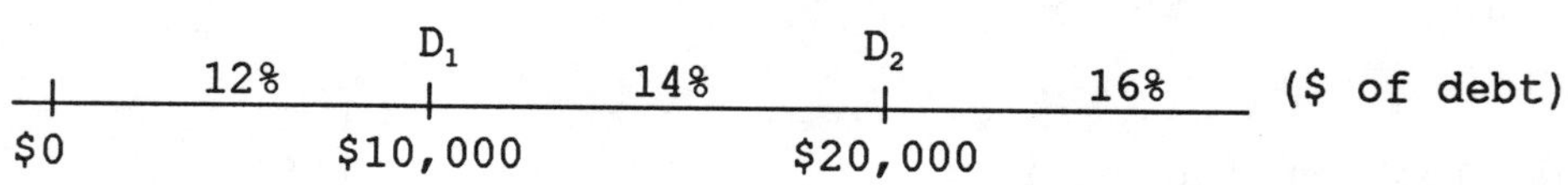

Now, look only at equity:

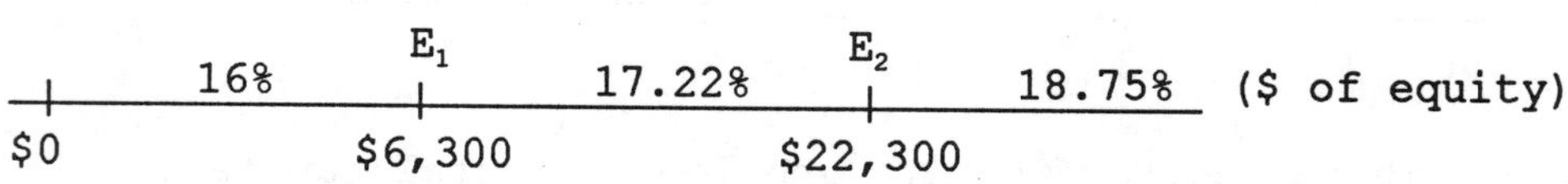

Retained earnings are forecast to be \$10,500(0.6) = \$6,300. The cost of retained earnings is as follows:

$$k_s = \frac{D_0(1 + g)}{P_0} + g = \frac{\$0.90(1.05)}{\$8.59} + 0.05 = 0.16 = 16.0\%.$$

The cost of new equity is as follows:

$$k_{e1} = \frac{D_0(1 + g)}{P_0(1 - F)} + g = \frac{\$0.90(1.05)}{\$8.59(1 - 0.10)} + 0.05 = 0.1722 = 17.22\%.$$

$$k_{e2} = \frac{\$0.90(1.05)}{\$8.59(1 - 0.20)} + 0.05 = 0.1875 = 18.75\%.$$

Now, combine debt and equity and look at total capital:

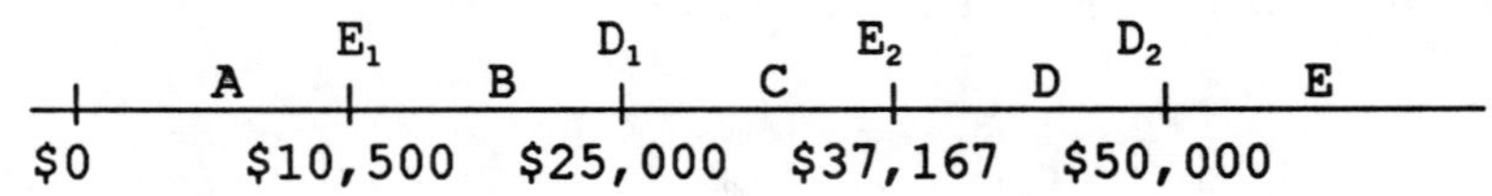

The break points are calculated as follows:

E_1 = \$6,300/0.60 = \$10,500.
D_1 = \$10,000/0.40 = \$25,000.
E_2 = \$22,300/0.60 = \$37,167.
D_2 = \$20,000/0.40 = \$50,000.

Now, determine the weighted average cost of capital for intervals A through E:

$$k_a = WACC = w_d(k_d)(1 - T) + w_s(k_s \text{ or } k_e)$$

A = 0.4(12%)(0.6) + 0.6(16.00%) = 12.48%.
B = 0.4(12%)(0.6) + 0.6(17.22%) = 13.21%.
C = 0.4(14%)(0.6) + 0.6(17.22%) = 13.69%.
D = 0.4(14%)(0.6) + 0.6(18.75%) = 14.61%.
E = 0.4(16%)(0.6) + 0.6(18.75%) = 15.09%.

Finally, graph the MCC and IOS schedules:

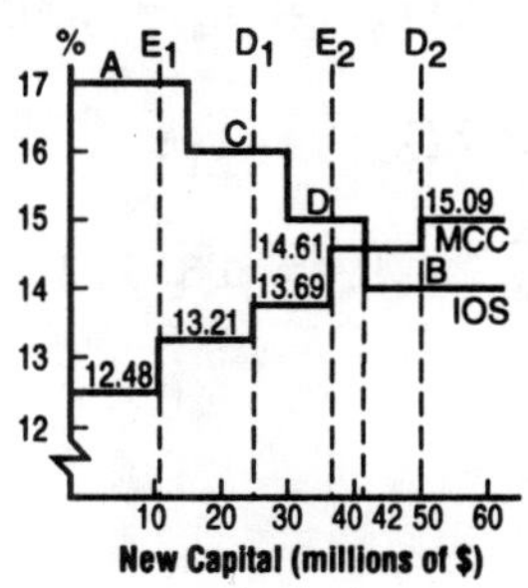

Therefore, the optimal capital budget is $42,000. Projects A, C, and D are accepted.

31. b. First, determine the risk-adjusted IRRs:

Project	Cost	IRR	Risk	Risk-Adjusted IRR
A	$15,000	17%	High	15%
B	20,000	14	Low	16
C	15,000	16	Average	16
D	12,000	15	Average	15

Now, regraph the IOS and MCC schedules:

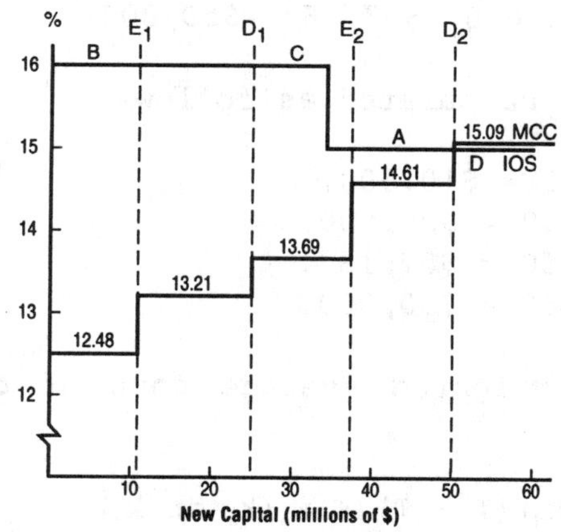

Note that Projects B and C are graphed first, and then the IOS can be ordered with A first or with D first. With A first, total cost of Projects B, C, and A is $50,000, which coincides with a break point. Clearly, Project D is not acceptable. Therefore, the optimal capital budget is $50,000.

32. c. At the intersection of the IOS and MCC schedules, k_a = WACC = 14%. Therefore,

$$w_d(k_d)(1 - T) + w_s(k_e) = k_a = \text{WACC} = 14\%$$

$$0.3(12\%)(0.6) + 0.7(k_e) = 14\%$$

$$k_e = 16.91\%.$$

Now, at equilibrium,

$$\hat{k}_e = k_e = \frac{D_1}{P_0(1 - F)} + g$$

$$0.1691 = \frac{\$2.00}{P_0(1 - 0.10)} + 0.06$$

$$0.1091 = \frac{\$2.222}{P_0}$$

$$P_0 = \$20.37.$$

33. c. 50% = Debt, 50% = Equity, NI = \$500, Retain 60%.

P_0 = \$32, D_0 = \$2.10, D_1 = \$2.27, g = 8%, and F = 25%.

RE = \$500(0.6) = \$300. RE_{BP} = RE/Equity ratio = \$300/0.5 = \$600.

At total capital of \$700, retained earnings will have been used up, so equity will come from new common stock, with a cost equal to:

$k_e = D_1/(P_0(1 - F)) + g$ = \$2.27/(\$32(1 - 0.25)) + 8% = 17.46%.

CHAPTER 20
LEVERAGE AND THE TARGET CAPITAL STRUCTURE

OVERVIEW

Capital structure theory suggests that some optimal capital structure exists which simultaneously maximizes a firm's stock price and minimizes its cost of capital. The use of debt tends to increase earnings per share, which will lead to a higher stock price, but at the same time, the use of debt also increases the risk borne by stockholders, which lowers the stock price. The optimal capital structure strikes a balance between these risk and return effects. While it is difficult to determine the optimal capital structure with precision, it is possible to identify the factors that influence it. The target may change over time as conditions vary, but, at any given moment, a well-managed firm's management has a specific structure in mind, and financing decisions are made so as to be consistent with this target structure.

OUTLINE

I. **Capital structure decisions involve a tradeoff between risk and expected return. There are two types of risk that are important in determining the target capital structure: Business risk is the riskiness of the firm's operations if the firm uses only common equity financing, while financial risk is the additional risk placed on common shareholders as a result of the firm's decision to use debt or preferred stock in its financing.**

A. Business risk is the uncertainty associated with forecasting and realizing future *operating income*. The element of uncertainty associated with business risk includes both the chance of not reaching a positive level of operating profits and the problems associated with fluctuating returns.

B. Operating income is also referred to as *earnings before interest and taxes (EBIT)*.

C. Business risk derives from a number of sources, the more important of which are the following:
1. Demand (unit sales) variability
2. Sales price variability
3. Input price variability
4. Inability to adjust sales prices for changes in input prices
5. Changing technology

6. Operating leverage (the extent to which operating costs are fixed)

D. Business risk varies not only from industry to industry but also among firms within a given industry. Furthermore, business risk can change over time.

E. If a firm uses no financial leverage, the variability of its ROE will be exactly equal to the variability of its EBIT. In that case, the firm's total risk is equal to its business risk; it has no financial risk.

II. Operating leverage is the degree to which a firm uses fixed costs in its production processes.

A. Firms that have a high percentage of fixed costs are said to have a high degree of *operating leverage.*

1. *Fixed operating costs* are operating costs that do not vary directly with sales but would be incurred even if a firm made no sales.
2. *Variable operating costs* are costs that vary directly with sales.
3. Interest charges are *financial* costs as opposed to *operating* costs; it will, therefore, influence financial leverage, but not operating leverage.

B. A high degree of operating leverage implies that a relatively small change in sales will result in a large change in operating income and ROE.

C. *Breakeven analysis* is a method of determining the point at which sales will just cover operating costs -- that is, the point at which the firm will break even. It also shows the magnitude of the firm's operating profits or losses if sales exceed or fall below that point.

1. As we develop the breakeven analysis here, the breakeven point before interest charges is shown. The reason for this emphasis is that, at this point, we are concerned with the firm's operating plan rather than its financing plan.

D. A *breakeven chart* shows both the breakeven sales in dollars and the breakeven sales in units needed to cover all operating costs, both fixed and variable.

E. The higher a firm's degree of operating leverage, the higher its breakeven point tends to be.

1. The *breakeven point* is the level of sales that just covers all operating costs, both fixed and variable. At this point Total revenues = Total costs, or QP = QV + F, where

Q = number of units produced and sold,
P = selling price per unit,
QP = level of sales in dollars,
V = variable cost per unit produced,
QV = variable operating costs in dollars, and

F = fixed operating costs.

2. The breakeven point stated in terms of units is

$$Q_{BE} = \frac{F}{P - V}.$$

3. The breakeven volume in dollars, S_{BE}, is calculated as:

$$S_{BE} = PQ_{BE}, \text{ or } S_{BE} = \frac{F}{1 - \frac{V}{P}}.$$

F. Breakeven analysis can shed light on three important types of business decisions:
   1. Breakeven analysis can help determine how large the sales of a new product must be for the firm to achieve profitability.
   2. Breakeven analysis can be used to study the effects of a general expansion in the level of the firm's operations.
   3. When the firm is considering modernization and automation projects, where the fixed investment in equipment is increased in order to lower variable costs, breakeven analysis can help management analyze the consequences of these projects.

G. In general, the higher a firm's fixed operating costs, the greater its operating leverage and its business risk (as measured by the variability of EBIT, net income, or ROE).

H. Production technology limits control over the amount of fixed costs and operating leverage.

I. However, firms do have some control over the type of production processes they employ. Therefore, a firm's capital budgeting decisions will have an impact on its operating leverage and business risk.

J. The firm's operating leverage, and hence the extent to which operating leverage will cause future operating profits to fluctuate, is an important factor in determining the firm's capital structure.

III. **Financial leverage refers to the firm's use of fixed-income securities such as debt and preferred stock, rather than common stock, in its capital structure.**

A. Capital structure policy involves a risk-return tradeoff. The *optimal capital structure* strikes a balance between risk and return such that the price of the stock is maximized, and, simultaneously the firm's overall cost of capital is minimized.

B. Financial risk is the additional risk placed on the common shareholders as a result of using financial leverage.
   1. By using financial leverage, the firm concentrates its business risk on the common stockholders.

IV. **The degree to which a firm employs fixed charge capital--debt and preferred stock--will affect its expected earnings per share, the riskiness of these earnings, and consequently the price of the firm's stock.**

A. EBIT does depend on operating leverage, but it does not depend on financial leverage.

B. Financial leverage will cause earnings per share to rise if the return on assets is greater than the cost of debt. However, the degree of risk associated with the firm will also increase as leverage increases.

C. As financial leverage increases, the cost of debt will also rise due to the increased risk of not being able to meet the fixed charges.

D. Financial leverage increases the potential return to common stockholders, but it also increases the potential variability in earnings per share.

E. A firm should choose that capital structure which maximizes the price of its stock. This capital structure is called the *optimal*, or *target*, *capital structure*.

F. Changes in the use of financial leverage will affect EPS and stock price.

G. At first, EPS will rise as the use of debt increases. Interest charges rise, but the number of outstanding shares will fall as equity is replaced by debt.

H. At some point EPS will peak. Beyond this point interest rates will rise so fast that EPS is depressed in spite of the fact that the number of shares outstanding is falling.

I. Risk, as measured by the standard deviation of EPS, rises continuously as the use of debt increases.

J. The expected stock price will at first increase with financial leverage, will then reach a peak, and finally will decline. This pattern occurs primarily as a result of corporate income taxes and bankruptcy costs.
   1. The optimal capital structure is found when the expected stock price is maximized.
   2. Management should set its target capital structure at this ratio of debt/assets.

K. The financial structure that maximizes EPS usually has more debt than the one which results in the highest stock price.

V. **According to the MM capital structure theory, because of the tax deductibility of interest on debt which provide tax shelter benefits, a firm can maximize its value by financing almost entirely with debt. However, the MM assumptions do not hold in the real world. In fact, there have been no**

empirical studies which have produced results enabling precise identification of a firm's optimal capital structure.

VI. **Operating leverage and financial leverage are interrelated. We can see how the two types of leverage interact through an analysis of the degree of leverage concept.**

A. *Degree of leverage* is a form of elasticity. It measures the percentage change in one variable, given a percentage change in another variable.
   1. Degree of leverage is a point concept. This means that it applies to percentage changes up or down in the quantity produced and sold from a specific starting level.

B. The *degree of operating leverage (DOL)* is the percentage change in operating income (EBIT) resulting from a given percentage change in sales.
   1. The formula used to calculate DOL at Point Q is (in units):

$$DOL_Q = \frac{Q(P - V)}{Q(P - V) - F},$$

   where:
   Q = units of output,
   P = sales price per unit,
   V = variable cost per unit, and
   F = fixed operating costs.

   2. The formula used to calculate DOL based on dollar sales is

$$DOL_S = \frac{S - VC}{S - VC - F},$$

   where:
   S = sales in dollars,
   VC = total variable costs, and
   F = fixed operating costs.

   3. To find the effects on EBIT of a particular percentage change in sales, multiply the percentage change in sales times the DOL.

C. In general, if a firm is operating at close to its breakeven level, the degree of operating leverage will be high, but DOL declines the higher the base level of sales is above breakeven sales.

D. Financial leverage affects earnings after interest and taxes, or the earnings available to common stockholders. The *degree of financial leverage (DFL)* is the percentage change in earnings available to common stockholders (EPS) associated with a given percentage change in EBIT.
   1. The formula for DFL is

$$DFL = \frac{Q(P - V) - F}{Q(P - V) - F - I} = \frac{EBIT}{EBIT - I},$$

where I is the total fixed financing charges.

2. To find the effects on income available to common stockholders, multiply the percentage change in EBIT by DFL. The greater the degree of financial leverage, the greater the impact of a given change in EBIT on EPS.

E. *Degree of total leverage (DTL)* combines DOL and DFL to show how a given change in sales will affect EPS. It is defined as the percentage change in earnings per share that results from a given percentage change in sales.

1. One formula for DTL is

$$DTL = \frac{Q(P - V)}{Q(P - V) - F - I}.$$

2. The degree of total leverage can also be found as

$$DTL = (DOL)(DFL), \text{ or}$$

$$DTL = \frac{S - VC}{S - VC - F - I}.$$

3. DTL shows the interrelationship between operating and financial leverage.
4. DTL is useful primarily for the insights it provides regarding the joint effects of operating and financial leverage on EPS.

VII. At the present time, financial theory does not allow us to specify a firm's optimal capital structure and it is evident that additional guidelines are needed. There are a number of factors which, in practice, have proven to be important considerations when actual capital structures are determined.

A. The lower the *times-interest-earned ratio (TIE)* the higher the probability that a firm will default on its debt and be forced into bankruptcy.

1. Management will be especially concerned about keeping TIE above 1.0, the point below which a firm's earnings will not cover its required interest payments.

B. A firm's capital structure can change because of merger activity.

1. The acquiring firm may issue debt to purchase the target firm's stock.
2. The new debt effectively changes the combined firm's capital structure.
3. The value enhancement resulting from the use of debt is sufficient to cover the premium offered for the stock and still provide a profit for the acquiring firm.

C. The following factors will all have some influence on the firm's choice of a target capital structure.

1. Sales stability. If sales are stable, a firm will be more likely to take on increased debt and higher fixed charges.
2. Asset structure. Firms whose assets can readily be pledged as collateral for loans will tend to operate with a higher degree of financial leverage.
3. Operating leverage. Lower operating leverage generally permits a firm to employ more debt.
4. Growth rate. Firms that are growing rapidly generally need large amounts of external capital. The flotation costs associated with debt are generally less than those for common stock, so rapidly growing firms tend to use more debt.
5. Profitability. A high degree of profitability would indicate an ability to carry a high level of debt. However, many profitable firms are able to meet most of their financing needs with retained earnings, and do so.
6. Taxes. Interest charges are tax deductible, while dividend payments are not. This factor favors the use of debt over equity for firms in high tax brackets.
7. Control. Management may not wish to increase the shares of stock outstanding for fear of losing voting control of the company.
8. Management attitudes toward risk. Managements vary in their attitudes toward risk. More conservative managers will use stock rather than debt for financing, while less conservative managers will use more debt.
9. Lender and rating agency attitudes. This factor will penalize firms that go beyond the average for their industry in the use of financial leverage.
10. Market conditions. At any point in time, securities markets may favor either debt or equity.
11. Firm's internal condition. Expected future earnings patterns and internal factors will influence management's choice of debt versus equity.
12. Financial flexibility. Most treasurers have as a goal to always be in a position to raise the capital needed to support operations, even under bad conditions. Therefore, they want to always maintain some *reserve borrowing capacity*.

VIII. There are wide variations in the use of financial leverage both among industries and among individual firms within each industry.

A. Generally, the least leveraged industries have the highest coverage ratios, while industries which finance heavily with debt have low coverage ratios.

DEFINITIONAL QUESTIONS

1. Business risk refers to the uncertainty about expected _________ _________, or ______.

2. Business risk represents the riskiness of the firm's operations if it uses no ______; financial risk represents the additional risk borne by common stockholders as a result of using ______.

3. The factors that influence a firm's business risk include the variability of (1) ______ in units, (2) ______ _________, and (3) _________ ______.

4. If a firm uses no __________ leverage, the variability in its ________ ____ ________ will be exactly equal to the variability of its EBIT.

5. Firms that have a high ratio of fixed to variable costs are said to operate with a high degree of _________ _________.

6. __________ __________ __________ are costs that do not vary directly with sales and therefore, will be incurred even if a firm made no sales.

7. __________ __________ is a method of determining the point at which sales will just cover costs.

8. At the __________ __________, total sales revenues and total operating costs are exactly equal.

9. Operating leverage refers to the use of __________ __________.

10. Financial leverage refers to the use of ____________ financing.

11. Determination of an _____________ capital structure requires consideration of both ______ and ______.

12. Common stockholders are compensated for bearing financial risk by a higher _______ _________.

13. Expected EPS generally ______ as the debt/assets ratio increases.

14. As financial leverage increases, the stock price will first begin to rise, but it will then decline as financial leverage becomes excessive because potential ____________ ______ become increasingly important.

15. The __________ _____ __________ is a form of elasticity that measures the percentage change in one variable given a percentage change in another variable.

16. The ________ ____ _________ __________ is defined as the percentage change in EBIT associated with a given change in sales volume.

17. The ______ ____ __________ __________ is defined as the percentage change in EPS associated with a given change in EBIT.

18. The ______ ____ ______ ___________ is defined as the percentage change in EPS associated with a given change in sales volume.

19. The ______ ratio and the ________-________-________ ratio give some indication of a firm's risk of default on its fixed charges.

20. Difficulties in determining the relationship between ____/____ ratios, _________ capitalization rates, and the degree of _________ _________ have made some managers reluctant to rely heavily on stock price analysis to help determine the optimal capital structure.

21. Conservative financial managers may try to maintain a target ____________ _________ that does not maximize the firm's _________ _________.

22. Some managers may be more concerned with _________ than with maximizing stock prices.

23. Debt has a ______ advantage over equity in that _________ is a deductible expense while _________ are not.

24. Management may prefer additional ______ as opposed to common stock in order to help maintain _________ of the company.

CONCEPTUAL QUESTIONS

25. Firm A has a higher degree of business risk than Firm B. Firm A can offset this by increasing its operating leverage.

    a. True   b. False

26. Two firms operate in different industries, but they have the same expected EPS and the same standard deviation of expected EPS. Thus, the two firms must have the same financial risk.

    a. True   b. False

27. Two firms could have identical financial and operating leverage yet have different degrees of business risk.

    a. True   b. False

28. As a general rule, the capital structure that maximizes stock price also

a. Maximizes the weighted average cost of capital.
b. Maximizes EPS.
c. Maximizes bankruptcy costs.
d. Minimizes the weighted average cost of capital.
e. Minimizes the required rate of return on equity.

29. In business terminology, if a firm has a high degree of operating leverage, other things held constant, it means that

a. a relatively small change in sales will result in a small change in operating income.
b. the firm uses more debt financing than equity financing.
c. a relatively large change in sales will result in a small change in operating income.
d. the firm will have relatively low breakeven point.
e. a relatively small change in sales will result in a large change in operating income.

30. Fixed operating costs consist of costs that do not vary directly with sales. Which of the following costs represent fixed operating costs?

a. Depreciation on plant and equipment.
b. Factory labor.
c. Raw materials.
d. Sales commission.
e. None of the above are fixed operating costs.

31. Which of the following is most *correct*?

a. If a firm is exposed to a high degree of business risk as a result of its high operating leverage, then it should probably offset this risk by using a larger-than-average amount of financial leverage. This follows because debt has a lower after-tax cost than equity.
b. Financial risk can be reduced by replacing common equity with preferred stock.
c. As explained in the text, one of the advantages of the degree of leverage concept is that it takes account of market risk, so if a firm's stockholders hold diversified portfolios of stocks, as opposed to holding the stock of only one firm, this fact is accounted for by the use of the degree of total leverage.
d. In the text it was stated that the capital structure which minimizes the WACC also maximizes the firm's stock price and its total value, but generally not its expected EPS. One reason given for why debt is beneficial is that it shelters operating income from taxes, while it was stated that a disadvantage of excessive debt has to do with costs associated with bankruptcy and financial distress generally.
e. All of the above statements are false.

32. A decrease in the debt ratio will normally have no effect on

a. Financial risk.
b. Total risk.
c. Business risk.
d. Systematic risk.
e. Firm-unique risk.

PROBLEMS

33. The Fisher Company will produce 50,000 10-gallon aquariums next year. Variable costs will equal 40 percent of dollar sales, while fixed costs total $100,000. At what price must each aquarium be sold for the firm's EBIT to be $90,000?

a. $5.00
b. $5.33
c. $5.50
d. $6.00
e. $6.33

34. Waber Incorporated believes that the annual demand for one of its new products will total 9,000 units. Waber's variable unit cost is $30. The depreciation on the production equipment and the rent on the building where production will occur all total $180,000 for the year. What is the minimum price Waber can charge for its new product and still break even?

a. $30.00
b. $40.00
c. $50.00
d. $55.00
e. $65.00

35. Refer to Problem 34. Suppose Waber can sell its product for $60 per unit. What will be the breakeven volume in dollars?

a. $180,000
b. $240,000
c. $300,000
d. $360,000
e. $390,000

(The following data apply to the next four questions.)

Brown Products is a new firm just starting operations. The firm will produce backpacks which will sell for $22.00 apiece. Fixed costs are $500,000 per year, and variable costs are $2.00 per unit of production. The company expects to sell 50,000 backpacks per year, and its effective tax rate is 40 percent. Brown needs $2 million to build facilities, obtain working capital, and start operations. If Brown borrows part of the money, the interest charges will depend on the amount borrowed as follows:

Amount Borrowed	Percentage of Debt in Capital Structure	Interest Rate on Total Amount Borrowed
$200,000	10%	9.00%
400,000	20	9.50
600,000	30	10.00
800,000	40	15.00
1,000,000	50	19.00
1,200,000	60	26.00

Assume that stock can be sold at a price of $20 per share on the initial offering, regardless of how much debt the company uses. Then after the company begins operating, its price will be determined as a multiple of its earnings per share. The multiple (or the P/E ratio) will depend upon the capital structure as follows:

Debt/Assets	P/E	Debt/Assets	P/E
0.0	12.5	40.0	8.0
10.0	12.0	50.0	6.0
20.0	11.5	60.0	5.0
30.0	10.0		

36. What is Brown's optimal capital structure, which maximizes stock price, as measured by the debt/assets ratio?

a. 10%
b. 20%
c. 30%
d. 40%
e. 50%

37. What is Brown's degree of operating leverage at the expected level of sales?

a. 1.00
b. 1.08
c. 2.00
d. 2.16
e. 3.00

38. What is Brown's degree of financial leverage at the expected level of sales?

a. 1.00
b. 1.08
c. 2.00
d. 2.16
e. 3.00

39. What is Brown's degree of total leverage at the expected level of sales and optimal capital structure?

a. 1.00
b. 1.08
c. 2.00
d. 2.16
e. 3.00

40. Bicycles Inc. currently sells 75,000 units annually. At this sales level, its net operating income (EBIT) is $4 million and the degree of total leverage is 2.0. The firm's debt consists of $20 million in bonds with a 10 percent coupon. Bicycles is considering a new assembly line which would entail an increase in fixed cost, resulting in a degree of operating leverage of 1.8. However, the firm desires to maintain the degree of total leverage at 2.0. Assuming that EBIT remains at $4 million, what dollar amount of bonds must be retired to accomplish adding the assembly line yet retain the old degree of total leverage?

a. $10 million
b. $12 million
c. $14 million
d. $16 million
e. $18 million

ANSWERS AND SOLUTIONS

1. operating income; EBIT
2. debt; debt
3. sales; sales prices; operating costs
4. financial; return on equity
5. operating leverage
6. Fixed operating costs
7. Breakeven analysis
8. breakeven point
9. fixed costs
10. debt (or fixed-charge)
11. optimal; risk; return
12. expected return
13. increases
14. bankruptcy costs
15. degree of leverage
16. degree of operating leverage (DOL)
17. degree of financial leverage (DFL)
18. degree of total leverage (DTL)
19. debt; times-interest-earned (or fixed charge coverage)
20. P/E; equity; financial leverage
21. capital structure; stock price
22. survival
23. tax; interest; dividends
24. debt; control

25. b. Increasing operating leverage will increase Firm A's business risk; therefore, Firm A should use less operating leverage.

26. b. The two firms would have the same total risk. However, they could have different combinations of business and financial risk.

27. a. Business risk consists of several elements in addition to operating leverage, for example, sales variability, and it does not depend on financial risk at all.

28. d. The capital structure that maximizes stock price does indeed minimize WACC.

29. e. High operating leverage (ie., high fixed operating costs) will create high business risk and a greater potential for large swings in EBIT and ROE.

30. a. The costs of plant and equipment will be incurred even if the firm produces no output. Therefore, depreciation of these assets is a fixed operating cost.

31. d. Statement a is false; if a firm is exposed to a high degree of business risk this implies that it should offset this risk by using a lower amount of financial leverage. Statement b is false; preferred stock is a fixed-income security, and as such, would increase financial risk. Statement c is false; the degree of total leverage is equal to the DOL × DFL -- which takes into account both business risk and financial risk. Statement d is the correct choice.

32. c. Business risk measures the riskiness of the firm's operation assuming no debt is used.

33. e.
$$\begin{aligned} EBIT &= PQ - VQP - F \\ \$90{,}000 &= P(50{,}000) - 0.4(50{,}000)P - \$100{,}000 \\ 30{,}000P &= \$190{,}000 \\ P &= \$6.33. \end{aligned}$$

34. c.
$$Q_{BE} = \frac{F}{(P - V)}$$

$$9{,}000 = \frac{\$180{,}000}{P - \$30}$$

$$\begin{aligned} P - \$30 &= \$20 \\ P &= \$50. \end{aligned}$$

35. d. $S_{BE} = \frac{F}{1 - (V/P)}$

$= \frac{\$180,000}{1 - (\$30/\$60)}$

$= \$360,000,$

36. b. The first step is to calculate EBIT:

Sales in dollars:	50,000($22)	$1,100,000
Less:	Fixed costs	500,000
	Variable costs: 50,000($2)	100,000
EBIT		$ 500,000

The second step is to calculate the EPS at each debt/assets ratio using the formula:

$$EPS = \frac{(EBIT - I)(1 - T)}{\text{Shares outstanding}}.$$

Recognize (1) that I = Interest charges = (Dollars of debt)(Interest rate at each D/A ratio), and (2) that Shares outstanding = (Assets - Debt)/Initial price per share = ($2,000,000 - Debt)/$20.00.

D/A	EPS	D/A	EPS
0%	$3.00	40%	$3.80
10	3.21	50	3.72
20	3.47	60	2.82
30	3.77		

Finally, the third step is to calculate the stock price at each debt/assets ratio using the following formula: Price = (P/E)(EPS).

D/A	Price	D/A	Price
0%	$37.50	40%	$30.40
10	38.52	50	22.32
20	39.91	60	14.10
30	37.70		

Thus, a debt/assets ratio of 20 percent maximizes stock price. This is the optimal capital structure.

37. c. $DOL = \frac{Q(P - V)}{Q(P - V) - F} = \frac{\$50,000(\$22 - \$2)}{\$50,000(\$22 - \$2) - \$500,000} = 2.00.$

38. b. $DFL = \frac{EBIT}{EBIT - I} = \frac{Q(P - V) - F}{Q(P - V) - F - I}$

$$= \frac{\$1,100,000 - \$100,000 - \$500,000}{\$1,100,000 - \$100,000 - \$500,000 - \$38,000}$$

$$= \frac{\$500,000}{\$462,000} = 1.08.$$

39. d. $$DTL = \frac{Q(P - V)}{Q(P - V) - F - I}$$

$$= \frac{\$1,100,000 - \$100,000}{\$1,100,000 - \$100,000 - \$500,000 - \$38,000}$$

$$= \frac{\$1,000,000}{\$462,000} = 2.16,$$

or DTL = (DOL)(DFL) = (2.00)(1.08) = 2.16.

40. d. $$DOL = \frac{Q(P - V)}{Q(P - V) - F} = 1.8.$$

But, Q(P - V) - F = EBIT = $4 million.

Therefore, [Q(P - V)]/$4 million = 1.8
Q(P - V) = $7.2 million.

Now, $$DTL = \frac{Q(P - V)}{Q(P - V) - F - I} = 2.0$$

$$\frac{\$7.2 \text{ million}}{\$4.0 \text{ million} - I} = 2.0$$

I = $0.40 million.

Therefore, the new interest payment must be $0.40 million. The current interest payment is 0.10($20 million) = $2.0 million. Thus, the interest payment must be reduced by $1.60 million by retiring bonds. This would require that $1.60/0.10 = $16 million of bonds be retired.

CHAPTER 21
DETERMINING THE DIVIDEND POLICY

OVERVIEW

Dividend policy involves the decision to pay out earnings as dividends or to retain and reinvest them in the firm. Any change in dividend policy has both favorable and unfavorable effects on the firm's stock price. The basic stock price model, $P_0 = D_1/(k_s - g)$, shows that if the firm adopts a policy of paying out more cash dividends, D_1 will rise, which will tend to increase the price of the stock. However, if cash dividends are increased, then less money will be available for reinvestment, the expected future growth rate will be lowered, and this will depress the stock price. The optimal dividend policy for a firm strikes that balance between current dividends and future growth which maximizes the firm's stock price.

A number of factors influence dividend policy: (1) investment opportunities available to the firm, (2) alternative sources of capital, and (3) stockholders' preferences for current versus future income. The residual dividend policy, where earnings are returned to finance capital projects that may be expected to earn a higher rate of return than required by investors with the residual amount to be paid as dividends, is discussed. Alternative dividend payment policies include: (1) constant, or steadily increasing, dollar dividends; (2) constant payout ratio; and (3) low regular dividends plus extras. It is simply not possible to state that any one dividend policy is correct, and hence it is impossible to develop a precise model for use in establishing dividend policy. Thus, financial managers must consider a number of factors when setting their firms' dividend policies.

OUTLINE

I. **Residual dividend policy is based on the premise that investors prefer to have a firm retain and reinvest earnings rather than pay them out in dividends if the rate of return the firm can earn on reinvested earnings exceeds the rate of return investors can obtain for themselves on other investments of comparable risk. Further, it is less expensive for the firm to use retained earnings than for it to issue new common stock.**

A. A firm using the residual policy would follow these steps:
1. Determine the optimal capital budget.
2. Determine the amount of equity capital required to finance the optimal capital budget, given a target capital structure.
3. To the extent possible, use retained earnings to supply the equity required.

4. Pay dividends only if more earnings are available than are needed to support the optimal capital budget.

B. Since both the IOS schedule and the earnings level vary from year to year, strict adherence to the residual dividend policy would result in considerable dividend variability. Thus, following the residual dividend policy would be optimal only if investors were not bothered by fluctuating dividends.

C. Firms use the residual policy to help set their long-run target payout ratios, not as a strict determinant of the payout in any one year.

II. Regardless of how dividend policy is determined, it is possible to identify several factors which influence dividend policy. These factors are grouped into four broad categories:

A. Constraints on dividend payments or on earnings retention
 1. Bond indenture provisions
 2. Impairment of capital rule
 3. Availability of cash
 4. Penalty tax on improperly accumulated earnings

B. Investment opportunities
 1. Location of the investment opportunity schedule
 2. Ability to accelerate or postpone projects

C. Availability and costs of alternative sources of capital
 1. Flotation costs of selling new stock
 2. Management control
 3. Capital structure flexibility--how steep is the average cost of capital schedule, and how much would it cost to substitute debt for equity?

D. Effects of dividend policy on the required rate of return
 1. Stockholder preference for current versus future income: *clientele effect*
 2. Risk of dividends versus capital gains
 3. Information content of dividends: *signaling*

III. In addition to the residual dividend policy, corporations tend to use one of three major dividend payment policies. Here are the actual dividend policies that firms follow in practice:

A. *Constant, or steadily increasing, dollar dividends per share.* A company which uses this procedure implies to shareholders that the regular dividend will at least be maintained and, accordingly, that earnings will be sufficient to cover it. Some other features of this policy are as follows:
 1. Dividends are increased only when earnings have increased and seem stable enough to maintain the new dividend level.

2. Dividend payments will be maintained, at least temporarily, even if earnings fall below the level of the dividend payment. Firms try very hard never to reduce the regular dividend.
3. Most corporations follow this type of policy.
   a. Stable dividends or a stable dividend growth rate will tend to stabilize a firm's stock price movements.
   b. Investors who rely on dividends for income normally prefer a stable dividend policy.
4. Because of these factors, many people think that a stable dividend policy (including a steady growth rate) will maximize the price of a firm's stock.

B. *Constant payout ratio*. Only a few firms pay out a constant percentage of their yearly earnings. This would normally result in an unpredictable dividend stream and would not please most investors.

C. *Low regular dividend plus extras*. This policy is often followed by firms with relatively volatile earnings from year to year. The low regular dividend can usually be maintained even when earnings decline, and "extra" dividends can be paid when excess funds are available.
   1. It represents a compromise between a stable dividend (or stable growth rate) and a constant payout rate.

IV. **Firms usually pay dividends on a quarterly basis in accordance with the following payment procedure:**

A. *Declaration date*. This is the day on which the board of directors declares the dividend. At this time they set the amount of the dividend to be paid, the holder-of-record date, and the payment date.

B. *Holder-of-record date*. This is the date the stock transfer books of the corporation are closed. Holders of record who purchased shares before the ex-dividend date will receive the announced dividend.

C. *Ex-dividend date*. This date is four business days prior to the holder-of-record date. Shares purchased after the ex-dividend date are not entitled to the dividend. This practice is a convention of the brokerage business which allows sufficient time for stock transfers to be made on the books of the corporation.

D. *Payment date*. This is the day when dividend checks are actually mailed to the holders of record.

V. **Many firms have instituted dividend reinvestment plans (DRIPs) whereby stockholders simply reinvest their dividends in additional shares of the corporation. Income taxes on the amount of the dividends must be paid even though stock rather than cash is received.**

A. There are two types of DRIPs: (1) plans which involve only "old" stock that is already outstanding and (2) plans which involve newly issued stock.

VI. Stock dividends and stock splits are often used to lower a firm's stock price, and, at the same time, to conserve its cash resources.

A. The effect of a *stock split* is an increase in the number of shares outstanding and a reduction in the par, or stated, value of the shares. For example, if a firm had 1,000 shares of stock outstanding with a par value of $100 per share, a 2-for-1 split would reduce the par value to $50 and increase the number of shares to 2,000.

1. The total net worth of the firm remains unchanged.

2. The stock split does not involve any cash payment, only additional certificates representing new shares.

B. A *stock dividend* requires an accounting entry transfer from retained earnings to the common stock and paid-in capital accounts and an accompanying pro-rata distribution of new shares to the existing stockholders.

1. Dollars transferred from retained earnings = (Number of shares outstanding)(Percentage of the stock dividend)(Market price of the stock).

2. Again, no cash is involved with this "dividend." Net worth remains unchanged, and the number of shares is increased.

C. Stock dividends and splits "cut a given amount of pie into smaller slices."

D. The rationale behind using stock splits and dividends to reduce share prices lies in the belief in an *optimal trading range* within which large numbers of investors will be able to purchase the stock, liquidity will be increased, and the price will be maximized.

E. Unless the total amount of dividends paid on shares is increased, any upward movement in the stock price following a stock split or dividend is likely to be temporary. The price will normally fall in proportion to the dilution in earnings and dividends unless earnings and dividends rise.

VII. Stock repurchases are an alternative to dividends for transmitting cash to stockholders.

A. There are two principal types of *repurchases*:

1. The firm may wish to distribute cash to its shareholders in the form of a repurchase rather than a cash dividend.

2. A firm may conclude that its capital structure is too heavily weighted with equity and may then decide to sell debt, using the proceeds to buy back its stock.

B. Stock that has been repurchased by a firm is called *treasury stock*.

C. Advantages of repurchases include:

1. Repurchases are viewed as positive signals by investors because it is often motivated by management's belief that the firm's shares are undervalued.
2. The per-share price of the stock after the buy-back should be higher than before, other things equal.
3. The stockholder is given a choice of whether to sell or to not sell his stock to the firm. The widening of the gap between the capital gains tax rate and the top rate on individuals' ordinary income makes stock repurchases more attractive to investors in high tax brackets.
4. If excess cash flow is thought to be only temporary, management may prefer to make the distribution in the form of a share repurchase rather than to declare an increased cash dividend that cannot be maintained.
5. Repurchases can be used to produce large-scale changes in capital structures.

D. Disadvantages of repurchase include:

1. Repurchases are not as dependable as cash dividends; therefore, the price of the stock may benefit more from cash dividends.
2. The selling stockholders may not be fully aware of all the implications of a repurchase.
3. The corporation may pay too high a price for the repurchased stock, to the disadvantage of remaining stockholders.
4. There is an "announcement effect" when a company repurchases its own shares. Management is basically making it known that the company does not have enough investment opportunities available yielding rates greater than its cost of equity capital.
5. A stock buy-back program is, in essence, the company reducing its size. The firm ends up with higher financial leverage and greater financial risk.

E. Stock repurchases are commonly made in one of three ways:

1. A publicly owned firm can simply buy its own stock through a broker on the open market.
2. The firm can make a *tender offer*, under which it permits stockholders to send in ("tender") their shares to the firm in exchange for a specified price per share, generally at a premium over the current market price.
3. The firm can purchase a block of shares from one large shareholder on a negotiated basis.

DEFINITIONAL QUESTIONS

1. The dividend residual policy assumes that the expected rate of return on capital projects will be ______________ than the investors' required rate of return.

2. A company may be forced to increase its ________ ratio in order to avoid a tax on retained earnings deemed to be unnecessary for the conduct of the business.

3. Some stockholders prefer dividends to ________ ________ because of a need for current ________.

4. If the ____ of a firm's stock increases with the announcement of an increase in dividends, it may be due to the _________ content in the dividend announcement rather than to a preference for dividends over capital gains.

5. The policy of using "extra" dividends is most appropriate for a firm with ________ earnings.

6. The stock transfer books of a corporation are closed on the __________-____-__________ date.

7. The ____-____________ date occurs four business days prior to the ____________-___-__________ date and provides time for stock transfers to be recorded on the books of the firm.

8. Actual payment of a dividend is made on the ________ date as announced by the ________ ______ ________.

9. Many firms have instituted ________ __________ plans whereby stockholders can use their dividends to purchase additional shares of the company's stock.

10. A stock dividend requires that an accounting transfer be made from ____________ ________ to the ___________ ___________ and __________-____ _________ accounts.

11. A stock split involves a reduction in the _____ _____ of the common stock, but no accounting transfers are made between accounts.

12. The assumption that some investors prefer a high dividend payout while others prefer a low payout is called the _________ effect.

13. The residual dividend policy is based on the fact that new common stock is ________ _____ than retained earnings.

14. Firms use the __________ __________ policy to help set their long-run target payout ratios, not as a strict determinant of the payout in any one year.

15. With the __________, or __________ __________, dollar dividends per share policy, a company implies to shareholders that the regular dividend will at least be maintained and, accordingly, that earnings will be sufficient to cover it.

16. A(n) __________ __________ __________ policy would normally result in an unpredictable dividend stream and would not please most investors.

17. The __________ __________ is the day on which the board of directors declares the dividend.

18. The rationale behind using stock splits and dividends to reduce share prices lies in the belief in a(n) __________ __________ __________ within which large numbers of investors will be able to purchase the stock, liquidity will be increased, and the price will be maximized.

19. Stock that has been repurchased by a firm is called __________ __________.

20. __________ __________ involves the decision to pay out earnings as dividends or to retain and reinvest them in the firm.

CONCEPTUAL QUESTIONS

21. An increase in cash dividends will always result in an increase in the price of the common stock because D_1 will increase in the stock valuation model.

    a. True   b. False

22. If investors are indifferent between dividends and capital gains, the farther to the left the IOS and MCC schedule intersect, the higher the dividend payout ratio should be.

    a. True   b. False

23. A stock dividend will affect which of the following balance sheet accounts?

    a. Common stock
    b. Paid-in capital
    c. Retained earnings
    d. Cash
    e. The accounts in a, b, and c will all be affected.

24. A stock split will affect the amounts shown in which of the following balance sheet accounts?

    a. Common stock
    b. Paid-in surplus
    c. Retained earnings
    d. Cash
    e. None of the above accounts.

25. Which of the following statements is most *correct*?

a. The residual dividend policy calls for the establishment of a fixed, stable dividend (or dividend growth rate) and then for the level of investment each year to be determined as a residual equal to net income minus the established dividends.
b. According to the residual dividend policy, for any given MCC schedule and level of earnings, the further to the right the IOS schedule cuts the MCC schedule, the lower the optimal dividend payout ratio.
c. According to the text, a firm would probably maximize its stock price if it established a specific dividend payout ratio, say 40 percent, and then paid that percentage of earnings out each year because stockholders would then know exactly how much dividend income to count on when they planned their spending for the coming year.
d. If you buy a stock after the ex-dividend date but before the dividend has been paid, then you, and not the seller, will receive the next dividend check the company sends out.
e. Each of the above statements is false.

26. Which of the following statements is most *correct*?

a. According to the text, the residual dividend policy is more appropriate for setting a company's long-run target payout ratio than for determining the payout ratio on a year-to-year basis.
b. Dividend reinvestment plans are popular with investors because investors who do not need cash income can have their dividends reinvested in the company's stock and thereby avoid having to pay income taxes on the dividend income until they sell the stock.
c. In the past, stock dividends and stock splits were frequently used by corporations which wanted to lower the prices of their stocks to an "optimal trading range." However, recent empirical studies have demonstrated that stock dividends and stock splits generally cause stock prices to decline, so companies today rarely split their stock or pay stock dividends.
d. Statements a, b, and c are all false.
e. Statements a, b, and c are all true.

PROBLEMS

27. Express Industries' expected net income for next year is $1.0 million. The company's target, and current, capital structure is 40 percent debt and 60 percent common equity. The optimal capital budget for next year is $1.2 million. If Express uses the residual theory of dividends to determine next year's dividend payout, what is the expected payout ratio?

a. 0%
b. 10%
c. 28%
d. 42%
e. 56%

28. Amalgamated Shippers has a current, and target, capital structure of 30 percent debt and 70 percent equity. This past year Amalgamated, which uses a residual theory dividend policy, had a dividend payout ratio of 47.5 percent and net income of $800,000. What was Amalgamated's capital budget?

a. $400,000
b. $500,000
c. $600,000
d. $700,000
e. $800,000

29. Hedden Products just declared a 10 percent stock dividend. Hedden's stock price on the date of the announcement was $50. Prior to the announcement there were 20 million shares outstanding. What is the dollar amount of retained earnings (in millions) after the stock dividend if retained earnings was $300 million before the transaction?

a. $200
b. $150
c. $100
d. $400
e. $250

30. The Aikman Company's optimal capital structure calls for 40 percent debt and 60 percent common equity. The interest rate on its debt is a constant 12 percent; its cost of common equity from retained earnings is 16 percent; the cost of equity from new stock is 18 percent; and its federal-plus-state tax rate is 40 percent. Aikman has the following investment opportunities:

Project A: Cost = $5,000,000; IRR = 22%.
Project B: Cost = $5,000,000; IRR = 14%.
Project C: Cost = $5,000,000; IRR = 11%.

Aikman expects to have net income of $7,000,000. If Aikman bases its dividends on the residual policy, what will its payout ratio be?

a. 22.62%
b. 14.29%
c. 31.29%
d. 25.62%
e. 18.75%

ANSWERS AND SOLUTIONS

1. greater
2. payout
3. retained earnings; income
4. price (or value); information
5. volatile
6. holder-of-record
7. ex-dividend; holder-of-record
8. payment; board of directors
9. dividend reinvestment

10. retained earnings; common stock; paid-in capital
11. par value
12. clientele
13. more costly
14. residual dividend
15. constant; steadily increasing
16. constant payout ratio
17. declaration date
18. optimal trading range
19. treasury stock
20. Dividend policy

21. b. A dividend increase could be perceived by investors as signifying poor investment opportunities and hence lower growth in future earnings, thus reducing g in the DCF model. The net effect on stock price is uncertain.

22. a. If investors are indifferent, firms should follow the residual dividend theory. Thus, the smaller the optimal capital budget, the higher the dividend payout ratio.

23. e. A stock dividend requires an accounting entry transfer from the retained earnings account to the common stock and paid-in capital accounts. There is no cash involved in a stock dividend.

24. e. A stock split will affect the par value and number of shares outstanding. However, no dollar values will be affected.

25. b. Statement a is false; the residual dividend policy calls for the determination of the optimal capital budget and then the dividend is established as a residual of net income minus the amount of retained earnings necessary for the capital budget. Statement b is correct. Statement c is false; a constant payout policy would lead to uncertainty of dividends due to fluctuating earnings. Statement d is false; if a stock is bought after the ex-dividend date the dividend remains with the seller of the stock.

26. a. Statement a is correct. Statements b, c, d, and e are false. Investors do not avoid income taxes on reinvested dividends and today companies still split their stocks and pay stock dividends.

27. c. The $1,200,000 capital budget will be financed using 40 percent debt and 60 percent equity. Therefore, the equity requirement will be 0.6($1,200,000) = $720,000. Since the expected net income is $1,000,000, $280,000 will be available to pay as dividends. Thus, the payout ratio is expected to be $280,000/$1,000,000 = 0.28 = 28%.

28. c. Of the $800,000 in net income, 0.475($800,000) = $380,000 was paid out as dividends. Thus, $420,000 was retained in the firm for investment. This is the equity portion of the capital budget, or 70 percent of the capital budget. Therefore, the total capital budget was $420,000/0.7 = $600,000.

29. a. Amount of transfer: $20,000,000(0.10)($50) = $100,000,000.

RE before stock dividend	$300,000,000
Less: Transfer	100,000,000
RE after transfer	$200,000,000

30. b. Maximum BP_{RE} = NI/Equity ratio = $7,000,000/0.6 = $11,666,667.

$WACC_1$ = 0.4(12%)(0.6) + 0.6(16%) = 12.48%.
$WACC_2$ = 0.4(12%)(0.6) + 0.6(18%) = 13.68%.

We see that the capital budget should be $10,000,000. We know that 60 percent of the $10,000,000 should be equity. Therefore, the company should pay dividends of:

Dividends = NI - Needed equity = $7,000,000 - $6,000,000 = $1,000,000.

Payout ratio = $1,000,000/$7,000,000 = 0.1429 = 14.29%.

CHAPTER 22
MERGERS, DIVESTITURES, HOLDING COMPANIES, AND LBOs

OVERVIEW

A merger involves the consolidation of two or more firms. Mergers can provide economic benefits through economies of scale, but they also have the potential for reducing competition; and, for this reason, mergers are carefully regulated by governmental agencies. Of the several rationales for mergers, perhaps the most common is the existence of synergy. When synergy is present, the value of the combined enterprise is greater than the sum of the values of the separate firms.

Merger analysis may be regarded as a specialized form of capital budgeting analysis, with the most difficult part of the analysis being the estimation of the incremental cash flows that would result from the merger. Investment banking firms have specialists who can assist both the acquiring firm and the target firm in the valuation process.

Divestitures, the opposite of mergers, also occur frequently. The reasons for divestiture are varied, and they range from the need for cash to governmental insistence (antitrust reasons). Holding companies are firms whose sole purpose is to own operating interests in the stock of other firms. The holding company structure has both advantages and disadvantages over the conventional divisional structure. Finally, the 1980s witnessed a huge increase in the number and size of leveraged buyouts, or LBOs, for the same reasons that mergers and divestitures occurred.

OUTLINE

I. **Although the driving force behind most mergers is the desire to increase, or at times to protect, shareholder wealth, the manner in which this is accomplished depends on the specific situation the firm faces.**

A. Synergistic effects account for the additional value driving many mergers.

1. If Companies A and B merge to form Company C, and if C's value exceeds that of A and B taken separately, then *synergy* is said to exist.
2. Synergism can arise from four sources:
   a. Operating economies
   b. Financial economies
   c. Differential management efficiency
   d. Increased market power

3. Operating and financial economies, as well as increases in managerial efficiency, are socially desirable. However, mergers to increase market power are both undesirable and illegal.

B. Tax considerations have stimulated a number of mergers.
   1. A highly profitable firm might merge with a firm which has accumulated tax losses so as to put these losses to immediate use.
   2. A firm with excess cash and a shortage of internal investment opportunities might seek a merger rather than pay the cash out as dividends, which would result in the shareholders paying immediate taxes on the distribution.

C. Sometimes a firm will become an acquisition candidate because the replacement value of its assets is considerably higher than its market value.
   1. For example, in the 1980s oil companies could acquire reserves more cheaply by buying out other oil companies than by exploratory drilling.

D. *Diversification* is often cited by managers as a rationale for mergers. Managers often claim that diversification helps to stabilize the firm's earnings and thus reduce corporate risk. Although diversification may bring some real benefits to the firm, stockholders can generally diversify more easily and efficiently than can firms by simply holding portfolios of stocks.
   1. For publicly held firms, diversification to reduce stockholder risk is generally not a valid motive for a merger.

E. The ability for management to maintain control has caused *defensive mergers*, which are designed to make a company less vulnerable to a takeover.
   1. These types of mergers are difficult to defend on economic grounds. There can be no question that many of these types of mergers have been designed more for the benefit of managers than for stockholders.

II. **There are four primary types of mergers: horizontal, vertical, congeneric, and conglomerate.**

A. A *horizontal merger* occurs when one firm combines with another in its same line of business.

B. A *vertical merger* exists when firms combine in a producer-supplier relationship.

C. A *congeneric merger* involves related enterprises but not producers of the same product (horizontal) or firms in a producer-supplier relationship (vertical).

D. A *conglomerate merger* occurs when completely unrelated enterprises combine.

E. Operating economies are dependent on the type of merger involved. Vertical and horizontal mergers generally provide the greatest synergistic operating benefits, but they are also the ones most likely to be attacked by the U.S. Department of Justice.

III. The high level of merger activity in the 1980s has been sparked by several factors.

A. The depressed level of the dollar relative to Japanese and European currencies, which made U.S. companies look cheap to foreign buyers.

B. The unprecedented level of inflation that existed during the 1970s and early 1980s, which increased the replacement value of firms' assets while a weak stock market reduced their market values.

C. The Reagan and Bush administrations' view that "bigness is not necessarily badness," which resulted in a more tolerant attitude toward large mergers.

D. The general belief among the major natural resource companies that it is cheaper to "buy reserves on Wall Street" than to explore and find them in the field.

E. Attempts to ward off raiders by use of defensive mergers.

F. The development of the junk bond market, which made it possible to use far more debt in acquisitions than had been possible earlier.

G. The increased globalization of business, which has led to increased economies of scale and to the formation of worldwide corporations.

IV. In most mergers, one company, the target company, is acquired by another, the acquiring company.

A. In a *friendly merger*, the management of the *target company* approves the merger and recommends it to their stockholders.

1. Under these circumstances a suitable price is determined and the *acquiring company* will simply buy the target company's shares.
2. Payment will be made either in cash, in shares of the acquiring company, or with bonds.

B. A *hostile merger* is one in which the target firm's management resists the takeover. The target firm's management either believes the price offered is too low or may simply want to remain independent.

1. Under these circumstances, the acquiring company may make a *tender offer* for the target company's shares. This is a direct appeal to the target firm's stockholders asking them to exchange their shares for cash, for bonds, or for stock in the acquiring firm.
2. The number of tender offers has increased greatly during the past several years.

V. **While merger analysis may appear simple, there are a number of complex issues involved.**

A. The acquisition decision involves both consideration of "strategic fit," or how well the proposed merger will fulfill or meet the corporate objectives, and financial value.

B. The acquiring firm must perform a capital budgeting analysis. If it appears that the target firm can be purchased for less than its intrinsic value, then the offer should be made. However, the target firm's shareholders must believe that a "fair" price is being offered. Otherwise, they will not tender their shares.

C. The process of estimating future cash flows is quite complex with an acquisition because one must take into account the effect of potential synergy and the new ownership.

D. Beyond estimating future cash flows, several other merger issues must be resolved:
   1. What effect, if any, the purchase will have on the acquiring firm's required rate of return on equity.
   2. What consideration will be used for the purchase--cash, stock, or some combination of both.
   3. Negotiating all the terms of the transaction as to best benefit the shareholders of both the target and the acquiring firm.

E. From a financial analysis standpoint, there are two basic types of mergers:
   1. An *operating merger* is one in which the operations of two companies are integrated in hopes of synergistic gains.
   2. A *financial merger* is one in which the merged companies will not be operated as a single unit and from which no significant operating economies are expected.

F. In a financial merger, the postmerger cash flows are simply the sum of the expected cash flows of the two companies if they continued to operate independently. However, if they are to be integrated, then accurate estimates of future cash flows are essential. In planning operating mergers, the development of accurate pro forma cash flows is the single most important aspect of the analysis.

G. The terms of a merger include two important elements:
   1. *Postmerger control* is of great interest to managers due to their concern for their jobs.
   2. The *purchase price* determines whether the shareholders of the acquiring company or the shareholders of the target company reap the greater benefits from the merger.

H. The larger the synergistic benefits, the more room there is for bargaining, and the higher the probability that the merger actually will be consummated.

VI. Virtually all acquisition valuation methods utilize a Discounted Cash Flow (DCF) methodology, under which two key items are needed: (1) a set of pro forma financial statements and (2) a discount rate to apply to the projected cash flows.

A. The various valuation approaches differ as to the relevant cash flows and appropriate discount rates used. The most widely used valuation method approaches the valuation of the entire firm and involves using yearly Free Cash Flow (FCF) estimates as the relevant cash flows.

B. In a complete merger evaluation, just as in a capital budgeting analysis, the component cash flow probability distributions would be specified, and sensitivity, scenario, and simulation analyses would be conducted.

C. The discount rate used in valuing a target firm is a weighted average cost of capital, determined using the average cost of equity and average cost of debt for firms comparable to the target firm--with the weights determined as the expected relative proportion of debt and equity in the target firm post-acquisition.

D. *Free Cash Flow estimates* are calculated as: Net Income + Depreciation + After-tax Interest - Investment Required.

1. After-tax interest is used to reflect the true cost of interest to the firm, net of the tax shelter effect of interest expense.

E. A *terminal value* must be determined using the perpetuity valuation model and this amount is considered with the free cash flow estimates in the acquisition valuation.

F. The present value of the expected Free Cash Flows and the terminal value is the maximum price that the acquiring firm should pay for the target company.

VII. Investment bankers play an important role in merger activities.

A. Investment bankers serve several critical functions in merger acquisitions:

1. Structuring and negotiating the merger.
2. Valuing the target firm.
3. Developing and implementing tactics.

B. The major investment banking firms have merger and acquisition (M&A) departments which help to match merger partners.

C. These same investment bankers can also help a firm fend off an unwanted suitor.

1. Sometimes a *white knight* will be lined up to acquire a firm that is trying to avoid being taken over by an unfriendly suitor.
2. Investment bankers can also recommend *poison pills,* which are actions that effectively destroy the value of the firm in the event of merger and hence drive off unwanted suitors.

D. Finally, investment bankers are used to help establish the offering price. Generally, both acquiring and target firms will use investment bankers to help establish a price and also to participate in the negotiations.

VIII. **Mergers are not the only ways in which resources of two firms can be combined. In fact, many companies are striking cooperative deals, or corporate alliances, which fall far short of merging. They are cooperative agreements between two firms that can range from simple marketing agreements to joint ownerships of a third corporation.**

A. Corporate alliances and partnering have become a dynamic element in the development of firms and markets. It is now often imperative for companies to partner to remain competitive in today's environment. By partnering, large and small firms can use their complementary strengths to take a new product or service from concept to the marketplace.
1. The process by which a new idea gets to the end-user is called the *value chain.*

B. The strongest form of corporate alliance is the *joint venture,* which involves the joining together of parts of companies to accomplish specific, limited objectives. Often a third corporation, which is jointly owned, is formed to accomplish the joint venture objective.

IX. **Although corporations do more buying than selling of productive assets, selling, or divestiture, does take place.**

A. The decision to sell an operating unit may be driven by either:
1. Strictly financial motives, such as a negative cash flow or the need to raise capital to pay outstanding debt obligations.
2. Strategic business motives, such as discontinuing an unrelated product line and concentrating on what the firm does best.

B. There are four primary types of divestitures:
1. A division may be sold intact to another firm. This is the most common form of divestiture.
2. A division may be sold to its managers. Such a managerial buyout results in the owners-managers reorganizing into a closely held firm.
3. A division may be set up as a corporation, with the parent firm's stockholders then being given stock in the new corporation on a pro rata basis. This type of divestiture is called a *spin-off.*
4. Sometimes, when a firm cannot find a buyer for an entire division, the division's assets must be sold off piecemeal. This is a liquidation.

C. There are a variety of reasons cited for divestitures:
   1. Sometimes the market does not appear to properly recognize the value of a firm's assets when they are held as part of a conglomerate. Thus, divestiture can occur to enhance firm value.
   2. Often, firms will need to raise large amounts of cash to finance expansion in their core business or to reduce an onerous debt burden, and divestitures can raise the needed cash.
   3. Sometimes, assets are just no longer profitable and must be liquidated.

X. **A holding company is a firm whose primary function is to hold the stock of other corporations, but has no operating units of its own. The holding company is often called the parent company, and the controlled companies are known as subsidiaries or operating companies. Holding companies may be used to obtain some of the same benefits that could be achieved through mergers and acquisitions.**

A. Advantages of holding companies include the following:
   1. *Control with fractional ownership*. Effective control of a company may be achieved with far less than 50 percent ownership of the common stock.
   2. *Isolation of risks*. Claims on one unit of the holding company may not be liabilities to the other units. Each element of the holding company organization is a separate legal entity.
   3. *Legal separation*. Certain regulated companies such as utilities and banks find it easier to operate as holding companies in order to separate those assets under the control of regulators from those not subject to regulation.

B. Disadvantages of holding companies include the following:
   1. *Partial multiple taxation*. Consolidated tax returns may be filed only if the holding company owns 80 percent or more of the voting stock of the subsidiary. Otherwise, intercorporate dividends will be taxed. Note, though, that 70 percent of the dividends received by the holding company may be deducted from taxable income.
   2. *Ease of enforced dissolution*. It is much easier for the Justice Department to require disposal of a stock position than to demand the separation of an integrated business operation.
   3. *"Management by financial statements" approach*. High level management decisions concerning the operating units are often made based on financial information with no insight or strategies regarding the firm's products, industry or competition. These short-sighted decisions often prove disastrous to the firm over time.

C. The holding company device can be used to control large amounts of assets with a relatively small equity investment. The substantial leverage involved in such an operation may result in high returns, but it also involves a high degree of risk.

XI. **The 1980s witnessed a huge increase in the number and size of leveraged buyouts, or LBOs.**

A. LBOs differ from ordinary acquisitions in several ways:
1. How they are financed.
2. Motivation for the transaction.
3. Future plans for the firm.

B. LBOs generally take place for purely financial reasons; with the equity group expecting "cash-out" and reap their profits by either selling the firm or taking it public within five years.

C. What makes an acquisition a leveraged buyout is the fact that it is purchased almost entirely with debt; a large portion of which is borrowed using the firm's assets as collateral. Generally, the newly formed company will have at least 80 percent debt, so the term "leveraged" is most appropriate.

D. The increase in LBOs occurred for the same reasons that mergers and divestitures occurred--the existence of potential bargains, situations in which companies were using insufficient leverage, and the development of the junk bond market.

E. A major risk facing LBO transactions, and the main reason that LBO transactions run into severe financial difficulties post-transaction, is that the massive debt load is determined assuming that the firm will maintain or increase their pre-transaction level of cash flow to service the debt. Consequently, recessionary periods or changes in the competitive environment which adversely impacts the firm's operations will render it unable to meet the interest payments on its debt.

DEFINITIONAL QUESTIONS

1. If the value of two firms, in combination, is greater than the sum of their separate values, then __________ is said to exist.

2. Synergistic effects may result from either ____________ economies or ____________ economies.

3. The Justice Department may be concerned about the ____________ implications of a proposed merger.

4. A(n) ____________ merger takes place when two firms in the same business combine, while the combination of a steel company with a coal company would be an example of a ___________ merger.

5. The merger of two completely unrelated enterprises is referred to as a(n) _______________ merger.

6. A firm which seeks to take over another company is commonly called the ____________ company, while the firm it seeks to acquire is referred to as the _________ company.

7. A merger may be described as "friendly" or "hostile," depending upon the attitude of the _____________ of the target company.

8. A(n) _________ ________ is a request by the acquiring company to the target company's _______________ to submit their shares in exchange for a specified price or specified number of shares of stock.

9. A(n) ____________ merger combines the business activity of the two firms with the expectation of ______________ benefits.

10. ____________ mergers do not combine the business operations of two firms, and no significant operating economies are expected.

11. Merger analysis is very similar to _________ ____________ analysis.

12. In valuing the target firm, the analysis focuses on the cash flows that accrue to the stockholders of the ___________ firm.

13. A pro rata distribution of stock in a new firm which was formerly a subsidiary is called a(n) _______-_______.

14. Unless a holding company owns at least _____ percent of the share of a subsidiary company, it may be subject to multiple ___________ on a portion of any intercorporate ____________.

15. Managers often claim that __________________ helps to stabilize the firm's earnings and thus reduce corporate risk and, as such, it is often cited by managers as a rationale for mergers.

16. The ability for management to maintain control has caused ____________ __________, which are designed to make a company less vulnerable to a takeover.

17. A(n) _____________ _________ involves related enterprises but not producers of the same product or firms in a producer-supplier relationship.

18. In a(n) ___________ _________, the management of the target company approves the merger and recommends it to their stockholders.

19. A(n) __________ _________ is one in which the target firm's management resists the takeover.

20. Sometimes investment bankers will line up a(n) ________ _________ to acquire a firm that is trying to avoid being taken over by an unfriendly suitor.

21. ________ ________ are actions that effectively destroy the value of the firm in the event of merger and hence drive off unwanted suitors.

22. ___________ ___________ are cooperative agreements between two firms that can range from simple marketing agreements to joint ownerships of a third corporation.

23. The strongest form of corporate alliance is the ________ __________, which involves the joining together of parts of companies to accomplish specific, limited objectives.

24. Although corporations do more buying than selling of productive assets, selling, or ______________, does take place.

25. A(n) _________ _________ is a firm whose primary function is to hold the stock of other corporations, but has no operating units of its own.

CONCEPTUAL QUESTIONS

26. In a financial merger, the expected post-merger cash flows are generally the sum of the cash flows of the separate companies.

a. True b. False

27. In the determination of the Free Cash Flow estimates, interest expense is explicitly excluded.

a. True b. False

28. The holding company device can be used to take advantage of the principle of financial leverage. Thus, the holding company can control a great deal of assets with a limited amount of top-tier equity.

a. True b. False

PROBLEMS

(The following data apply to the next five problems.)

TransCorp, a large conglomerate, is evaluating the possible acquisition of the Chip Company, a transistor manufacturer. TransCorp's analyst projects the following postmerger incremental cash flows (in millions of dollars):

	1994	1995	1996	1997
Net sales	$200	$230	$250	$270
Cost of goods sold	114	124	127	132
Selling/administrative expenses	20	25	30	32
Depreciation	16	16	18	18
EBIT	$ 50	$ 65	$ 75	$ 88
Interest	10	12	13	14
EBT	$ 40	$ 53	$ 62	$ 74
Taxes (40%)	16	21	25	30
NI	$ 24	$ 32	$ 37	$ 44
Investments for growth	$ 12	$ 13	$ 14	$ 15

The acquisition, if made, would occur on January 1, 1994. All cash flows above are assumed to occur at year end. Chip currently has a market value capital structure of 10 percent debt, but TransCorp would increase the debt to 50 percent if the acquisition were made. Chip, if independent, pays taxes at 30 percent, but its income would be taxed at 40 percent if consolidated. Chip's current market-determined beta is 1.00. Its estimated post-merger beta is 1.50. The marginal cost of debt (post-merger) is 10 percent.

The cash flows above include the additional interest payments due to increased leverage and asset expansion, and the full taxes paid by TransCorp on the Chip income stream. The risk-free rate is 8 percent and the market risk premium is 4 percent. Also, assume after the fourth year that Chip's cash flows are expected to grow at a constant rate of 3 percent.

29. What is the appropriate discount rate for valuing the acquisition?

a. 10.00%
b. 15.00%
c. 19.00%
d. 21.75%
e. 23.35%

30. What is Chip Company's terminal value (in millions) to TransCorp?

a. $697.07
b. $726.45
c. $775.33
d. $815.17
e. $888.98

31. What is the value (in millions) of the Chip Company to TransCorp?

a. $429.08
b. $486.13
c. $552.49
d. $613.97
e. $697.06

32. Chip has 15 million shares outstanding. Chip's current market price is $32.50. What is the maximum price per share that TransCorp should offer?

a. $32.50
b. $35.66
c. $38.33
d. $43.96
e. $46.47

33. TransCorp should offer Chip's stockholders $32.625 per share.

a. True b. False

ANSWERS AND SOLUTIONS

1. synergy
2. operating; financial
3. antitrust
4. horizontal; vertical
5. conglomerate
6. acquiring; target
7. management
8. tender offer; stockholders
9. operating; synergistic
10. Financial
11. capital budgeting
12. acquiring
13. spin-off
14. 80; taxation; dividends
15. diversification
16. defensive mergers
17. congeneric merger
18. friendly merger
19. hostile merger
20. white knight
21. Poison pills
22. Corporate alliances
23. joint venture
24. divestiture
25. holding company

26. a. In a financial merger, no synergistic effects are anticipated.

27. b. Free Cash Flows are calculated as: Net Income + Depreciation + After-tax Interest - Investment Required.

28. a. This statement is true.

29. a. $k_s = 8\% + (4\%)1.5 = 14\%$; $k_d = 10\%$.
$WACC = 0.5(10\%)(0.6) + 0.5(14\%) = 10\%$.

30. d. Determine the yearly Free Cash Flows:

	1994	1995	1996	1997
Net income	$24	$32	$37	$44
+ Depreciation	16	16	18	18
+ After-tax Int.[a]	6	7.2	7.8	8.4
- Investments	12	13	14	15
FCFs	$34	$42.2	$48.8	$55.4

Terminal value = $55.4(1.03)/(0.10 - 0.03) = $57.06/0.07 = $815.17.

[a] Interest(1 - T) = Interest(0.6).

31. e. Total value = $\$34/(1.10)^1 + \$42.2/(1.10)^2 + \$48.8/(1.10)^3 + (\$55.4 + \$815.17)/(1.10)^4$

= $697.06031.

32. e. $\frac{\$697,060,310}{15,000,000} = \$46.47.$

33. b. It does not make sense to offer Chip's shareholders just a little above the current market price. Enough shares would not be tendered to gain control, the expenses would be for nought, and other firms could be induced to make competing bids.

CHAPTER 23
INTERNATIONAL FINANCIAL MANAGEMENT

OVERVIEW

International financial management is not a separate set of issues from domestic or traditional financial management, but does involve a number of risks and complexities not confronted domestically. These complexities, different laws, different methods, different markets, different interest rates, and most of all different currencies, require specific knowledge of how these foreign financial markets work, and how the modern firm must adapt its financial management practices. There is an important distinction between a firm which only imports and exports, an international firm, and a firm which not only conducts direct import/export business but also has foreign affiliate and subsidiary operations, a multinational firm.

International financial management means that all the standard financial activities and decisions within a firm (capital budgeting, capital structure, raising long-term capital, working capital and cash flow management, and so on) will be complicated by the differences in markets, languages, cultures, governments, laws, and especially currencies of conducting business internationally. This management requires many different activities from the domestic financial management practices described up to now. All firms, no matter how domestic they may seem in structure, are influenced by exchange rate changes. The financial management of a firm which has any dimension of international activity, must pay special attention to these issues if the firm is to succeed in its international endeavors.

OUTLINE

I. **Because most international business activities require at least one of the two parties to first purchase the country's currency before purchasing any good, service, or asset, a proper understanding of exchange rates and exchange rate markets is very important to the conduct of international business.**

A. The price of one country's currency in terms of another country's currency is called a foreign currency *exchange rate*.

B. The order in which the foreign exchange rate is stated is sometimes confusing.
1. The *direct quotation* on any currency is the form when the home currency is stated first, while an *indirect quotation* refers to when the home currency is stated last.
2. The two quotations are *reciprocals* of one another.

C. A *spot* transaction is the exchange of currencies for immediate delivery.
   1. Although it is defined as immediate, in practice, settlement actually occurs two business days following the agreed upon exchange.

D. *Forward exchange rates* are contracts which provide for two parties to exchange currencies on a future date at an agreed upon exchange rate.
   1. Forwards are typically traded for the major-volume currencies for maturities of 30, 90, 120, 180, and 360 days (from the present date).
   2. The primary purpose of a forward contract is to allow a firm to lock-in a future exchange rate.

E. Any exchange of currency which is not under the control of a government is interpreted to be a better indication of the currency's true market value.

F. With only a few exceptions, most currencies are quoted in direct form quotes versus the U.S. dollar.
   1. The major exceptions are those currencies at one time or another associated with the British Commonwealth, including the Australian dollar and the British pound sterling.

G. Any currency's value can be stated in terms of any other currency. When the exchange rate for a currency is stated without using the U.S. dollar as a reference it is referred to as a *cross-rate*.
   1. If one of the exchange rates changes due to market forces, the others will have to adjust in order for the three cross-rates to all be once again aligned.
   2. If they are out of alignment, it would be possible to make a profit simply by exchanging one currency for a second, the second for a third, and the third back to the first. This is known as *triangular arbitrage*.

H. The market for foreign currencies is a worldwide market which is informal in structure. The market for currencies is composed of thousands of telecommunications links between financial institutions around the globe, and is therefore open 24 hours a day.
   1. Because there is no one exchange, no one floor, no world central bank, there is no single agreed upon exchange rate between all financial institutions.

I. A *money market* is traditionally defined as a market for deposits, accounts, or securities which have maturities of one year or less. The international money markets, often termed the *Eurocurrency markets*, constitute an enormous financial market which is in many ways outside the jurisdiction and supervision of world financial and governmental authorities.
   1. A *Eurocurrency* is any foreign currency-denominated deposit or account at a financial institution outside the country of the currency's issuance.

a. Because eurocurrencies are not controlled by governments, the financial institutions pay no deposit insurance, hold no reserve requirements, and are normally not subject to any interest rate setting restriction with respect to these accounts.

2. The interest rate which is used most often in international loan agreements is the Eurocurrency interest rate on U.S. dollars in London between banks: *LIBOR*, the London Inter-Bank Offer Rate.
3. Only well-known international firms, financial or non-financial, have access to the quantities of capital necessary to operate in the Euromarkets.

J. A currency is said to sell *forward at a discount*, if the forward contract possesses a rate for purchasing the currency which is cheaper than the present spot rate.

1. A currency is said to sell *forward at a premium*, if the forward contract possesses a rate for purchasing the currency which is more expensive than the present spot rate.

K. The *purchasing power parity* exchange rate is simply that rate which equalizes the price of the identical product or service in two different currencies.

1. The future spot exchange rate is simply the present spot rate multiplied by the ratio of the two expected rates of inflation.
2. The currency with the higher rate of inflation generally loses value relative to the lower-inflation currency, it *depreciates*.

L. The international monetary system has seen many changes since the beginning of the 20th century.

1. The major Western countries exchanged currencies on a gold standard until the outbreak of World War I in 1913. Under the *gold standard* each currency was convertible into a specific weight of gold, thereby "fixing" the rates at which one currency is exchanged for another currency.
2. After World War I, each country ended convertibility of their currency into gold because of rapid depletions in gold stocks due to investor fear of loss of currency value. With the onset of World War II, world trade came to a standstill.
3. In 1944, the Bretton Woods Agreement established stable exchange rates which allowed the re-opening of world markets. All currencies were fixed in value versus the U.S. dollar (they could generally vary by plus or minus 1 percent), and the U.S. dollar itself was convertible into gold.
4. As the economies of Europe and Asia once more flourished, the demands of the world economy forced continuing outflows of gold from the U.S. as other countries exchanged U.S. paper money for gold. In 1971, the world was effectively shifted to a *floating exchange rate system* in which governments no longer dictated currency values.

II. **Traditional capital budgeting exercises, when conducted domestically, discount expected future net cash flows by the weighted average cost of**

capital for the firm if the project is of the same risk as the firm. International capital budgeting, however, must also address the issue of whether the added risk introduced by cross-border investments, including the risk components of currency values, potential government restrictions on the movements of capital, or even the potential political stability of the country in which the investment is to take place, should be captured in the analysis by adding a risk premium to the discount rate used. Others believe that the additional risk of international projects should be captured in the estimation of the net cash flows themselves, and through added sensitivity analysis.

A. The primary theoretical distinction between a domestic capital budget and a multinational capital budget is the project evaluation from the parent's viewpoint will focus on whatever cash flows, either operational or financial, which find their way back to the parent firm in U.S. dollars.

B. The steps in the multinational capital budgeting process are as follows:

1. Estimate the annual net cash flows of the project in the foreign currency.

2. Forecast the movement of the exchange rate during the project's life.

3. On the basis of Steps 1 and 2, calculate the annual net cash flow in the home currency.

4. Now apply the firm's cost of capital as the discount rate, to determine the net present value of the project.

C. The higher risk of an international investment as compared to a domestic investment arises from the different countries, their laws, regulations, and potential for interference with the normal operations of the investment project, and obviously currencies, all of which are unique to international investment.

1. The risk of international investment is considered greater than that for domestic investment because the proposed investment will lie within the jurisdiction of a different government.

2. The other major distinction between a domestic and a foreign investment is that the viewpoint or perspective of the parent and the project are no longer the same.

3. Any individual investment can be judged only on the basis of the future cash flows which it generates in the investor's own currency.

III. **The choice of what proportions of debt and equity to use in international investments is usually dictated by either the debt-equity structure of the parent firm, or the debt-equity structure of the competitive firms in the foreign country--host country to the investment.**

A. Because international investments are subject to higher risks from political sources or financial sources, the parent firm would ideally prefer to risk little of its own capital and instead fund the foreign subsidiary with large quantities of debt.

B. It is the proportion of profits which are to be returned to the parent versus profits which are to be retained and reinvested in the project or firm, which often leads to conflict between the host-country authorities and the multinational firm's parent.

C. A foreign affiliate can raise debt capital from the following sources:
1. Parent.
2. Parent firm's home-market through a bank loan or bond issue, or a bank loan or bond issue in the host-country market.
3. Third-country bank loan, bond issue, Euro-syndicated credit or Euro-bond issue.

D. The larger firms internationally will often have their own financial subsidiaries, companies purely for the purpose of acquiring the capital needed for the entire company's continuing growth needs.

IV. **The maintenance of proper liquidity, the monitoring of payments, and the acquisition of additional capital when needed, requires a great degree of organization and planning in international operations today.**

A. Firms possess both operating cash flows and financial cash flows. *Operating cash flows* are those which arise from the everyday business activities of the firm, while *financial cash flows* arise from the funding activities of the firm. The proper management of these cash flows is critical to the success or failure of the international business.

B. The structure of the firm dictates in what ways cash flows and financial resources can be managed. The trend in the past decade has been for the increasing centralization of most financial and treasury operations. The centralized treasury often enjoys significant economies of scale.

C. There are a number of operating structures which aid the multinational firm in managing its cash flows:
1. *Cash pooling*. A large firm with a number of units operating both within an individual country and across countries may be able to economize on the amount of firm assets needed in cash if operated through one central pool.
2. *Netting*. Coordination between units simply requires some planning and budgeting of intra-firm cash flows in order that two-way flows are "netted" against one another, with only one smaller cash flow having to be undertaken as opposed to two.
3. *Leads and lags*. The timing of payments between units of a multinational is somewhat flexible.
4. *Reinvoicing*. Multinational firms with a variety of manufacturing and distribution subsidiaries scattered over a number of countries within a region may often find it more economical to have one office or subsidiary taking ownership of all invoices and payments between units.
5. *Internal banks*. An internal bank within the firm actually buys and sells payables and receivables from the various units. This frees the

units of the firm from struggling for continual working capital financing, and allows them to focus on their primary business activities.

V. **Internationally, financial trust is pushed to its limit. An order from a foreign buyer may constitute a degree of credit risk which the producer--the exporter--cannot afford to take. The exporter needs some guarantee that the importer will indeed pay for the goods. Arrangements which provide guarantees to exports are important to countries and companies wishing to expand international sales. This is accomplished through a sequence of documents surrounding the letter of credit.**

VI. **There are three types of foreign currency exposures which firms possess to varying degrees: transaction exposure, economic exposure, and translation exposure.**

A. *Transaction exposure* is the risk associated with a contractual payment of foreign currency. This is the most commonly observed type of exchange rate risk.
   1. Two conditions are necessary for it to exist:
      a. A cash flow denominated in a foreign currency.
      b. The cash flow occurs at a future date.
   2. The risk is that the exchange rate between the present date and the settlement date will change.
   3. Management of transaction exposure is usually accomplished by either natural hedging or contractual hedging.
      a. A *hedge* is an asset or a position whose value moves in the equal but opposite direction of the exposure.
      b. *Natural hedging* is the term used to describe how a firm might arrange to have foreign currency cash flows coming in and going out at roughly the same times and same amounts.
      c. *Contractual hedging* is when the firm uses financial contracts to hedge the transaction exposure. The most common foreign currency contractual hedge is the *forward contract*.

B. *Economic exposure* is the risk to the firm of its long-term cash flows being affected, positively or negatively, by unexpected future exchange rate changes.
   1. Measuring economic exposure is subjective, and for the most part is dependent on the degree of internationalization present in the firm's cost and revenue structure, as well as potential changes over the long run.
   2. Management of economic exposure is being prepared for the unexpected. It can be accomplished through diversification: *diversification of operations* and *diversification of financing*.

C. *Translation exposure* is the risk that arises from the legal requirement that all firms consolidate their financial statements of all worldwide operations annually.

1. The process of translation is dictated by financial accounting standards. The proper method for translating foreign financial statements is given in FASB 52.
2. If a foreign subsidiary is operating in a foreign currency functional environment, most assets, liabilities, and income statement items of foreign affiliates are translated using current exchange rates (the exchange rate in effect on the balance sheet date). It is often referred to as the *Current Rate Method*.
3. Translation exposure under FASB 52 results in no cash flow impacts under normal circumstances.

D. Transaction exposure and economic exposure are true exposure in the financial sense because they both present potential threats to the value of a firm's cash flows over time.

E. Translation exposure is a problem which arises from accounting so, for the most part, little in the way of real resource use should be devoted to the management of a purely accounting-based event.

F. Exchange rate movements are inherently random, therefore some type of mutual risk-sharing arrangements may prove useful.

VII. **One of the most significant developments in international finance in the 1980s was the development of the interest rate and currency swap market. These markets have allowed firms to arbitrage the differences between markets, using their comparative advantage of borrowing in their home-market, and swapping for interest rates or currencies which are not as readily accessible.**

A. The *interest rate swap*, often called the "plain vanilla swap," allows one firm to use its good credit standing to borrow capital at low fixed rates and exchange its interest payments with a slightly lower credit-rated borrower who has debt-service payments at floating rates. Each borrower ends up making net interest payments at rates below those they could have achieved on their own.

B. The *currency swap* is the equivalent of the interest rate swap, only the currency of denomination of the debt is different.
1. The initial borrower is responsible for covering any shortfall or non-payment by the swap party. This risk, termed *counterparty risk*, is an increasing concern in the interest rate and currency swap markets as more and more firms utilize these markets to manage their debt structures.

C. Although the currency or interest rate swap markets are not sources of capital, they are very important ways to change the characteristics of capital. As more and more firms attempt to expand internationally, the swap market is expected to grow in significance as a means of managing the international financial risks and exposures of the firm.

DEFINITIONAL QUESTIONS

1. ______________ __________ ___________ is not a separate set of issues from domestic or traditional financial management, but does involve a number of risks and complexities not confronted domestically.

2. A firm which only imports and exports is referred to as a(n) ____________ firm, while a firm which not only conducts direct import/export business but also possesses foreign affiliate and subsidiary operations, is referred to as a(n) ______________ firm.

3. The price of one country's currency in terms of another country's currency is called a foreign currency __________ ______.

4. The ________ quotation on any currency is the form when the home currency is stated first, while a(n) __________ quotation refers to when the home currency is stated last.

5. A(n) _______ transaction is the exchange of currencies for immediate delivery.

6. _________ __________ ________ are contracts which provide for two parties to exchange currencies on a future date at an agreed upon exchange rate.

7. The primary purpose of a forward contract is to allow a firm to lock-in a(n) _________ __________ _______.

8. When the exchange rate for a currency is stated without using the U.S. dollar as a reference it is referred to as a(n) ________-_______.

9. If exchange rates are out of alignment, it would be possible to make a profit simply by exchanging one currency for a second, the second for a third, and the third back to the first. This is known as ____________ ___________.

10. The international money markets, often termed the _____________ __________, constitute an enormous financial market which is in many ways outside the jurisdiction and supervision of world financial and governmental authorities.

11. A(n) ______________ is any foreign currency-denominated deposit or account at a financial institution outside the country of the currency's issuance.

12. The interest rate which is used most often in international loan agreements is the Eurocurrency interest rate on U.S. dollars in London between banks known by its acronym _______, the _________ ______-______ ________ _______.

13. A currency is said to sell forward at a(n) __________, if the forward contract possesses a rate for purchasing the currency which is cheaper than the present spot rate.

14. A currency is said to sell forward at a(n) __________, if the forward contract possesses a rate for purchasing the currency which is more expensive than the present spot rate.

15. The ____________ ________ _________ exchange rate is simply that rate which equalizes the price of the identical product or service in two different currencies.

16. When a currency with a higher rate of inflation generally loses value relative to a lower-inflation currency, it is said to ____________.

17. Under the _______ ___________, each currency was convertible into a specific weight of gold, thereby "fixing" the rates at which one currency is exchanged for another currency.

18. In 1971, the world was effectively shifted to a ___________ ___________ _______ _________ in which governments no longer dictated currency values.

19. ___________ ___________ is the risk associated with a contractual payment of foreign currency.

20. A(n) ________ is an asset or a position whose value moves in the equal but opposite direction of the exposure.

21. _________ _________ is the term used to describe how a firm might arrange to have foreign currency cash flows coming in and going out at roughly the same times and same amounts.

22. ______________ ___________ is when the firm uses financial contracts to hedge the transaction exposure.

23. ___________ ___________ is the risk to the firm of its long-term cash flows being affected, positively or negatively, by unexpected future exchange rate changes.

24. ______________ ___________ is the risk that arises from the legal requirement that all firms consolidate their financial statements of all worldwide operations annually.

25. The ___________ _______ _______, often called the "plain vanilla swap," allows one firm to use its good credit standing to borrow capital at low fixed rates and exchange its interest payments with a slightly lower credit-rated borrower who has debt-service payments at floating rates.

CONCEPTUAL QUESTIONS

26. The cost of capital is generally lower for a foreign project than for an equivalent domestic project since the possibility of exchange gains exists.

    a. True　　b. False

27. As sources of capital, currency and interest rate swap markets are very important ways to change the characteristics of capital.

    a. True　　b. False

28. A currency swap is the equivalent of an interest rate swap except that the currency of the denomination of the debt is different.

    a. True　　b. False

29. The primary theoretical distinction between a domestic capital budget and a multinational capital budget is the project evaluation from the parent's viewpoint will focus on whatever cash flows, either operational or financial, which find their way back to the parent firm in U.S. dollars.

    a. True　　b. False

PROBLEMS

30. The "spot rate" for Greek drachmas is 0.0313 U.S. dollars per drachma. What would the exchange rate be expressed in drachmas per dollar?

    a. 0.0313 drachmas per dollar
    b. 3.1300 drachmas per dollar
    c. 31.9489 drachmas per dollar
    d. 319.4890 drachmas per dollar
    e. 400.0000 drachmas per dollar

31. The U.S. dollar can be exchanged for 942.1432 Italian lire today. The Italian currency is expected to appreciate by 10 percent tomorrow. What is the expected exchange rate tomorrow expressed in lire per dollar?

    a. 836.1935 lire per dollar
    b. 841.3167 lire per dollar
    c. 847.9289 lire per dollar
    d. 958.2334 lire per dollar
    e. 965.9813 lire per dollar

32. You are considering the purchase of a block of stock in Galic Steel, a French steel producer. Galic just paid a dividend of 10 francs per share; that is, D_0 = 10 francs. You expect the dividend to grow indefinitely at a rate of 15 percent per year, but because of a higher expected rate of inflation in France than in the United States, you expect the franc to depreciate against the dollar at a rate of 5 percent per year. The exchange rate is currently 5 francs per U.S. dollar, but this ratio will change as the franc depreciates. For a stock with this degree of risk, including exchange rate risk, you feel that a 20 percent rate of return is required. What is the most, in dollars, that you should pay for the stock?

a. $20.90
b. $31.70
c. $46.00
d. $53.60
e. $60.34

33. Refer to Question 32. Now assume that the franc is expected to appreciate against the dollar at the rate of 1 percent per year. All other facts are unchanged. Under these conditions, what should you be willing to pay for the stock?

a. $20.90
b. $31.70
c. $46.00
d. $53.60
e. $60.34

ANSWERS AND SOLUTIONS

1. International financial management
2. international; multinational
3. exchange rate
4. direct; indirect
5. spot
6. Forward exchange rates
7. future exchange rate
8. cross-rate
9. triangular arbitrage
10. Eurocurrency markets
11. Eurocurrency
12. LIBOR; London Inter-Bank Offer Rate
13. discount
14. premium
15. purchasing power parity
16. depreciate
17. gold standard
18. floating exchange rate system
19. Transaction exposure
20. hedge
21. Natural hedging
22. Contractual hedging
23. Economic exposure
24. Translation exposure
25. interest rate swap

26. b. The cost of capital is generally higher because of exchange risk and sovereign risk.

27. b. Currency and interest rate swap markets are not sources of capital.

28. a. This statement is correct.

29. a. This statement is correct.

30. c. The exchange rate for drachmas per dollar would be the reciprocal of the exchange rate of dollars per drachma: 1/(0.0313 dollars per drachma) = 31.9489 drachmas per dollar.

31. c. 942.1432(0.90)/$1.00 = 847.9289 lire per dollar.

32. a. First, the valuation equation must be modified to convert the expected dividend stream to dollars:

$$D_t = D_0(1 + g)(ER),$$

where ER = exchange ratio. ER = 1/5 today, but if francs depreciate at a rate of 5 percent, it will take more francs to buy a dollar in the future. The value of ER at some future time (t) will be

$$ER_t = \text{Dollars/Francs} = 1/[5(1.05)^t].$$

Therefore, D_t in dollars may be calculated as follows:

$$\begin{aligned} D_t \text{ (in dollars)} &= (10 \text{ francs})(1 + g)^t(ER_t) \\ &= \$10(1.15)^t/[5(1.05)^t] \\ &= \$2(1.15)^t/[(1.05)^t] \\ &= \$2(1.15/1.05)^t \\ &= \$2(1.0952)^t. \end{aligned}$$

Thus, if the dividend in francs is expected to grow at a rate of 15 percent per year, but the franc is expected to depreciate at a rate of 5 percent per year against the dollar, then the growth rate, in dollars, of dividends received will be 9.52 percent. We can now calculate the value of the stock in dollars:

$$\hat{P}_0 = \frac{D_1}{k_s - g} = \frac{\$2(1.0952)}{0.20 - 0.0952} = \frac{\$2.1904}{0.1048} = \$20.90.$$

33. e. Solve the problem as above: $ER_t = 1(1.01)^t/5$.

$$\begin{aligned} D_t \text{ in dollars} &= (10 \text{ francs})(1 + g)^t[(1.01)^t/5] \\ &= (\$10/5)(1.15)^t(1.01)^t \\ &= \$2(1.1615)^t. \end{aligned}$$

Thus, the franc dividend is expected to increase at a rate of 15 percent per year, and the value of these francs is expected to rise at the rate of 1 percent per year, so the expected annual growth rate of the dollar dividend is 16.15 percent. We can now calculate the stock price:

$$\hat{P}_0 = \frac{D_1}{k_s - g} = \frac{\$2(1.1615)}{0.20 - 0.1615} = \frac{\$2.3230}{0.0385} = \$60.34.$$

